LIBRARY OF
AND
MONEY BANKING
HISTORY

# THE GROWTH OF CAPITAL

*Also by* ROBERT GIFFEN

*In REPRINTS OF ECONOMIC CLASSICS*

Stock Exchange Securities [1887]

# THE

# GROWTH

## OF

# CAPITAL

BY

ROBERT GIFFEN

[ 1889 ]

REPRINTS OF ECONOMIC CLASSICS

AUGUSTUS M. KELLEY · PUBLISHERS

*NEW YORK 1970*

First Published 1889

( London: George Bell & Sons, *York Street, Covent Garden*, 1889 )


Reprinted 1970 by
AUGUSTUS M. KELLEY · PUBLISHERS
REPRINTS OF ECONOMIC CLASSICS
*New York   New York   10001*


. . . . . . . . . . . .

*I S B N   0 678 00664 4*
*L C N   67 29505*

. . . . . . . . . . . .

PRINTED IN THE UNITED STATES OF AMERICA
*by* SENTRY PRESS, NEW YORK, N. Y. 10019

THE

# GROWTH OF CAPITAL.

BY

## ROBERT GIFFEN.

LONDON:

GEORGE BELL AND SONS, YORK STREET,

COVENT GARDEN.

—

1889.

# CONTENTS.

# APPENDIX.

# CONTENTS.–Continued.

NOTE.—The following pages were written for the most part in 1887, or early in 1888, and should be read as speaking from those dates. The completion of the book has been prevented till now, by a pressure of official work, leaving but scanty leisure. The delay, however, makes comparatively little difference in what is spoken of as the present time, as there was no great change in the Income Tax Returns for a few years after 1885, although a considerable change seems probable in the present year, and next year.

December, 1889.

# THE
# GROWTH OF CAPITAL.

## CHAPTER I.

### INTRODUCTORY

In the present essay I propose to resume and continue the notes on accumulations of capital in the United Kingdom, contained in a paper which I read to the Statistical Society in January, 1878, and since reprinted in the first series of my "Essays in Finance."\* An additional period of ten years can now be dealt with, and the later compared with the earlier results.

In entering on the task I desire to recall attention to the special object in view. This is to discuss the

---

\* See " Essays in Finance," first series, fourth edition. London : Geo. Bell and Sons. 1886.

accumulations of capital or growth of capital in a given period. For various reasons economists desire to know the rate of accumulation in a country—to compare the rate of taxation, for instance, with the gross and with the taxable income, to ascertain in what forms mainly the wealth of the country is growing, to compare the growth of capital itself with the growth of population, and so on. It is recognised, however, that only approximate results are obtainable. Imagination shrinks from the task of framing a catalogue or inventory of a nation's property as a valuator would make it : the idea of a valuation of the whole property of a country, as if a country could really be valued as a going concern, is itself a violent hypothesis; yet only from such inventories from time to time could the growth of wealth in the same country between two different dates be ascertained, while such growth being expressed in money might itself require correction if for any reason it did not happen to correspond with the growth in things. In the absence of such complete inventories, however, it is thought that an approximation can be made to the results aimed at by valuing the leading items of national property in some definite way, and that this approximation may be tolerably useful as a basis for comparing the growth between two different periods, and for comparing one country with another, although the incompleteness of each inventory itself may be fully recognised. According to well-known statistical experience, the comparison of the growth or increment may be reasonably successful if the same method is followed on each occasion in working out the data for the comparison, although these data themselves may be unavoidably incomplete.

I must insist on this point all the more, because, since my former paper was written, attention has, in fact, been withdrawn from the special object in view, and it has been thought, apparently, that such estimates of property can be used for miscellaneous purposes in a way which I believe most dangerous, and that they can be made with a degree of accuracy which I believe to be impossible. Country has been compared with country, and period with period, in the most reckless fashion, without any attention to the comparability of the data. Such figures have even been used officially for the purpose of discussing the relative incidence of taxation on different kinds of property, real and personal being the kinds distinguished. I desire to record an emphatic protest against the employment of a method, which appears good enough for a special purpose in the absence of anything better, for purposes of a totally different kind, where a different degree of accuracy, which the figures are not susceptible of, may be necessary. Whether estimates of property, and the different kinds of it, can be made for such a purpose as discussing the incidence of taxation, or the like practical objects, is a point at least on which I reserve my own opinion. At any rate, those who make such estimates are bound *in limine* to justify their method, and to prove that the necessary degree of accuracy for the purpose they have in view is obtainable. For any such purpose as that now in hand, comparatively rough estimates are all that are required, and comparatively rough estimates are all that it is proposed to make.

An explanation at the outset as to the method followed may also be allowed. The object being to ascertain the accumulations of capital, and not primarily the amount of capital itself at a given time, it is an obvious suggestion that the problem may be attacked directly. Why not, it is said, reckon up the savings annually as they are made in the different forms in which they are made ? This point was glanced at in my former paper, and reasons were given for the method actually followed ; but this question of method is of some importance, and, perhaps, demands somewhat fuller illustration.

The objection to the method of merely recording investments as they are made, instead of valuing the whole property of the country at different dates, is first of all, its incompleteness. It is difficult, if not impossible, if we follow it, to take any account of the regular annual investment by individuals in their own business or properties, which must always be the most important form of saving—far more important in amount than the visible public investments. Next, even if it could be complete, this method makes no allowance for bad investment, for the waste of capital which is possible, (the invest-ment so-called having been merely a form of throwing money into the sea), and it makes no allowance for the depreciation or loss of capital in old investments which have become obsolete or use-less. By valuing property at different times as it stands, any inclusion of capital which has been merely wasted, or which has depreciated, is avoided. At each date only effective capital is reckoned. No doubt in many cases the valuation may represent a greater sum than has actually been invested, even when allowance is made for changes in prices ; but the element of judiciousness in investments is as much to be allowed for as any other in a question of the amount of property in a country, and this is really a reason for the method and not against it. For these two reasons mainly, then, the method of valuing property at different times is to be preferred to the method of counting up investments as they are made. It is the more complete method of the two, including all kinds of private as well as public investment, and it allows, as the other cannot do, for loss and depreciation of old investments. There is a third reason in its favour. The figures when obtained by it can be compared with those obtained from the annual records of investments, and this comparison is useful in many problems, of which the amount of free savings coming on the general investment markets —*i.e.*, the Stock Exchange—and the proportion that amount bears to the whole savings of a country is one.

Of course, however, the exact meaning attached to the word accumulation must always be kept in mind by those who engage in the discussion. No method can be quite perfect. If we record merely investments as they are made, without considering whether they are judicious or not, and disregarding altogether the loss and depreciation of old investments, we get a fact which may be useful in some discussions, though not in others ; and may call it, if we so please, the annual accumulation of capital. If we wish, however, to compare effective capital or property at one time with effective capital or property at another, we must proceed by the method of periodic stocktaking and valuation, and call the difference between the valuations at different times allowing for changes of prices, the accumulation of capital. The amounts to be dealt with in either case might not in some cases differ greatly from each other, but the different senses in which the words may be used, and the possibility of differences in the amounts of the accumulations as differently defined and ascertained, should, of course, be kept in mind.

There is yet another preliminary point. The method of estimating the property in the country at different times, which was followed in my former paper, it will be remembered, was to take the income returned for assessment to the Income Tax, capitalise the different portions of that income derived from capital—land, houses, and so on,—at so many years' purchase, and then make an estimate for other property in the country where the income was not got within the sweep of the Income Tax net. A similar method, it may be repeated in passing, as mentioned in the former paper, was first employed by Mr. Newmarch in the *Economist* in 1873. Mr. Newmarch by various calculations had arrived at the opinion that to obtain an idea of the annual accumulation in the country the amount of the Income Tax assessments might be multiplied by 20, and the difference between the totals at different dates would represent the accumulation. It was with some pleasure I noticed afterwards that Mr. Newmarch in the last paper he read to the Statistical Society adopted the more detailed plan of my former paper and practically accepted the figures, substituting them for those he had formerly used. In such a method, then, to come to the point I wish now to make, a great deal turns upon the number of years' purchase assigned to each description of income, and the question arises, when valuations at different dates are compared, or when the valuations of different countries are compared, how far is it expedient or necessary to vary the number of years' purchase as regards particular descriptions of property ? In my former essay this difficulty was evaded. Dealing with one country only, the question of assigning a different number of years' purchase because of a comparison with other countries, or between different parts of the same country, did not arise; while I assumed that as the tendency had rather been in the interval compared, for all classes of income to be valued, as time went on, at a greater number of years' purchase, the rate of interest falling in the interval, the effect of ignoring this element would be for the figures stating the accumulation of capital to err rather by defect than by excess, which it was desirable to avoid. Now, however, the question of the number of years' purchase may require discussion. Since 1875 the capital value of many sorts of income, the number of years' purchase for which it will sell, has undoubtedly risen. As regards other kinds of income, however, such as the rent of land, the number of years' purchase at which the same nominal rental will pass in the market, has undoubtedly diminished. The question seems, therefore, not quite so simple as it was. On what basis should changes of the kind be dealt with theoretically if the general totals are likely to be seriously affected ? It is proposed also, as will be seen, to compare different parts of the United Kingdom with each other as well as to make more extended comparisons with foreign countries. Here the element of the number of years' purchase must be dealt with explicitly. In some references a few years ago which I made to the capital of Ireland I assumed that landed property in that country ought to be valued at a smaller number of years' purchase of the rental than landed property in the rest of the United Kingdom, and I found to my astonishment that some critics assumed the contrary. Because in capitalising the lands of the United Kingdom I had assumed so many years' purchase *on the average*, therefore it was to be assumed, I was told, when one part of the kingdom was put against another, that the valuation of each description of property in each part should be at the same number of years' purchase! Such a procedure, in my opinion, would be most absurd. But whatever may be the right conclusion, the subject at any rate, owing to the different circumstances with which I have now to deal, as compared with what was the case formerly, and owing also to the wider scope of the paper, will require the most careful attention.

Another point of some difficulty, which was glided over in my former paper, though not altogether *sub silentio*, has also become too serious to be passed over now in a similar manner. This is the difficulty caused by changes of prices, and—to come to the period now specially under review, viz., the period 1875-85—the difficulty caused by the fall of prices in that interval. The valuations being of property, and the money value of all kinds of property depending on the prices of commodities directly or indirectly, anything which changes the prices must change the valuation. Changes of prices between two different dates, where they are at all serious, have accordingly to be allowed for in estimating the growth of capital by the difference in the two valuations; and the practical difficulty in handling the figures, it will be seen, is somewhat formidable. The point will be dealt with in its order when it arises, but it has to be mentioned at the outset to give all interested warning of a discussion which must take up a great deal of space. It is a purely unavoidable complication of our task.

# CHAPTER II.

—

## THE VALUATION OF 1885.

The first step to be taken, following the method of the former paper, is to look at the valuation of the nation's property at the present time.

For this purpose the accompanying Table (A), (see p. 11), has been drawn up in a form precisely similar to that of a similar table in 1875. The classifications of the items of the nation's property follows closely as far as possible that of the Income Tax returns, and additions are then made for property which is not accounted for as connected with any income dealt with by the Income Tax. The Table of 1875, it may be mentioned, is followed so closely that the list of items is word for word the same.

The table speaks very much for itself, but a few observations may be made before we pass to the proper subject of this essay—viz., the recent accumulations of capital.

I have first of all, then, to draw attention to the fact that it has been thought necessary in one or two cases to vary the number of years' purchase

[CONTINUED ON P. 12.]

## TABLE A.

Amount of Income in Income-tax Returns, derived from Capital, Number of Years' Purchase at which the same may be Capitalised, and Approximate Amount of Capital; together with Estimate of remaining Income and Capital of the Country.

[000's omitted in amount columns.]

| — | Income. | Years' Purchase. | Capital. | Years' Purchase & Capital at Years' P'rchase Employed for 1875, where a Change has now been made. |
|---|---|---|---|---|
| | £ | | £ | £ |
| Under Schedule A. | | | | |
| Lands | 65,039, | 26 | 1,691,313,* | 30 | 1,951,170 |
| Houses | 128,459, | 15 | 1,926,885, | ... | ... |
| Other profits | 877, | 30 | 26,310, | ... | ... |
| Schedule B. | | | | |
| (Farmers profits) | 65,233, | 8 | 521,864, | 10 | 652,330 |
| Schedule C. | | | | |
| (Public funds less home funds)... | 21,096, | 25 | 527,400, | ... | ... |
| Under Schedule D. | | | | |
| Quarries | 933, | 4 | 3,732, | ... | ... |
| Mines | 7,603, | 4 | 30,412, | ... | ... |
| Ironworks | 2,265, | 4 | 9,060, | ... | ... |
| Gasworks | 5,026, | 25 | 125,650, | 20 | 100,520 |
| Waterworks | 3,260, | 20 | 65,200, | ... | ... |
| Canals, &c. | 3,546, | 20 | 70,920, | ... | ... |
| Fishings | 618, | 20 | 12,360, | ... | ... |
| Market tolls, &c. | 590, | 20 | 11,800, | ... | ... |
| Other public companies | 34,789, | 20 | 695,780, | 15 | 521,835 |
| Foreign and Colonial securities, &c. | 9,859, | 20 | 197,180, | 15 | 147,885 |
| Railways in United Kingdom... | 33,270, | 28 | 931,560, | 25 | 831,750 |
| „ out of United Kingdom | 3,808, | 20 | 76,160, | ... | ... |
| Interest paid out of rates, &c. ... | 5,041, | 25 | 126,025, | ... | ... |
| Other profits | 1,435, | 20 | 28,700, | ... | ... |
| Trades and professions—one-fifth of total income of £180,000,000 | 36,096, | 15 | 541,440, | ... | ... |
| Total under Income-tax ... | 428,843, | ... | 7,619,751, | ... | 7,661,894 |
| Trades and professions omitted, 20 per cent. of amount assessed, or £36,000,000, of which one-fifth is ...) | 7,219, | 15 | 108,285, | ... | ... |
| | 960,† | 15 | 14,400, | ... | ... |
| Income of non-Income-tax paying classes derived from capital | 67,000, | 5 | 335,000, | ... | ... |
| Foreign investments, not in Schedules C and D | 50,000, | 10 | 500,000, | ... | ... |
| Moveble property not yielding income, e.g., furniture of houses, &c., works of art, &c. | ... | ... | 960,000, | ... | ... |
| Government and local property, say | ... | ... | 500,000, | ... | ... |
| | 554,022, | ... | 10,037,436, | ... | 10,079,579 |

* This is the result of capitalising lands in Ireland at 15 years' purchase, and in England and Scotland at 28 years' purchase. The average for the United Kingdom is an infinitesimal fraction over 26 years' purchase.      † Estimate of income escaping assessment by raising of limit of exemption in 1876.

from that which was employed in the former paper
for 1875, and that where this is done it is noted in
supplemental columns what the figures would have
been if the number of years' purchase formerly used
had been retained.  The general effect, it will be
seen, is that while there are alterations in the relative
amounts of particular items of capital *inter se,* the
final totals arrived at are not materially different, in
consequence of the changes made in the number of
years' purchase, from what they would have been if
no such changes had been made.  The total valuation
now arrived at is 10,037 millions, and if no change
had been made in any case in the number of years'
purchase the total would have been 10,079 millions.

The next remark to be made is on the magnitude of the sum total arrived at.  The round figure
of 10,000 millions is about $13\frac{1}{2}$ times the amount of
the National Debt, and gives a sum of about £270 for
every person in the United Kingdom, equal, at an
average of five persons per family, to about £1,350
per family.  If the valuation is at all moderate, the
figure shows how much on the average each family in
the United Kingdom possesses.

Of course, there are "averages" and "averages."
An average may be made up of items where the preponderant numbers individually nearly correspond
with it, or it may be made up of items where the
preponderant numbers are greatly under it, a minority
throwing it up.  There is no doubt that, as regards
the distribution of wealth in the United Kingdom the
average is made up most unevenly.  For convenience'
sake the figures are reduced to so much per head or'
per family, but the actual distribution is a different
matter.

Coming to the different items, the *first* to notice is the valuation of lands constituting about one-sixth of the total valuation. The income of £65,039,000 capitalised at 26 years' purchase shows a capital of £1,691,000,000.

The question will perhaps be raised whether 26 years' purchase, looking at the uncertainty of rentals, and the unsaleability of land on the basis of actual rentals, is not too high, although it is a great reduction upon the number of 30 years which was employed with general approval in my former paper. It is a great point, however, in such investigations to beware of panic figures, and of extreme quotations characteristic of a transitional and uncertain period. It is too soon yet to tell at what rent land in the United Kingdom will settle after the revolutionary circumstances of the last ten years, the adjustments required by the new circumstances being still in progress. We may be sure, however, looking at the low rate of interest for money, that the number of years' purchase, when a settlement is made, will in no case be so low as 26, while there is much land at present, which, for residential and other reasons, has not participated in the extreme fall of values of which we have heard so much. The figure of 26 years, therefore, is suggested as a safe mean in the present exceptional and transitional circumstances, and in the present uncertainty regarding the income on which the valuation is based.

It may be added also that, in fixing the number of 26 years, special regard is had to the peculiar circumstances of Ireland, where it has not been thought safe to assume a higher average than 15 years on the nominal Income Tax assessment of about

£10,000,000, which must be largely nominal only.
The average assumed for England and Scotland is 28
years, by which a large allowance is made for residential and other land which has not yet participated
in the extreme fall to which much land has been
subject.

To prevent misconstruction, moreover, I have to
remind those interested that the valuation is made
as for the year ended 31st March, 1885, when the
extreme depreciation of agricultural produce lately
witnessed had not yet taken place.

2. The second item to be noticed is that of
"Houses." The total income here is over 128 millions, and at 15 years' purchase the capital is 1,927
thousand millions—nearly one-fifth of the total valuation. "Houses" thus constitute the most important
item in the valuation, being more important than
lands which at the time of my former paper had still
the undoubted pre-eminence, being nearly a fourth
of the total.

The value of "Houses" alone, per head of the
population of the United Kingdom is about £54,
equal to £270 per family, at five persons per family.

To prevent misconstruction, it should be understood
that the item of "Houses" in Schedule A in the Income Tax Returns, includes not merely dwelling
houses, as might at first be supposed, but messuages
and tenements generally, that is factories, workshops,
warehouses, &c., these appearing to constitute about
a fifth part of the total, according to the returns of
Inhabited House Duty ; and on the other hand, it
does not include "Farm Houses" which are comprised
with the item of lands. Deducting on the one-side,
however, messuages which are not dwelling houses,

and adding on the other side the separate value of
farm houses, if it could be separated, the total housing
of the people of the United Kingdom would not
probably be far short of the figures above stated.

3. The third item I have to remark on is that of
Schedule B. (Farmers' Profits), where the income,
£65,233,000, is substantially the same as that of
lands in Schedule A. This income, at 8 years' purchase, the figure assumed, brings out a capital of
£522,000,000.

In this case the figure of 8 years is substituted for
that of 10 years which was employed for 1875,
and in making the substitution I have been influenced by the uncertainty of the income, and the
exceptional and transitional circumstances, which
appeared to necessitate a similar substitution as
regards the capital value of lands in Schedule A.
In normal circumstances I should consider 10 years'
purchase the safer number to use on the basis of
rental, so as to obtain a total of capital corresponding to Schedule B.

On the reading of my former paper, Major Craigie
expressed the opinion that 10 years' purchase was too
high, and he suggested a lower figure, which would
have amounted to about 7 years' purchase of the
rental of that time. Now he suggests, as I understand, a figure which would amount to about 5 years'
purchase of the rental last returned.

The point is of very small importance for the
special object of this paper. The difference in the
number of years' purchase assigned hardly makes
any appreciable difference in the accumulation of
capital in the interval. The total difference in
income under Schedule B, between 1875 and 1885,

is about £1,500,000 only, and at 10 years' purchase this would represent a diminution of £15,000,000 in capital, at 7 years' a diminution of £10,500,000—figures quite insignificant in comparison with the immense accumulations here in question, while the difference between them is only £4,500,000—a still smaller figure in the comparison.  Even the total farming capital, whether we take it at 300, 500, or 700 millions, is comparatively a small item in a valuation of 10,000 millions.  There is a good rule about "de minimis," which is as applicable in statistics as in other matters, or even more applicable. It would be very foolish for those of us who are not agriculturists to waste time, in a question like this, on discussions about agricultural capital.

As the point has been raised, however, I have thought it interesting to look into the matter a little, and have a few observations to make, a small fraction of what I could write, if necessary ; but I must refrain from introducing matter not germane to the main topic.  What seems to have misled Major Craigie, as I believe, is a misconception on two points.  He does not allow, first of all, for the necessity of dealing with agricultural capital, in a question like the present, in such a way that all the capital needed for the occupation, whoever owns it, is comprised.  This is the general method used with reference to railway and other income in the Income Tax Schedules.  A railway is not looked at from the point of view of the ordinary shareholder who really runs it, practically borrowing from the preference share and debenture holders to enable him to do so, but the whole value of the undertaking and its equipment is included.  The same with gas works and other business, and with trades and professions. If this had not been done, then it would have been necessary to make a special item of that floating capital which bankers and other capitalists handle and lend in various ways to the active agents in industrial enterprise. Dealing with agricultural capital, then, in the same way a little reflection will show that it must include three main items :—(1) The value of one year's crops, or thereabouts ; (2) the value of the live-stock; and (3) the value of the farming machinery and tools. At one period of the year, viz., harvest time, there must be practically a year's crops on the field or in stock, if not more ; the live-stock and equipment are always there, and *somebody owns them.* On this basis, however, in 1875, a much larger figure than Major Craigie's £476 millions must have been arrived at. Sir James Caird, not long after, in his book on the landed interest, valued the annual crops in the United Kingdom at 260 millions, and the live-stock at the same amount—total 520 millions ; while the farm equipment in machinery and tools could not then be put at less than about £1 per acre, making another 50 millions*—total 570 millions for the cultivated area alone. In such a matter, of course, being an outsider, I can only follow agricultural authority as regards the data, and the data undoubtedly show that Major Craigie's former estimate was too low for such a purpose as that of the present valuations. Besides all this something should be allowed for the tenants' unexhausted improvements, and any beneficial interest he may have through his rent not being a rack-rent.

The other point where Major Craigie appears to

---

* See " The Book of the Farm," vol. ii., pp. 443-5, edition 1871.

have misconceived the problem we must deal with here, is in not attending sufficiently to the nature of Schedule B, which is called for brevity's sake the "Farmer's Profits" Schedule, but which is strictly and technically the occupation of land. Even if Major Craigie was right, therefore, in his estimate of 476 millions for farmers' capital, he had still to consider what other occupation of land there might be under Schedule B. There are 30,000,000 acres here to be dealt with, no doubt for the most part mountain and waste, but still worth something, and possessing occupation capital. I need only mention one item— viz., woods and plantations—to show what a huge hiatus there may be here. Of these there are nearly 3,000,000 acres in the United Kingdom, and one has only to read the recent reports and evidence of the Select Committees of the House of Commons on Forestry to perceive that in spite of the fall in timber, as in other things, compared with former times, the woods and plantations have a considerable annual value and a still more considerable capital value to correspond, which would not, from the mode of valuation, be comprised in the income and capital under lands in Schedule A. This capital I should be disposed to estimate even now at something like 60 or 70 millions sterling, while in 1875, with much higher prices then prevailing, it was probably not less than 100 millions sterling, making with the capital of the cultivated area above mentioned a total of 670 millions, which was just about the figure in my former paper. It may be urged that timber goes with the land, and is included in the valuation of the land, but this is not so according to the method of the Income Tax

returns. The real income from woods and plantations is not included in Schedule A, but only an
assumed agricultural or prairie value. In a stricter
account other items would have to be included, so
that even if the 100 millions for woods and forests
only is a little excessive the aggregate of 670 millions would not be far out. The bulk of the 670
millions is in any case sufficiently accounted for, and
there are not materials, I fear, for more exact valuation. In this way it is easy to see that the criticisms
of Major Craigie have been based partly on miscon-
ceptions of the problem. His figures were altogether too low as an estimate of capital under
Schedule B, partly from his narrow construction of
the term capital itself, and partly from his ignoring
the large capital under Schedule B, which was capital
of the occupation of land certainly, but not farmers'
capital at all.

The point, as I have explained, is of small importance for the present paper ; but perhaps the digres-
sion may be permitted for the sake of the explanations
of method that have arisen upon it. In such a
general valuation, it is, above all, important to leave
out nothing of substantial consequence. It would
not do to construe the word capital very narrowly in
a given case, and thus leave out something which is
not included anywhere else, so that it is left out
altogether.

For the present time, I have not *data* on the same
authority to refer to, but the recent valuations by
Mr. Howard and Mr. Turnbull as to agricultural
crops, and a portion of the property, show approximately that the present valuation of a little over
£520,000,000 cannot be far off the mark. The

crops sold off the farm are valued by Mr. Howard at a little over £200,000,000,* and while this is the value of the crops in the final form, so that it may be said part of it is the value of the live stock in another form, Mr. Howard's calculations show that the value of the crops before any part is converted into meat or dairy produce cannot be far short of this figure. Then the value of the live stock, exclusive of horses, is put by Mr. Turnbull at £150,000,000,* to which, if we add horses, farm implements, &c., at about £50,000,000 each, we have a further sum of £250,000,000—total £450,000,000, exclusive of the value of woods and other items under Schedule B, the importance of which has already been discussed. Without making exact calculations, it is easy to see that the sum of £520,000,000 for occupation capital under Schedule B—a wider term than agricultural capital, though the item is popularly spoken of as agricultural capital only—cannot be far off the mark, even if a stricter mode of valuation is followed than what is possible on the basis of Income Tax figures.

4. The next item to comment upon is that of "Public Funds less Home Funds," which shows an income of £21,096,000, and at 25 years' purchase a capital of £527,000,000.

I have some remarks to make on this item in connection with the general subject of foreign investments, and I propose afterwards to bring together with this view the various items in the Income Tax assessments which deal with such foreign income; but let me refer just for a moment here to the fact that the "Home Funds," included in Schedule C, are

---

* All these valuations also are at lower prices than were ruling in 1885.

here omitted in valuing the general property of the country. The reason I gave for this omission was stated as follows in my paper in 1878 :—

" As regards the second deduction, it will only be proper, I think, that in such a computation as this, we should not reckon the National Debt twice over,* and that would be the effect of our capitalising the whole of Schedule C. The National Debt is a mortgage upon the aggregate fortune of the country. As we may assume it to be practically all held at home, we may reckon up our whole estate without deducting the debt, whereas we should have to deduct it if it were held by foreigners ; but while we do not deduct the debt from the total of our estate, neither can we add it without falling into error."

And I desire to call attention here very specially to the fact that this omission was, and is, made. In these figures, the capital represented by the National Debt is not represented as part of the property of the community, though, of course, to each individual holding a portion of the National Debt the holding is property.

What I have done is clear enough, and I believe that, on the whole, the reason assigned is a good one. But I should not censure very much any one who included the National Debt as a part of the capital of the community. The general reason for such a course would be that as the debt is a charge upon the resources of the community, the money expression of all the other capital of the community is less than it would otherwise be by the amount of the debt. If there were no National Debt, lands, houses,

---

* The phrase, " twice over," is a slip. It would have been more accurate to say that the National Debt is not reckoned at all, which is the obvious meaning of the passage.

and every other description of property would exchange for rather more than they now do.  The debt
in this view represents a certain distribution of part
of the capital of the country, and we do not get a
complete view of the capital unless we include it.
Where the Debt is all held at home the point may
be of importance in making comparisons with other
countries, or in making comparisons between different
dates in the same country where the amount of the
Debt has changed much in the interval.  I am bound
to admit that in my view there is something in this
reasoning, though it seems a strange thing at first
sight to talk of debt as capital.  Practically, however, for the reasons above given, I have thought it
safer not to include the debt, and as regards the
United Kingdom, at least, the debt not having much
changed in recent years, the point is not of much
importance in dealing with the question of the
accumulations of capital in a given period.

5. The next observation I have to make on the
table is with reference to the items of quarries, mines,
and ironworks, which are all taken at four years'
purchase, as they were in my former paper.  It has
been suggested since that a larger number of years'
purchase ought to be taken, as the assessments com-
prise royalties as well as the ordinary profits of mines.
Royalties, however, are only a mode of distributing
profit, and experience has shown, I think, the wisdom
of a low valuation.  As will be seen afterwards, the
income from mines and ironworks has dwindled
enormously since 1875 ; it is only now a fraction of
what it was.  Four years' purchase in 1875, as experience has proved, was almost too high.

It may be pointed out also that the result of

capitalising mines and iron works, at four years' purchase, gives only a slightly higher result than the mode of dealing with ordinary business income (trades and professions) afterwards adopted. This plan is to assume that only a fifth of the income is derived from capital, and then to capitalise this fifth at fifteen years' purchase. Fifteen years' purchase of a fifth is equal to three years' purchase of the whole. Mines and ironworks at four years' purchase are thus still valued at more and not less than ordinary business income.

6. The next point to notice, is the number of years' purchase for Gas works, where 25 years have been substituted for 20, which was the years' purchase assigned in 1875. This may seem an unwarrantable change, in the face of the sensation caused by the electric light, and the consequent fear that gas would lose its value. In this and other cases of joint-stock property, however, I have only followed the market somewhat tardily. It may be doubted whether even now sufficient allowance has been made for the fall in the rate of interest. Assuming it to be right in principle to vary the number of years' purchase, as the market varies, this change in detail seems fully justified.

I pass over other minor items in the list—waterworks, canals, &c., fishings, market tolls, &c., where no alteration is made in the number of years' purchase compared with that formerly used ; and

7. I come to three cases where such a change is made, viz., Other Public Companies, Foreign and Colonial Securities, &c., and Railways in the United Kingdom. In the two former cases, the number of years' purchase is raised from 15 to 20, and in the

latter from 25 to 28. It will be for those who take
an interest in such matters to consider whether this
is an adequate, or an insufficient, or an excessive
allowance for the fall in the rate of interest in the
interval. In the case of railways the change is equal
to an average fall in the rate of yield to investors on
railway securities from 4 to £3 11s. 6d. per cent. ;
and in the case of other public companies, &c., to
an average fall as from £6 13s. 4d. to 5 per cent.
The changes, however, correspond to the greater proportionate improvement of credit which seems to
have taken place in what were formerly considered
securities of inferior grade, though really not substantially much inferior. High-class securities have
improved enormously, but as they have risen in price
investors have naturally turned to lower-priced investments where there seemed still some chance of
5 or 6 per cent., and in many of these at any rate,
including foreign securities of all but the first-class,
and excluding the bogus class, there has been an
immense improvement.

The result no doubt is, as we shall see when we
come to make comparisons, to bring out a remarkable
increase of capital in railways and public companies,
without a fully corresponding increase of income ;
and what value is to be placed on an increase of
capital thus arising, as well as on the corresponding
decrease in the case of lands already adverted to, will
be one of the main points for discussion.

8. The remaining items of property corresponding
to income included in the Income Tax assessments
call for little remark. It would have been justifiable,
I think, to increase the number of years' purchase
applied to railways out of the United Kingdom, as it

has been increased in the case of foreign securities, but I have been afraid of exaggerating. A larger number of years' purchase might also be assigned to the "Interest paid out of rates," but this has been avoided for the same reason. As to the method followed in dealing with Trades and Professions, I need only repeat what was said in my former paper. I have here followed Mr. Dudley Baxter's calculations —viz., to assume that one-fifth of the income is derived from capital, and then to capitalise at 15 years' purchase. This is especially a figure where no exactness is possible. Trades and professions include to some extent the salaries of clerks and other employés where there is no corresponding capital; but they are, no doubt, made up for the most part of really trading and professional incomes, where capital is indispensable to the income, but where the income as undoubtedly is mainly dependent on personal exertions. If a better plan can be suggested for dealing with this part of the Income Tax, I shall gladly follow it.

9. Coming last of all to the items of capital either arising from incomes below the Income Tax limit or being property of another kind, I have to notice, to begin with, the first two of these items—viz., trades and professions, which ought to have been assessed and are not, and incomes of trading and professional persons below the Income Tax limit, which are capitalised at five years' purchase. These are, of course, very rough estimates indeed, designed to prevent the complete omission of something which ought to have been dealt with somehow. Here, again, I have been guided by Mr. Dudley Baxter, who explains in his Essay on National Income his mode

of estimating the two kinds of income which lay
intermediate between incomes comprised in the
Income Tax assessments on the one side and working
class incomes on the other. The only point I have to
notice here is the special inclusion of a certain income
which has fallen below the Income Tax limit since
1875 by the raising of the lower limit of the Income
Tax since that date. On this head, however, I may
refer simply to what is said in the table and the notes.
The point could not be passed over.

10. The next item to notice is that of foreign investments not in Schedules C or D, where a large
amount of income—viz., £50,000,000—is taken note
of, and capitalised at 10 years' purchase. Wonder is
expressed at so much foreign income escaping taxation, but, in spite of all that has been done since
1875 to get hold of such income for the revenue—
and a great deal, I think, has been done—I must
appeal to a few broad considerations to justify the
figure put down, as I did in my former paper, to
justify a similar figure.

The best way to look at the matter is to put
together all the foreign income which the Income
Tax authorities get hold of, and compare them with
other known facts :—

|  | Thousands. |
|---|---|
|  | £ |
| Public Funds (Schedule C) ... ... ... ... ... ... | 21,096 |
| Foreign and Colonial Securities (Schedule D) ... ... | 9,859 |
| Railways out of United Kingdom (Schedule D) ... ... | 3,808 |
|  | 34,763 |
| Foreign Investments not in Schedules C or D ... ... | 50,000 |
|  | 84,763 |

It is obvious that the £34,763,000 is too small, whatever may be thought of the proposed addition of £50,000,000 for the income "omitted." I have to submit, however, on this last head the table in the Appendix (Table I), showing from an analysis of Stock Exchange lists how probable it is that the income from foreign public securities alone coming to English people is enormously larger than the sum of £34,763,000 which the Income Tax authorities get hold of, while there is an immense investment besides through private channels and by mercantile houses with partners and establishments abroad. It should be explained, moreover, that a great deal of this income may escape assessment to the Income Tax in no improper way. The partners residing abroad of firms which are really English, but which are domiciled abroad, are perhaps under no obligation to return the income, though their wealth and income are English wealth and income, and much profit that may be made by such partners may be eventually brought home as capital and not as income, and so escape assessment.

11. The next item is that of movable property not yielding income, which is assumed to amount to half the valuation of houses. This does not pretend to be much more than a guess, though it was not arrived at without some data. It has since been very generally accepted. In any case it is a rough figure, and is affected, of course, by the circumstance that the item "houses" in the Income Tax assessments does not correspond exactly with dwelling houses.

12. The last item of all, is that of government and local property. Here again the figure is somewhat rough. But army property, navy property, and

public buildings of all kinds are government property, which must come to something, while local property of every kind cannot now be less than three hundred millions. It has increased on a moderate calculation from the amount of local loans, and the amount annually repaid, by about 100 millions at least, in the ten years specially under review. The figure here inserted certainly cannot err much by excess.

Large as the figures are, therefore, the estimate of 10,000 millions as the property of the United Kingdom valued as a going concern does not seem unreasonable. Of this sum again, nearly 8,500 millions must be reckoned as income yielding, the corresponding income being about 552 millions. The figures are truly bewildering, but it is quite certain that some such figures are about the mark. Valued as a going concern at the current prices of the individual items of the property, the business carried on by the community within the British Isles, with the property of every kind they possess, would exchange for all this money.

# CHAPTER III.

## THE RECENT PROGRESS.

Our special business, however, is not with the valuation of the national estate at the present time, but with the accumulation of capital in recent years. For that purpose, instead of the 30 years' comparison which was all that was possible when I wrote ten years ago, it is now possible to make a comparison in the same detail for two ten-yearly periods.

I shall begin, however, by comparing 1885 with 1875, which can be compared in the minutest detail, and then go on to compare 1865-75 with 1875-85, which cannot be done in quite so much detail. For this purpose I have copied in full the valuation for 1875, which appeared in my former paper, and I have also prepared a comparative table showing, with less detail, the increase in 1875 over 1865, and the increase in 1885 over 1875. (See valuation of 1875, p. 30, and Comparative Table, 1865-75-85, pp. 43.) Comparing 1885 with 1875 only, as may be done by looking at the accompanying table (p. 30), and referring

[CONTINUED ON P. 31.]

## TABLE B.

*Amount of Income in Income Tax Returns, derived from Capital; Number of Years' Purchase at which the same may be Capitalised, and Approximate amount of Capital; together with Estimate of remaining Income and Capital in the Country.* [*Year 1875—Extracted from Paper on Recent Accumulations of Capital in the United Kingdom. Read before Statistical Society, January, 1878. " See Essays in Finance," 1st Series, p. 176.*]

[000's omitted in amount columns.]

| | Income. | Years' P'rchase | Capital. |
|---|---|---|---|
| Under Schedule A— | £ | | £ |
| Lands | 66.911, | 30 | 2,007,330, |
| Houses | 94,638, | 15 | 1,419,570, |
| Other Profits | 883, | 30 | 26,490, |
| Schedule B— | | | |
| (Farmers' profits) | 66,752, | 10 | 667,520, |
| Schedule C— | | | |
| (Public funds less home funds) | 20,767, | 25 | 519,175, |
| Under Schedule D— | | | |
| Quarries | 916, | 4 | 3,664, |
| Mines | 14,108, | 4 | 56,432, |
| Ironworks | 7,261, | 4 | 29,044, |
| Gasworks | 2,630, | 20 | 52,600, |
| Waterworks | 1,869, | 20 | 37,380, |
| Canals, &c. | 1,007, | 20 | 20,140, |
| Fishings | 207, | 20 | 4,140, |
| Market Tolls, &c. | 842, | 20 | 16,840, |
| Other public companies | 25,647, | 15 | 384,705, |
| Foreign and colonial securities, &c. | 6,836, | 15 | 102 540, |
| Railways in United Kingdom | 26.215, | 25 | 655,375, |
| „ out of United Kingdom | 1,330, | 20 | 26,600, |
| Interest paid out of rates, &c. | 2,647, | 25 | 66,175, |
| Other profits | 1,120, | 20 | 22,400, |
| Trades and professions—one-fifth of total income of £175,000,000 | 35,000, | 15 | 525,000, |
| Total under Income Tax | 377,586, | ... | 6,643,120, |
| Trades and professions omitted, 20 per cent. of amount assessed, or £35,000,000, of which one-fifth is | 7,000, | 15 | 105,000, |
| Income of non-income-tax paying classes derived from capital | 60,000, | 5 | 300,000, |
| Foreign investments not in Schedules C or D | 40,000, | 10 | 400,000, |
| Movable property not yielding income, e.g., furniture of houses, &c., works of art, &c. | ... | ... | 700,000, |
| Government and local property, say | ... | ... | 400,000, |
| | 484,586, | ... | 8,543,120, |

back to the table for 1885 (on p. 11), the general
result is that the capital of the United Kingdom,
which appeared in 1875 to be about 8,500 millions,
is now estimated by an exactly similar process at
10,037 millions in 1885. The increase between the
two dates is 1,489 millions, or almost exacly 17½ per
cent. The increase is not so great as in the previous
decade, for if the increase had continued at the former
rate of 40 per cent. in ten years, the total estimated
capital in 1885, instead of being over 10,000 millions,
would have been just under 12,000 millions, and
the increase would have amounted to 3,420 millions
instead of being 1,489 millions only. Still the figures
are very large, and for the present we may postpone
any discussion of the relative rate of growth in 1865-75
and the more recent period.

The more prominent details, apart from the special
questions to be presently discussed, do not seem to
require much comment. I shall make a few observations on the principal items in their order.

1. No one will be surprised at the reduction shown
in the item of lands. The income assessed has fallen
from £66,911,000 to £65,039,000, and as the number
of years' purchase assigned is also less, there is a
corresponding reduction of capital amounting to
£316,000,000 on a total of £2,007,000,000, or over
15 per cent.

If there is any surprise at all it will be that the
reduction is not much greater. The fall in the value
of agricultural produce, and the consequent fall in
rents, have been notorious. The wonder will be that
the income from lands in these returns, and consequently the capitalised value, according to the method
of estimating here followed, have not fallen more.

In explanation, I have to suggest the following reasons why the reduction of income and capital here shown should not correspond to the popular impression of what has been going on :—

*(a.)* The valuation follows somewhat slowly the change in the property itself, and the maximum valuation of lands, before the fall of prices began to have effect, was not reached until after 1875, the fall of prices not beginning to tell until about 1881. Comparing the maximum reached after 1875, viz., £69,549,000 in 1880, with the figure of £65,039,000 for 1885, the apparent reduction of income is not merely 2·8 per cent., but nearly 7 per cent. And the apparent reduction of capital value, owing to the diminution in the number of years' purchase, would, of course, be greater still. Even this reduction is still small compared with the popular impression ; but, allowing that the reduction still lags behind the actual change in the property, as the valuation of 1875 lagged behind the enhancement of value still going on then, we may expect that later returns will show a greater change.

(*b.*) To some extent the figures of the Income Tax Valuation as regards lands have been stereotyped. In past times, it may be allowed, they did not show the real variation in money income that took place from period to period ; and as they did not show the increase, neither have they shown the decrease. This is especially the case as regards Irish land, where Griffith's valuation seems to have been followed year after year, although it was much under the rents of 1875, and is not now nearly so much under them.

A defect of this kind in the Income Tax Valuations is, of course, a drawback to the use of them in showing the accumulations of capital in different periods, and if it were general throughout the returns would make it hardly possible to use them at all ; but there is no reason to believe the defect to be at all general.

(c.) A large amount of "lands" has practically a residential as distinguished from an agricultural value, and the capital value of such lands will not change as that of merely agricultural land changes.

(d.) The income from different sorts of agricultural land has diminished in very varying degrees, while the effect on landlords' rent has also been partially mitigated by the fact that tenant farmers, as a rule, in England have not been rackrented, that they have had virtually a beneficial interest in their holdings, and that the loss by agricultural depression has not consequently fallen so exclusively on landlords' rent as it would otherwise have done.

All these are reasons for the item of lands not showing as great a diminution in these returns as it might have been expected to do. The diminution of rent should not have so much effect as is commonly supposed, and the effect in any case is partly postponed. The result will be that when we come to deal with another period of ten years, the increase, if there is an increase, will not appear so great as it would otherwise do ; and the decrease, if there is a decrease, will appear to be more than it will really be, reckoning from the present date—i.e., 1884-85.

2. The next item to comment upon is houses, which show a very large increase—quite as great, nearly, though this is anticipating a little, as the increase between 1865 and 1875. The capital of houses is now much more than lands, being just

under £2,000 millions, and the increase in the decade has been £507 millions, or nearly 36 per cent. Houses, as already noticed, are now the main item in the whole valuation.

Part of the increase may be due to more stringent valuation, a remark which applies to all the heads of the Income Tax ; but, on the whole, the progress in houses seems to correspond fairly well with pro·gress in the country.

We should have expected, perhaps, as the result of the fall of prices, that the increase would not have been quite so great. It is to be observed that the greater part of the increase took place in the first five or six years of the decade, when almost all values were still swelling rapidly. In the last four or five years it has been at a slower rate.

3. The next important item is that of Schedule B —farmers' profits, as it is popularly called, though it includes, as already explained, a good deal more than farmers' profits. Here the decrease corresponds to that of the item "lands," the two valuations being, in fact, substantially the same, and being expressly, according to law, made upon rental in the absence of a formal claim by the farmer, to be assessed after the method of Schedule D, which is practically never made.

Here the change calls for little remark. The reduction of capital in the ten years is from £667,000,000 to £522,000,000, or between 20 and 25 per cent. It seems doubtful whether the diminution in agricultural capital has not been more. One hears of the tenant farmers having lost three rents, or about £200,000,000. I have to suggest, however, as is done regarding lands, that the years 1875 and 1885 do not correspond precisely to the maximum and minimum years which mark the whole change from better to worse in agriculture. Farther, the loss to the farmer is not the same thing for our present purpose as the loss of agricultural capital itself. The tenant farmer's loss may well have been borne in part out of current income, or out of other funds of his own, or at the expense of creditors. The things constituting the capital, the live-stock, &c., may have remained, and in fact, seem to have largely remained, and are only now valued at lower prices. In putting the present figures in the Table, therefore, I must not be understood as under-valuing the amount of the farmer's losses.

Of course, the loss is brought out very largely in the comparison by changing the number of years' purchase, but for this good reason has been shown.

4. The next item of Public Funds less Home Funds, Schedule C, calls for more mark. The change in the ten years is immaterial. The change to notice here is in connection with foreign investments generally, which will be dealt with later.

5. The next items I have to notice are mines and ironworks, which show a great reduction. The income in the case of mines falls in the ten years from £14,108,000 to £7,603,000, or very nearly 50 per cent.; and there is a proportionate reduction in the estimated capital from £56,432,000 to £30,412,000. In the case of ironworks the reduction in income is from £7,261,000 to £2,265,000, and in capital from £29,044,000 to £9,060,000; or a reduction of 69 per cent.

As compared with the general capital of the country the investments in mines and ironworks are not large, and the changes unimportant, but in themselves they are immense. A more fluctuating industry there could hardly be. There is no doubt of these industries having been specially inflated about 1875.

I have already dealt with the suggestion which has been made, since my former paper was written, that the number of years' purchase assigned to the income from mines and ironworks, viz., four years, is too low —that part of the income consists of royalties which are worth a greater number of years' purchase. I may now add that possibly there may be a reason for assigning a larger number of years' purchase in a period of comparatively low income, and a smaller number when the income has been inflated from any cause, but the amounts involved are too small to make the question worth while.

6. The next items are those of gasworks, water-works, canals, &c., fishings and shootings, which are all of a minor character compared with the main items in the Income Tax assessments, but which all show very considerable increase in the ten years, apart from the change in the number of years purchase, viz., gasworks 91 per cent., waterworks, &c., 74½ per cent., canals, &c., 252 per cent., and fishings and shootings 198½ per cent. Part of the increase is no doubt due to transfers from other heads, but there must still be considerable real increase, corresponding to the increase in such an item as houses. I believe the *etcetera* in the case of canals, &c., where the increase is so remarkable, is specially important. It would be a mistake to suppose that canals in particular, which have been so long stationary or declining, have picked up between 1875 and 1885 to the remarkable extent stated.

7. Markets tolls, &c., show a considerable diminution in the ten years, owing, no doubt, to the gradual extinction in this country of all forms of *octroi*. In any case the item is unimportant.

8. The next item to comment upon is that of "other public companies," which shows a remarkable increase of 35·6 per cent. in the income and of 81 per cent. in the capital, the change in the income being from £25,647,000 to £34,789,000, and in the capital from £384,705,000 to £695,780,000. The change in the capital is, of course, largely due to the increased number of years' purchase, but taking the increase on the income only it is still immense. Part of it, we may believe, is due not only to the continuous creation of public companies for new enterprise, which is a process constantly going on, but to the conversion of private firms into limited companies, which has been a marked feature of Stock Exchange business in recent years, and which may help to account, therefore, for the slow increase in "Trades and Professions" to be presently noticed.

9. The next item is that of Railways in the United Kingdom, which show an increase in income in the ten years from £26,215,000 to £33,270,000, and in capital from £655 millions to £931 millions. A large part of the increase of capital is, of course, due to the increase in the number of years' purchase assigned; but even without this enhancement the change would have been very great, as the figures of capital at the present time would then have stood at 832 millions. Here the figures may be compared with the railway returns themselves, which give for, practically, the same dates, viz., the calendar years 1874 and 1884 an increase in income from £26,643,000

to £33,305,000, and in capital from £610 millions to £801 millions. The figures as to capital in the two statements do not correspond, an important difference being made by the change in the number of years' purchase employed in the calculation. Nothing more need be said, however, than what has already been said generally, or will be said later on. The magnitude of railway capital, in reference to capital generally, could not be shown without taking note of its selling value. In any case, it may be pointed out, the Railway Return itself does not contain figures of actual investment. The record of actual investment in railways would show even a smaller figure than that shown by the Railway Return of capital itself. The real investment of railway capital, whether profitable or not, is not the difference in nominal capital shown between 1874 and 1884, amounting to 191 millions, but probably not more than 170 millions, the actual new cash outlay in the interval.

10. The item of interest paid out of rates shows a large increase, though the amount in comparison with the figures here dealt with is, of course, not large. Possibly if this item were larger the question might arise whether it should not be dealt with in the same way as the interest on the National Debt; but the item as yet seems hardly large enough to make it worth while to raise the discussion.

11. The last important item in connection with the Income Tax assessments themselves is that of "Trades and Professions." Here the total income capitalised, according to the method and for the reasons stated in my former paper, is only a portion of the net income assessed, but the proportion maintained is the same, and as the result the increase shown in the income capitalised is from £35,000,000 to £36,096,000, and

in the capital at 15 years' purchase from £525,000,000 to £541,000,000 ; or 3·1 per cent.

This is a very small increase, but a partial explanation has already been suggested in connection with the item of Public Companies, viz., that private firms of late years have been converted in an increasing degree into public companies.

It may also be pointed out that this item has specially suffered between 1875 and 1885 by the change in the lower limit of the Income Tax, and that in all probability the income under this head but for this change would have been £960,000 more than is here estimated ; this sum of £960,000, it will be observed, being specially taken account of in the lower and supplementary part of the above Table, which deals with income and capital not represented by any Income Tax assessment.

12. Apart from the observations already made, and the special remarks on foreign investments which I have reserved to the last, and which apply, strictly speaking, to all parts of the Table, the lower and supplementary part of the Table appears to call for little remark. The estimates of the income of non-income tax paying classes derived from capital, of movable property not yielding income, and of government and local property, are put in almost *pro formâ* and to round off the estimates, and not with any idea that any very exact figures can be stated. The increase of capital altogether under these heads is £513,000,000, out of a total increase of £1,489,000,000, and deducting about £50,000,000 for capital, which would have appeared in the upper part of the Table but for the change in the lower limit of the Income Tax, it is little over £450 millions, or little more than a fourth part of the total increase of capital.

So far as I have been able to do so, I have endeavoured to deal with these rough estimates in a safe manner, and so as not to exhibit too great an accumulation in a given period ; but no one is more sensible than I am that a more exact valuation, if it were possible, might alter the figures somewhat, besides giving information which would be most useful and would enable us to discuss interesting points with minute accuracy, which must now be left undiscussed altogether. Whether, for instance, movable property not yielding income increases at a greater or less rate than other property would be a most interesting point. At present, by the method followed, equality in the rate of increase is assumed, and although this may not be material in a question of the accumulation of capital generally, it would, of course, be most interesting in its own place. I know of no method, however, upon existing data, by which statisticians could attack the problem. The limits of the information available by the method here followed must be distinctly recognised.

I come, then, to the question of foreign investments, which affects many items in the Tables. Putting all the items together, the comparison between 1875 and 1885 is as follows :—

|  | 1875. | 1885. | Increase. |
|---|---|---|---|
|  | Mlns. | Mlns. | Mlns. |
| Public Funds, less House Funds (Schedule C) ... ... ... ... | 20·7 | 21·1 | 0·4 |
| Foreign and Colonial Securities (Schedule D) ... ... ... ... | 6·8 | 9·8 | 3·0 |
| Railways out of United Kingdom (Schedule D) ... ... ... ... | 1·3 | 3·8 | 2·5 |
| Foreign Investments not in C or D (estimated) ... ... ... ... | 40·0 | 50·0 | 10·0 |
|  | 68·8 | 84·7 | 15·9 |

It cannot be said upon these figures that the estimate of the increase of foreign investments between
1875 and 1885 is at all excessive. The total increase
of income assumed is under 16 millions sterling, which
would represent, at 20 years' purchase, more than the
average, a capital of 320 millions only, or 32 millions
per annum. Allowing for all the capital called in
from abroad, of which we have heard so much, it
must be admitted, I think, that the foreign investments between 1875 and 1885 were more than some
30 millions per annum. I have only to refer on this
head to a table which was appended to my essay
on the "Use of Import and Export Statistics,"
which was read to the Statistical Society in March,
1882*, and which I propose to continue in the journal
of the Statistical Society, a summary being here given
in the Appendix. (See Appendix II.) From this
summary it appears that the actual new issues in
the ten years 1876-1885 of Colonial Government
Loans, Municipal Loans, Foreign Government Loans,
and Railway Issues were as follows : —

|  | Millions. £ |
|---|---|
| 1876 ... ... ... ... ... ... ... ... | 25·6 |
| 1877 ... ... ... ... ... ... ... ... | 18·8 |
| 1878 ... ... ... ... ... ... ... ... | 25·9 |
| 1879 ... ... ... ... ... ... ... ... | 23·1 |
| 1880 ... ... ... ... ... ... ... ... | 29·9 |
| 1881 ... ... ... ... ... ... ... ... | 44·0 |
| 1882 ... ... ... ... ... ... ... ... | 45·2 |
| 1883 ... ... ... ... ... ... ... ... | 48·7 |
| 1884 ... ... ... ... ... ... ... ... | 48·9 |
| 1885 ... ... ... ... ... ... ... ... | 51·7 |
| Total ... ... ... ... ... ... | 361·8 |

* See "Essays in Finance," second series, second edition. London :
Geo. Bell and Sons. The table here referred to is printed in the "Statistical Society's Journal " for June, 1882.

—a larger amount than the sum arrived at by capitalising the assumed addition to the income from foreign investments between 1875 and 1885. In addition there were issues of miscellaneous companies and mining companies to a large amount. Besides all this there is the private investment, which must be very large. Of course the period between 1875 and 1885 includes the period of the foreign loan collapses, but the table in the Appendix (Table I.), it will be observed, which compares with a similar table for 1875, is constructed in such a way as to allow for all such collapses. After all, the collapse of Turkish and Peruvian loans and a few minor issues were as nothing to the great business of the market, the collapse at a later date in American railway issues being substantially more serious. Making all allowances, then, the increase here reckoned for the ten years is by no means excessive.

So much for the comparison between 1875 and 1885. I have next to call attention to the accompanying Table (see Table on p. 43), which exhibits the comparative results above dealt with in a more condensed form, and places alongside, in addition, the comparative results for the ten years preceding for which it is impossible to give so many details. The comparison between the progress shown in 1865 and 1875, and the progress now shown, is instructive, both as regards the total amounts and the details.

Between 1865 and 1875 the increase in total capital was from 6,113 millions to 8,548 millions, an increase of 2,435 millions, or 40 per cent. ; whereas now the increase is from 8,548 to 10,037 millions, or 1,489 millions and $17\frac{1}{2}$ per cent. only. Both in amount and percentage the increase in the second

[CONTINUED ON P. 44.]

## TABLE C.

*Approximate Amount of Capital or Property in United Kingdom in 1865, 1875, and 1885, compared.*

| | 1865. | 1875. | 1885. | Increase in 1865-75. | | In. or Dec. in 1875-85. | |
|---|---|---|---|---|---|---|---|
| | | | | Am'unt. | Per C'nt. | Am'unt. | Per Cent. |
| | Mlns. | Mlns. | Mlns. | Mlns. | | Mlns. | |
| — | £ | £ | £ | £ | % | £ | % |
| Lands.......................... | 1,864 | 2,007 | 1,691 | 143 | 8 | −316 | − 15·7 |
| Houses ...................... | 1,031 | 1,420 | 1,927 | 389 | 38 | 507 | 35·7 |
| Farmers' profits ............ | 620 | 668 | 522 | 48 | 8 | −146 | − 21·9 |
| Public funds less home funds ..................... | 211 | 519 | 527 | 308 | 146 | 8 | 1·5 |
| Mines........................... | 19 | 56 | 31 | 37 | 195 | − 25 | − 45 |
| Ironworks ..................... | 7 | 29 | 9 | 22 | 314 | − 20 | − 69 |
| Railways ..................... | 414 | 655 | 932 | 241 | 58 | 277 | 42 |
| Canals ....................... | 18 | 20 | 71 | 2 | 11 | 51 | 255 |
| Gasworks ..................... | 37 | 53 | 126 | 16 | 43 | 73 | 138 |
| Quarries...................... | 2 | 4 | 4 | 2 | 100 | ... | ... |
| Other profits.................. | 55 | 84 | 116 | 29 | 53 | 32 | 38 |
| Other Income-tax income, principally trades and professions and public companies ...... | 660 | 1,128 | 1,664 | 468 | 71 | 536 | 47·5 |
| | 4,938 | 6,643 | 7,620 | 1,705 | 35 | 977 | 14·7 |
| Trades and professions omitted.. | 75 | 105 | 108 | 30 | 40 | 3 | 3 |
| Income from capital of non-income-tax paying classes ... | 200 | 300 | 349 | 100 | 50 | 49 | 16 |
| Foreign investments not in Schedule C and D............... | 100 | 400 | 500 | 300 | 300 | 100 | 25 |
| Movable property not yielding income.......................... | 500 | 700 | 960 | 200 | 40 | 260 | 37 |
| Government and local property, say........................ | 300 | 400 | 500 | 100 | 33 | 100 | 25 |
| | 6,113 | 8,548 | 10,037 | 2,435 | 40 | 1,489 | 17.4 |

ten years is considerably less than in the first ten. Omitting the supplementary items which are not directly based on Income Tax assessments the difference is just as remarkable. The increase between 1865 and 1875 was from 4,938 millions to 6,643 millions, an increase of 1,705 millions, or 35 per cent.; between 1875 and 1885 it is from 6,643 to 7,620 millions, an increase of 977 millions, or about 15 per cent. A little difference would be made in the latter period by adding in about 50 millions of capital representing income transferred from the higher to the lower part of the Table in consequence of the change in the lower limit of the Income Tax, but the difference would not be very material. The rate of increase in the later period would still be less than half what it was in the earlier period.

Looking at the comparison in more detail, the first broad fact noticeable appears to be that, whereas between 1865 and 1875 every item of capital shows an increase—in some cases very little in proportion, but in others a great deal—yet between 1875 and 1885 there are, as already noticed, a good many items of decrease. Lands, Schedule B, and mines and ironworks are all cases of actual decrease—in some cases of very great decrease between 1875 and 1885,—although in each case in the previous period there was an increase, and that increase in the case of mines and ironworks was very large, amounting to 195 and 314 per cent. respectively. Next, it is to be noticed that the rate of increase generally between 1875 and 1885, where there is an increase, is much less, with one or two exceptions, than in the previous ten years, and where the increase is now at an equal or greater rate, it is owing, in part, to the increase in the number of years' purchase at which the income has been capitalised. The following comparison brings the facts on this head to a point :—

*Increase per Cent. of certain Items of Capital in 1865-75 and 1875-85 compared.*

|  | 1865-75. | 1875-85. |
|---|---|---|
| Houses ... ... ... ... ... ... ... ... ... | 38 | 35·7 |
| Public Funds, less House Funds ... ... ... | 146 | 1·5 |
| Railways, United Kingdom ... ... ... ... | 58 | 42·0* |
| Canals, &c. ... ... ... ... ... ... ... ... | 11 | 255 |
| Gasworks ... ... ... ... ... ... ... ... | 43 | 138·0* |
| "Other Profits" ... ... ... ... ... ... ... | 53 | 38·0 |
| Other Income Tax Income ... ... ... ... | 71 | 47·5* |
| Trades and Professions omitted ... ... ... | 40 | 3·0 |
| Income of non-Income Tax paying Classes ... | 50 | 16·0 |
| Foreign Investments, &c. ... ... ... ... ... | 300 | 25·0 |
| Moveable Property not yielding Income ... | 40 | 37·0 |
| Government and Local Property ... ... ... | 33 | 25·0 |

In all directions, therefore, there is a diminution in the rate of increase in the later as compared with the earlier period. The two exceptions are those of canals, &c., and gasworks, where the amounts are too small to be material, and where, in one case, at least—that of canals, &c.—the apparent increase is not improbably due to transfers, and in the other the increase is largely due to the increased number of years' purchase at which the income is capitalised. The broad fact that the change in the rate of increase in the two periods extends throughout almost all the items of the comparison, a decrease in some cases being substituted for an increase, and in others a less rate of increase shown, is not to be qualified in any way. The decrease shown in the general totals is made up of minor changes, all in the same direction.

* In these cases part of the enhancement of capital is due to the increase of the number of years' purchase at which the whole or part of the income is capitalised.

The only apparent exception to the general change is formed by "Houses," and in the corresponding item of capital in the supplementary part of the table, viz., moveable property not yielding income, where the estimate is based on the assumption that such property bears a certain proportion to the capital value of the houses. Here it will be seen the rate of increase in 1865-75 is fairly well maintained in 1875-85. The maintenance of the former rate, however, as regards these two large items, implies, of course, that the general reduction on other heads must be somewhat more than the average of the above totals.

As regards these two special items, again, the point already noticed, that in the last half of the last decade the rate of increase here has slackened greatly, would require serious consideration in forming any conclusions as to the present growth of property in the country as far as its money expression is concerned. There is nothing, indeed, to alter the general impression given by the figures that in the last decade, as compared with the previous decade, something must have happened to diminish the rate of accumulation of capital as expressed in money. The increase in the last decade is not inconsiderable, and if comparison were not made with a preceding decade of a different character would be accepted at once as completely satisfactory, but the comparison cannot but be made and the causes of the difference must be sought for.

The discussion of this comparison and their causes should be one of the most interesting topics of a paper like the present.

Before entering on it, however, let me notice very briefly the other general question which has been

suggested as to varying the number of years' purchase in comparing different periods. In the above
Table, contrary to the practice in 1875, I have in
some cases taken a different number of years' purchase at the two dates compared. Formerly, however, one of my reasons for the contrary course was
to avoid any error by way of excess in estimating the
increase of capital between the two dates. It seems
to be expedient now, in view of the apparent
diminution in the rate of increase of capital, to
avoid any error by way of defect by taking note of
variations in the number of years' purchase, and this
I have accordingly done.

Theoretically there would seem to be no good
argument against altering the number of years' purchase from period to period according to market
changes. Such a course would appear to be absolutely
indispensable if changes in the relative amounts of
property in different categories are to be taken note
of. Possibly with little change in aggregate wealth
between two dates there may be great changes in its
distribution, through a community setting higher
store by one species of it relatively to others at one
time than at another. In the present case, too, it is
notorious that as regards two large branches of property there have been great changes in the last
decade in the common estimates of their value. On
the one hand land sells for a smaller number of years'
purchase of the actual rent than it did. On the
other hand Stock Exchange securities of all descriptions, but especially the highest and the next higher
classes, such as the public funds, colonial securities,
and the like, as above explained, have been rising in
value. There is another reason of a general kind for

varying the number of years' purchase. There is reason to believe that in the last decade the rate of interest on capital has been steadily declining, and this means that the number of years' purchase for which old securities will exchange has increased. Capital has to be invested for a smaller and smaller return. But while this means that, as far as income is concerned, wages and salary receivers get a larger and larger proportion of the whole income of a community, yet accumulated or fixed capital, in relation to commodities or circulating capital, bears a higher value than before, and we do not take note of this change in capital, which is really a mode of accumulation, unless we take note of the change in the number of years' purchase.

Practically, however, I do not, as a rule, vary the number of years' purchase in comparing 1875 with 1885 any more than in comparing 1865 with 1875, when there was perhaps less reason for making a change. I have only made the change in one or two cases where there seemed an obvious necessity. As regards land, for instance, it would be pedantic not to have made a change in view of the fact that the nominal rent in the Income Tax returns has ceased to be the real rent, and that for the present at least the selling value of land is much less than it was. It is quite true that as yet the whole affair is in transition. Land is speculatively depreciated because of the uncertainty as to what the rent is to be reckoned at. When things are more settled it seems quite possible, and even probable, that land will participate in the general tendency of all income from property to pass for an increasing number of years' purchase. But the blow that has been dealt

at land is too big to pass altogether unnoticed even
in this transitionary period: As regards other securities, such as those of the Stock Exchange, again,
the change in the direction of an enhancement of the
years' purchase they command is so great that it
would be pedantic not to recognise the relative
transference of capital. What the community loses
in one direction it gains in another. The increase
of the exchangeable value of a security is an increase
of its real power as capital.

I have further to call attention to what was
noticed at the outset, that the aggregates are little
changed by these changes in the number of years'
purchase ; the items only are changed.

In comparing the different parts of the United
Kingdom with each other, and the United Kingdom
with other countries, we must return to this question of the number of years' purchase, but for the
present we need only notice that the few changes
in the above table appear sufficiently justified by the
special reasons stated.

We come, then, to the practical discussion of the
causes of the change in 1875-85, as compared with
1865-75, in the rate of accumulation of property in
the United Kingdom as expressed in money. How
far is there a change in the rate of accumulation of
things to correspond ? How far is it due to a mere
change in money values ?

The question is not quite a new one. In a very
interesting book, written more than sixty years ago,
called " The Present State of England," by Mr. Joseph
Lowe, which is well-known to students of the litera-
ture of Political Economy, though I must confess, for
my own part, that I was ignorant of it when I wrote

my former paper in 1878, this very question is explicitly treated. Mr. Lowe, in giving an account of English resources, treats in one part of the book of the capital valuation of the country. He employs as his basis the estimate of Mr. Colquhoun (a writer who was most unjustly decried, I think, by M'Culloch), for about the year 1812, and then makes a correction of them by allowing for the fall of prices in the interval. This correction is the more remarkable because Mr. Lowe, in making it, allows for the relative importance of different commodities, applying, correctly in fact, the principle of an index number and discussing with much good sense, the historical index number of Sir George Evelyn, who was the first, so far as I know, to employ the method. I shall have to notice Mr. Lowe's results afterwards, but for the present I am only pointing out that the point I am raising is not really novel, and that it has been present to the minds of former statistical inquirers.* Mr. Lowe also suggested the expediency of a tabular standard of value for making payments which is now exercising not a few minds, and will probably do so for a long time to come, until a solution is found, as the importance of some such standard for deferred payments, let alone statistical inquiries like the present, is beyond all question.

It must be obvious, to begin with, that some correction must be made in the present case for the change in money. On the one hand, the fact of a great reduction of prices between 1875 and 1885 is notorious. On the other hand, it is equally most unlikely that the rate of accumulation of things in

* See Chapters 8, 9, and 10, and Chapters 3, 8, and 10 of Appendix to Mr. Lowe's book.

this country should have changed so much in the period 1875-85, as compared with 1865-75, as is represented by the diminution in the rate of growth of the Income Tax assessments, or by the diminution in the rate of growth of capital from about 44 to $17\frac{1}{2}$ per cent., or even, to take the upper part of the above table only, from 35 to 15 per cent. An inspection of the table in detail abundantly confirms this impression. In cases where there is absolute diminution of money capital, such as lands, farmers' profits, mines, and ironworks, there has been notoriously a great fall of prices; while, in regard to the two latter classes of property at least, there has been simultaneously a great increase of production, so that the apparent diminution of property shown must be nominal, not real.

But the question of the amount of correction raises very difficult points. What articles are to be taken as typical of things in general? and how is the fall of prices to be ascertained between two given dates? What should be the precise effect of such a fall on general valuations of property? Even if these particulars could be ascertained as between two given dates, how are they to be applied to valuations of property based on Income Tax assessments, which necessarily lag behind the real changes in the market values of the income valued, and the money amount of the income itself? It is plain, on a consideration of these questions, that we can only correct in a very rough manner.

As regards the fall of prices itself, I should be disposed to put it, comparing either period 1865-75 with the period 1875-85, or the year 1875 with the year 1885, at about 15 per cent. There are three general index numbers which we may compare for this purpose, and this is the mean of the result which they give, while the mean itself does not vary greatly from either result.

The first of these index numbers is the well-known *Economist* index No., which gives the following results :—

| Period. | Average Index No. |
|---|---|
| 1865-75 ... ... ... ... ... ... ... ... | 2,866 |
| 1875-85 ... ... ... ... ... ... ... ... | 2,419 |
| Reduction ... ... ... ... ... | 447 |
| | = 15½ % |

| Year. | Average Index No. |
|---|---|
| 1875 ... ... ... ... ... ... ... ... | 2,778 |
| 1885 ... ... ... ... ... ... ... ... | 2,098 |
| Reduction ... ... ... ... ... | 680 |
| | = 24½ % |

The next is Mr. Sauerbeck's, which gives the following results :—

| Period. | Average Index No. | Year. | Average Index No. |
|---|---|---|---|
| 1865-75 ... ... ... | 101 | 1875 ... ... ... ... | 96 |
| 1875-85 ... ... ... | 85 | 1885 ... ... ... ... | 72 |
| Reduction ... | 16 | Reduction ... ... | 24 |
| | = 16 % | | = 24½ % |

The third is that of Mr. Soetbeer, which gives the following results :—

| Period. | Average Index No. | Year. | Average Index No. |
|---|---|---|---|
| 1865-75 ... ... ... | 128·43 | 1875 ... ... ... ... | 129·85 |
| 1875-85 ... ... ... | 120 75 | 1885 ... ... ... ... | 108·72 |
| Reduction ... | 7·68 | Reduction ... ... | 21·13 |
| | = 6 % | | = 16 % |

And the mean of all these reductions is :—

|   | Period. | Year. |
|---|---|---|
| 1 ... ... ... ... ... ... ... ... ... | 15½ | 24½ |
| 2 ... ... ... ... ... ... ... ... ... | 16 | 24½ |
| 3 ... ... ... ... ... ... ... ... ... | 6 | 16 |
| Mean ... ... ... ... ... ... ... | 12½ | 21½ |

Mean of periods and years 17 per cent.

I am not sure but that a smaller and more carefully formed index No., based on a few articles only,
according to the plan followed by Mr. Lowe, would
not be just as serviceable ; but no very different
results would be produced.

With the above may also be compared the fall in
silver, amounting between 1875 and 1885 to a fall
from 56⅞d. to 50⅝d., or 12 per cent.

It is most important in fact to keep in mind that
we are not dealing here with the whole fall of prices
which has occurred since what is called the appreciation of gold began, but only with what has occurred
in a particular period of ten years. I should be
disposed to place the fall in the interval covered by
the present essay at about 15 per cent., which
is a little under the mean of 17 per cent. above
stated.

The correction of the capital figures, however,
would depend on a further estimate as to how far
the income tax assessments lag behind the real
changes in the amount of income dealt with, or the
money value of that income. There is undoubtedly
some lagging behind, as in the income of lands and
other items, but I am disposed to think not so much
in general as would at first sight be supposed, public
companies and other bodies being, of course, assessed

exact on their profits. At any rate, if changes in average prices are to be the test, I should be disposed to correct the comparative valuation between 1875 and 1885 either by a deduction of 15 per cent. from the valuation of the former period or by a similar addition to the valuation of the latter period.

On the whole I think also the average prices of staple articles are a good test. As I have explained in an address to the British Association in 1887 at Manchester,* money income of every kind of property necessarily depends on price. Some property is dependent directly; all property is dependent indirectly, and the valuation on the whole must vary directly as the variation of average prices of staple articles, or what may be called the price-level.

If the matter is considered for a moment, the necessity for this result will appear. As regards all properties held and worked by their owners, without payment of wages or rent, the effect of the fall of prices is instantaneous. The money return is so much less than it would otherwise be to the extent of the fall of price. If an owner has money wages to pay, but no rent, he is even worse off at first than an owner who has everything in his own hands. The prices change quicker than the wages, and the margin of income which has to be valued in valuing the property is reduced in even greater proportion than the prices of the articles produced. The case cannot be different where rent or mortgage charges or equivalent payments have to be made. Such payments are only a mode of distributing the net income; the corpus of the net income itself must be affected

* See " The Recent Rate of Material Progress in England." London: Geo. Bell and Sons.

in precisely the same way as if it were in one hand only, and were not distributed to different individuals. Hence, in fact, the complaints that some owners have had their margins swept away altogether, and that mortgagees or rent chargers have had to suffer.

The only doubts that can apparently be raised arise from the great bulk of mortgage or similar property, which seems to be unaffected by considerable changes of price, and the mass of Stock Exchange securities of different kinds, particularly public funds, which appear equally unaffected. It has to be considered, however, that the comparison is not between mortgages at one time and at another, but between what they are at the different times and what they would have been if there had been no change of prices. The same mortgage interest or rent-charge continues to be paid with as great a margin apparently as before. But the explanation is that the property has really become more productive—that continual efforts to maintain its money value, in spite of the fall of prices, have been successful. The margin has not been increased as it would otherwise have been. Similarly, as regards Stock Exchange securities, if they are in the nature of mortgages, the same explanation applies; while if they are in the nature of residual margins, the margin may have been maintained, in spite of the fall in prices, by greatly increased production. It is less than it would otherwise have been, though it may not be less on a comparison with a previous period. The only exception I can think of is in the case of public funds where the funds are held by one community, and the debt is that of another community. The former is so much richer, the latter so much poorer, than it would otherwise be by the fall of prices. There is a real as well as a nominal change corresponding to the fall of prices. By such a change between 1875 and 1885 a community like England should have benefited. There need be no reduction in this part of its capital, as far as old securities are concerned, as compared with what it would otherwise have been owing to the fall of prices. But looking at matters broadly, the differences thus possible seem too small to be allowed for.

Correcting, then, the valuations of 1875 and 1885 as above suggested, we should find that, by reducing the valuation of 1875 by 15 per cent., the total would be about $7\frac{1}{2}$ thousand millions instead of $8\frac{1}{2}$ thousand millions, upon which an increase to a little over 10 thousand millions is very nearly 40 per cent., thus approaching the increase in the previous decade. Applying the correction to the 1885 figures and adding 15 per cent. to them, the total would be $11\frac{1}{2}$ thousand millions, rather more, which again is an increase of nearly 40 per cent. upon $8\frac{1}{2}$ thousand millions.

So much difference is apparently made in the valuation by a difference of 15 per cent. in the level of prices only.

The correction of course cannot pretend to any exactness. It only serves to fix in our minds that probably there is less difference in reality in the growth of wealth in the country in the two periods 1865-75 and 1875-85 than would seem at first sight. The necessary correction for prices makes most of the difference.

A question of a different sort is suggested. Is there any means of deducing from these figures, what, in point of fact, is the normal rate of growth in the country in wealth, from which a variation upwards or downwards in the actual money figures would imply an average rise or fall in prices, or change in the purchasing power of money?

So far as the remarks already made go, the answer would appear to be that if, allowing for the fall of prices since 1875, the rate of growth has been about 40 per cent., which was about the rate of growth in the ten years before, during which no allowance seemed required for the fall of prices, then the normal growth must be taken to be about 40 per cent. in ten years. This would, however, raise the question whether in the decade 1855-65 in which prices rose greatly, and in which the growth of the Income Tax assessments was nevertheless only 28 per cent., the actual advance in wealth measured by things can have been so great as it has since been. The comparison might be carried further back, and the figures of 1845 compared with those of 1815, from which it would appear that the fall of prices in that interval must have been enormous if wealth had really grown in the interval as it has since done —such a fall of prices in fact as it is difficult to believe in. The question is not without practical interest, as it is difficult not to believe that the real growth of wealth in the country must have been tolerably steady all through, in which case the normal growth cannot be so great as 40 per cent., assuming prices to be steady.

To elucidate the problem a little I have thought it would be interesting to insert the accompanying statement of the growth of Income Tax assessments from period to period since 1815. (See Table p. 59.)

This can only be done for England, and Wales, and
for Scotland, the Irish figures, which are in any case
less important, not going back so far.

The effect of this table is that, while the increase
of population all through has been tolerably uniform,
the average annual rate of increase of Income Tax
assessments has been :—

|  | England. | Scotland. |
|---|---|---|
|  | % | % |
| 1815-45 ... ... ... ... ... ... ... ... ... | 1·1 | 1·7 |
| 1845-55 ... ... ... ... ... ... ... ... ... | 1·5 | 2·5 |
| 1855-65 ... ... ... ... ... ... ... ... ... | 2·7 | 1·7 |
| 1865-75 ... ... ... ... ... ... ... ... ... | 3·7 | 4·1 |
| 1875-85 ... ... ... ... ... ... ... ... ... | 1·1 | 1·4 |
| Mean ... ... ... ... ... ... ... | 2·0 | 2·3 |
| Mean (exclusive of 1815-45) ... ... | 2·25 | 2·42 |

From this, assuming the state of prices to have
been in 1885 much the same after 40 years' interval
as they were about 1845, the normal rate of growth
of wealth would come out as nearly 2¼ per cent. per
annum, from which it would also follow that, in spite
of the assumption made in my former paper that
the growth between 1865-75 was not swollen by any
general rise in prices, yet that some such augmentation
must have occurred. Part of the increase of capital then
dealt with in 1875 must have been a money increase
only, and even part of the increase between 1855 and
1865, the total enhancement of prices thus apparent
being about 15 per cent., which corresponds fairly
well with Mr. Jevons' estimates in 1862 of the depreciation of gold. It is impossible to reason on the
subject at all finely, owing to changes in the strin-
gency of valuation; but either the mean above stated,

[CONTINUED ON P. 60.]

*Statement showing the gross amount of property and profits assessed to the Income Tax in England and Wales and Scotland in the undermentioned years, the amount and proportion of the increase in each such year over the previous year mentioned, and the average annual rate per cent. of increase in each period :—*

| Years. | Amount Assessed. | Increase over Previous Year. | | Average Annual Rate of Increase. | Average Annual Rate of Increase of Population. |
|---|---|---|---|---|---|
| | | Amount. | % | % | % |

ENGLAND AND WALES.

| Years. | Amount Assessed. Thousand £ | Increase over Previous Year. Thousand £ | % | % | % |
|---|---|---|---|---|---|
| 1815... ... ... | 156,735 | | | | |
| 1845... ... ... | 220,465 | 63,730 | 40·7 | 1·1 | 1·4 |
| 1855... ... ... | 256,008 | 35,543 | 16·1 | 1·5 | 1·2 |
| 1865... ... ... | 335,175 | 79,167 | 30·9 | 2·7 | 1·2 |
| 1875... ... ... | 481,775 | 146,600 | 43·7 | 3·7 | 1·3 |
| 1884... ... ... | 530,538 | 48,763 | 10·1 | 1·1 | 1·4 |

SCOTLAND.

| Years. | Amount Assessed. | Increase over Previous Year. | % | % | % |
|---|---|---|---|---|---|
| 1815... ... ... | 14,293 | | | | |
| 1845... ... ... | 23,832 | 9,539 | 66·7 | 1·7 | 1·1 |
| 1855... ... ... | 30,544 | 6,712 | 28·2 | 2·5 | 0·8 |
| 1865... ... ... | 36,195 | 5,651 | 18·5 | 1·7 | 0·7 |
| 1875... ... ... | 53,935 | 17,740 | 49·0 | 4·1 | 1·0 |
| 1884... ... ... | 61,118 | 7,183 | 13·3 | 1·4 | 1·1 |

as a whole, underrates the normal growth of wealth,
measured by things and not by money, or there must
have been an inflation of money values, of prices, and
of property as the result of prices, between 1855 and
1875. The subject can hardly be followed out in
this connection. It can only be studied properly in
connection with changes in wages as well as prices.
But the experience of many years proves, at least,
that the recent growth of the Income Tax is far
below the normal rate of the past forty years, and
that it can only be explained by the fall of prices,
which alters all the valuations. The growth between
1875 and 1885 has, in fact, got back to the rate
between 1815 and 1845, when there was an enormous
fall of prices.

There is yet another conclusion to be drawn from
the figures which has a bearing on the larger question
of the appreciation of the standard. It is sometimes
argued that when prices fall there need have been
no change in the money—it is only the commodities
that need have changed. It is assumed that a line
can be drawn at a given date, and that the increase
of commodities or money can be measured as from
that date. But if it is at all correct to assume that
throughout the whole period covered by the above
table commodities have been increasing with comparative steadines, yet, nevertheless, there have been
great changes from time to time in the money growth
of property in the country owing to changes of prices,
then these changes of prices themselves, when long
periods are surveyed, must be properly held to be
determined by changes in money and not in commodities. Dynamically, commodities do not change
all through ; their increase is constant ; but dynami-

cally money does change : it moves at one time in such a way as to keep prices in equilibrium, or even make them, and all property valuations with them, rise ; at another time it either diminishes or only grows so slowly that all money prices and property valuations with them fall. This result can only be described as due to changes in money. The opposite view, ascribing the change in a given period to commodities, is the result of a study of the subject for a short period beginning with what is an impossibility in such a subject—a statical equilibrium. Viewing a long period dynamically, it is beyond all question that the commodities are comparatively steady and only the money changes.*

This is not a paper on money; but, having said so much, I may be permitted to add that if in future commodities are to progress as they have done in the past, then unless money changes dynamically, prices must continue to fall, and income tax and property valuations must increase more slowly than they otherwise do, or even diminish. An income tax increasing ten per cent. only in ten years will be a very different thing, as the Chancellor of the Exchequer recognises, from one which increases 40 per cent. in the same period.

---

In making these comparisons in my former essay I took occasion to notice also the official figures of the Legacy and Succession Duty Returns, showing from time to time a growth in property corresponding to

---

* See for a fuller explanation on this head the paper on "Recent Changes in Prices and Incomes Compared," read last year and published in Statistical Society's Journal, December, 1888.

what is shown in the Income Tax Returns. It appears unnecessary to do so now, the superiority of the Income Tax figures for such a purpose being universally admitted. There has also been a change in the last few years in regard to the Legacy Duty, which makes the figures no longer comparable. The Probate Duty figures must be substituted, and these cannot be carried very far back with the needful detail.

# CHAPTER IV.

## DISTRIBUTION OF WEALTH BETWEEN ENGLAND, SCOTLAND, AND IRELAND.

WRITING in 1878, I made no attempt to show the distribution of wealth between the communities of England, Scotland, and Ireland, which compose the United Kingdom. I regard any attempt at such a comparison very doubtfully, indeed. The people constituting the United Kingdom are closely intermixed in their business relations. Property in one part of the kingdom is held by people resident in another part; there are not a few whose domicile is by no means certain, who are as fixed in Scotland or Ireland as they are in England, leading, in fact, a dual existence, part "in the country," in Scotland or Ireland, and part in the metropolis; so that for the purposes of a comparison like the present, they cannot be classed as distinctly and exclusively English or Scotch or Irish. There is, moreover, a considerable amount of foreign property belonging to people in all parts of the United Kingdom, but assessed exclusively in the metropolis. An exact division between England, Scotland, and Ireland, represent-

ing the wealth of each section, as the table above
given represents the wealth of the United Kingdom,
is accordingly impossible.

I have been encouraged, however, to make an
attempt at separation, as useful, for certain political
computations, as helping, if properly done, to show
the relative strength of the metropolitan community,
that of England, in comparison with the comparatively outlying communities of Scotland and Ireland.
In doing so we must make the assumption that, on
the whole, the foreign income, and certain other
income, must be assigned exclusively, or mainly to
the metropolitan community because it really belongs
to the people of the United Kingdom in their metropolitan and even cosmopolitan capacity, and on a
division, if such a thing were conceivable, would
most probably go with the metropolis.

For the rest it will probably be convenient to
follow the divisions of the Income Tax assessment
generally, and credit to each community the property
locally situated, although we know, for instance, that
railway shares and other property in Ireland and
Scotland are held in England and *vice versa*. The
presumption is that this mode of division will not
assign too little to Scotland and Ireland ; it will even
assign to these countries so much in excess as to be a
set-off against any defect that may arise through the
whole or larger part of the metropolitan or cosmopolitan capital, as above explained, being assigned to
England.

I have accordingly to refer to the Tables in the
Appendix in which such a division between England,
Scotland, and Ireland is attempted. (See Tables,
Appendix III.). These Tables follow exactly the

model of Table A. inserted above (Chap. II.), so that it will be easy to compare the details of each section with the similar details for the United Kingdom as well as for each other.

The general effect is striking enough. The preponderance of England is manifest. Scotland is a long way behind. Ireland is comparatively insignificant. If we include the element of population, Scotland is not far behind England in the amount per head, but Ireland is a long way behind.

In the following short Table a comparison is made both of total amounts and amounts per head :—

*Property in England, Scotland, and Ireland, and the amount per head of population compared. [The calculations are made on the population of 1887.]*

|  | Property. | Per Cent. of Total. | Property per Head. |
|---|---|---|---|
|  | Mln. £. |  | £ |
| England ... ... ... ... | 8,617 | 86·0 | 308 |
| Scotland ... ... ... ... | 973 | 9·7 | 243 |
| Ireland ... ... ... ... ... | 447* | 4·3 | 93 |
| Total ... ... ... ... | 10,037 | 100 0 | 270 |

England, in fact, on this showing, possesses rather more than 8½ tenths of the wealth of the United Kingdom ; Scotland about a tenth ; and Ireland less than half a tenth. The wealth of the metropolitan community is equal to about £308 per head ; of Scotland to £243 per head, or rather less than the average of the United Kingdom ; and of Ireland to about one-third of the average, or about £93 per head only.

* In roughly estimating in 1886, in a paper on "The Economic Value of Ireland to Great Britain," I put the total capital of Ireland at about 400 millions. The present figure I should still think too high if a strict account were taken, but I have followed here the method explained in the text of distributing the Income Tax income which gives some advantage to Ireland. The present is also a more detailed statement than that of 1886.

A rapid survey reveals in a moment how these great differences arise. Apart from land in Schedules A and B, Ireland possesses very little of the great elements of capital which constitute the wealth of the United Kingdom. Its total capital connected with Income Tax income is only about 400 millions, and of this about 230 millions arises from land in Schedule A, or the occupation of land in Schedule B, leaving only 170 millions as the whole capital of the Irish people in connection with the other Schedules. The income in Ireland under Schedule A for land and houses is valued at a smaller number of years' purchase than similar income in Great Britain, a point which will be discussed presently; but this is not the case with other income. Ireland is, in fact, singularly destitute of all the constituents of wealth under Schedule D; its total income under this head in the appended tables above the Income Tax limit being about £4 millions only, as against a similar income in the whole of the United Kingdom of £148 millions; so that Ireland, as regards Schedule D, is one-thirty-seventh only of the United Kingdom. It is in this way, then, that the difference between Ireland and the rest of the United Kingdom arises.

No doubt some difference is also made by the difference in the number of years' purchase at which certain property in Ireland is valued, as compared with similar property in the United Kingdom. Land in Ireland is valued at 15 years' purchase only, as compared with 28 years' purchase in England and Scotland; and houses in Ireland are valued at 12 years' purchase only, as compared with 15 years' purchase in England and Scotland. Even, however, if we applied the same number of years' purchase in Ireland as in England and Scotland, the valuation of wealth in Ireland would still lag far behind in its proportion to that of its neighbours. About £140 millions would be added to its total capital, and the amount would remain under 600 millions, about a seventeenth, in place of a twenty-third, part of the wealth of the United Kingdom.

There is, however, I contend, no justification for estimating income from Irish land and houses at a similar number of years' purchase as similar property in the United Kingdom. We should get a false idea of Irish wealth and relative resources if we did so.

The reason as regards houses, the smaller item, is plain. The average rent of houses in Ireland is much below what it is in England or Scotland, and the lower the rent, at any rate when it is very low, the smaller number of years' purchase it is worth. I need hardly add that many of the so-called houses in Ireland for which rent is paid are merely huts, and not properly comparable with the houses of a more advanced community. The property is not of the same kind.

The reason as regards land is, first, that from the exceptional difficulty of collecting small rents, land in Ireland being in smaller holdings than in Great Britain, there is more difference in Ireland between gross and net rental than in England and Scotland. The capital value is really less because the net income on the same gross figures is not really so large. Next and even more important the income from land in Ireland, like all other income to some extent but even in greater degree, is rendered insecure by the political agitator, and its capital value

is consequently less than it would be if politics were
more stable.· The difference is a real loss to the
insecure community. It means that the general
credit of the community in proportion to its income
is less than that of a more stable community with
the same income ; it can do less with what seems the
same property than a more stable community can.
Individually the loss is marked enough. The same
amount of income in the one community actually
exchanges for less than it does in the other. The
test of the market proves that it is not the same
thing.

Fifteen years' purchase for the income of Irish
land may seem too little ; but the rental itself in the
Income Tax returns, it must be remembered, is a
little exaggerated above the reality, as many Irish
landlords only too well know. The net ascertained
and paid rental may sell for more than fifteen years'
purchase, though according to recent reports of sales
not for very much more ; but the nominal rental
here in question is as moderately valued at 15 years'
purchase as the similar rental in England and Scotland at 28.

Another point is raised by these comparative
valuations. If the rent of land in Schedule A, it is
said, cannot be valued at more than 15 years' purchase, ought not the capital value of tenant-right to
be included under Schedule B, the tenant in Ireland
possessing a property of a kind which is not possessed by the tenant in England or Scotland, and
which is, in fact, saleable? The answer to this is in
part that it will be found something is in fact
credited to Irish agricultural capital under Schedule
B which is not credited to the same capital in Eng-

land and Scotland, because Irish occupation capital
in proportion to rent, apart from tenant-right, is not
so large as in England or Scotland, and yet the same
number of years' purchase is applied. But I object
to including the capital value of tenant-right, except
to a very moderate degree, as being, in fact, not a
positive quantity which can come into comparisons
like the present, the so-called capital value of tenant-
right being largely a fine which the excessive land
hunger compels farmers to pay to live, and not a real
capital asset which would be available on a large
scale in the open market. Even if sales of tenant-
right, therefore, were better recorded than they are,
and the means existed for forming averages over Ireland, I should doubt the propriety of allowing for
this capital value to more than a moderate extent—
to such an extent, for instance, as would include the
cost of the houses which tenants have built, and
other substantial improvements in the way of drain-
age and manuring they have made. The fine paid
for the right to live is not to be reckoned, at any
rate in comparison with a country where no such
fines are paid, and where the rental is unquestionably
a simple bargain between landlord and tenant, the
tenant professedly having nothing but the occupation capital.

It is fair also to add, I think, that Irish capital is
not only greatly less than it would otherwise be,
owing to the political insecurity of the country, but
it is also lessened by the excess of its population
above what is needed for the most fitting agriculture. Rent is below what it is in England for similar
qualities of land, because the land has to support a
larger cultivating population, and rent of course is

only possible after the cultivating population, according to the scale of living it is able to maintain, has
been supported. With a different arrangement for
cultivation, requiring a smaller population, rent might
be increased on the one hand, and the comfort of the
cultivating population on the other, in which case
the capital value of the land would undoubtedly be
much increased. The possibility of a great increase
of Irish capital, as soon as the political and economic
causes of its being so small as it is are removed,
must accordingly be recognised. Political insecurity
and over - population combined probably make its
capital less than it would otherwise be even now
by from two to three hundred millions sterling, the
mischief being about equally divided between the
two causes of evil specified. Whatever figure we
may place upon it the loss must be very great.

I have referred very little in these remarks to the
case of Scotland, because it is so much on all fours
with that of England. It is not a contrast to England. As showing the difference, however, between
a politically insecure country and one that is every
way secure, and between a country with an excessive
cultivating population and one free from that evil,
it may be pointed out that while Scotland, as regards
land, has rather less income than Ireland, though not
so very much less in spite of its smaller area, yet
with a population of just under four millions, as compared with nearly five in Ireland, it has more than
twice the capital—973 millions, as compared with
447 in Ireland—and that this difference largely arises
in connection with Schedule D. The income in Scotland from capital under Schedule D dealt with in
the tables in the Appendix is in fact about 15 millions

sterling as compared with 4 millions from the same sources in Ireland. No contrast could be more striking.

The main lesson of the whole comparison is, however, that already given, viz., the predominance of the metropolitan community of England. Reckoning by wealth England should have 86 per cent. of the representation of the United Kingdom, or 576 members out of 670. Scotland by the same rule should have about 64 only; and Ireland no more than 30. These are very different figures from those which actual politics have established, or which the exact proportions of population would give, though even the latter would give a smaller representation to the weaker parts of the community than is now given. But for all that they point to a real weakness, I believe, in our present constitutional arrangements. It is neither wise nor prudent to make so complete a divorce as has now been made between the real strength of different parts of the population of the United Kingdom and the representation in Parliament. There should be a representation of forces in Parliament, if we had perfectly just arrangements, and not merely a counting of heads. Nothing can be more absurd to the mind of any student of politics, who knows how forces rule in the long run, than the system now established as between the metropolitan community of England and its companions in sovereignty by which one of the companion communities, and that the least entitled to privilege, obtains most disproportionate power.

# CHAPTER V.

---

## HISTORICAL RETROSPECT.

ANOTHER comparison to be made is that between the figures of the present time and more distant periods. It will of course be impossible in such comparisons, to show the same details as in the recent years, when we have the benefit of Income Tax Returns on the same basis for several periods, but the older totals at least, and possibly some of the main details may be compared with these of the present time. In certain respects, I am inclined to think, the figures we are using are more serviceable and more trustworthy, when the right precautions are taken, for extended historical comparisons than for any other purpose. The great intervals of time and the great differences in the figures, in these extended historical comparisons, bring out certain facts with marvellous clearness, which could not be brought out in any other way.

It is most interesting to find that the inquiry as to past valuations of aggregate property takes us back to a period in which statistical studies in this country to a certain extent originated, and to authors who

are well-known as among the founders of the study,
which they called by the name of Political Arithmetic.
The period is the latter part of the 17th century, and
the authors are Sir William Petty and Sir William
Davenant, both of whom devoted no little attention
to this very question of the valuation of aggregate
property, including the connected subject of aggregate income. In fact one of the main objects of their
" Political Arithmetic" was to obtain an idea of the
resources of the country, and of their growth, partly
for purposes of taxation, and partly for comparison
with the resources and growth of England's depen-
dents or neighbours at the time; Ireland, France, and
Holland, being the chief countries considered. The
subject has only been intermittently studied in the
same form since, but those who began, we may believe,
had a good idea of what they were about, and it is all
the more instructive, therefore, for us to go back in
this matter to the earliest promoters of formal statistical knowledge in this country.

I do not propose, of course, to go through the entire
work of these two authors on this head. It will be
sufficient to notice briefly the leading estimates, in
which a great deal of their work is summed up, only
premising that those who care to pursue the study
will find that the estimates now to be used, and compared with those of the present time, were not hap-
hazard guesses, but were based on available data,
carefully considered and built upon. There are
certain points of difference between the two authors
which I shall endeavour to explain, but this would,
of course, be impossible if they had not themselves
used what were largely common data, and shown how
their sums were done. I may add that the estimates

can practically be used, so as to form a third statement for the year 1600 good enough for comparative purposes. First, however, I shall notice the various statements of the two authors separately.

Sir William Petty, as the founder of Political Arithmetic, and as the author of the statement earliest in date, the date as near as I can judge being 1679, ought first to be noticed. He makes many statements and calculations as to population, taxable recources, income and property, in his numerous essays in Political Arithmetic, but for our present purpose, these are summed up in his little " Verbum Sapienti." The result of the calculation there given, may be summarised as follows :—

*Statement of the Income and Capital of the people of England anno circa 1679, summarised from Sir William Petty's Verbum Sapienti*

[In mlns. stg.]

|  | Income. | Capital. |
|---|---|---|
|  | £ | £ |
| Total ... ... ... ... ... ... ... ... ... | 40 | 250 |
| Land ... ... ... ... ... ... ... ... ... | 8 | 144 |
| Houses ... ... ... ... ... ... ... ... ... | 2½ | 30 |
| Shipping ... ... ... ... ... ... ... ... | ... | 3 |
| Stock of Cattle, &c. ... ... ... ... ... ... | ... | 36 |
| Coined Gold and Silver ... ... ... ... ... | ... | 6 |
| Wares, Merchandise, Plate, and Furniture ... | ... | 31 |
| Income from above sources, exclusive of Land and Houses, and from personal services ... | 29½ | ... |

Sir William Petty, in his essay, proceeds to capitalise the income from personal services as well as the income from property by a process which appears to me not quite correct as introducing a figure, not on all fours with the others in his statement, and which would not at any rate be comparable with statements made up on the basis of the Income Tax returns, according to the method followed in the present paper. I have, therefore, omitted this additional computation in the above summary, but those who are interested can easily read for themselves in the original. The above figures, if at all near the mark, appear to be strictly comparable with those of the present time.

The enormous difference between two centuries ago and the present time is at once palpable. Taking the population of England as little over five millions when Sir William Petty wrote (his own figure of 7 millions appearing somewhat excessive), the above figures would give something less than £8 per head of income, and £50 per head of capital for the whole people; the capital now, as we have seen, being approximately £270 per head, and the income being probably not less than about £34 per head. The difference is so enormous that the largest possible corrections would still show an enormous advance between two centuries ago and the present time The difference, it may be said, would not be so great if we allowed for the greater purchasing power of money two centuries ago. But as far as I can judge no allowance, or little allowance, should be made on this head. Great masses of articles are much lower in money price now than they were then, and the staple article, wheat, is also rather cheaper.

The items may be more conveniently noticed in connection and comparison with Sir William Davenant's figure to be presently considered. It may be mentioned, however, that the land rent in the above statement works out at 18 years' purchase, and that this figure of 18 years' purchase is explicitly adopted by the author, while only 12 years' purchase is allowed for house rent. The other items are all arrived at on consideration and for reasons given. Lands and houses were of course at the time in question much more in proportion to the total wealth of the country than they are now, so that the preponderance here given to them is *prima facie* reasonable. The data regarding them at the time were also fairly complete and trustworthy, there being assessments for the 4s. tax, since become the land tax, and for other taxes, while the more exact knowledge as to London and some parts of the country on many points could be made use of by a simple rule of proportion to supplement the less complete knowledge on the same points as to remoter parts of the country.

Coming next to the estimate of Sir William Davenant, the first remark to make is that in using his figures we must associate with him another well-known name, that of Mr. Gregory King. Sir William Davenant's figures, when we look into them, are found to be, and are, in fact, expressly acknowledged to be those of Mr. Gregory King, though Sir William Davenant discusses them very fully in adopting them. Whether Gregory King was employed by Sir William Davenant is not quite clear; but the connection was, at any rate, very close, and I shall therefore treat the figures as those of Sir William Davenant and Gregory King together, taking them directly from Gregory King's essay. This essay is reprinted in full in another book well-known to economic students, Mr. Chalmers' "Resources of the Nation," published at the end of last and the beginning of the present century, in which the material history of England and the Empire is traced throughout the eighteenth century, that is, from Gregory King's time downwards, with the addition of various notes for earlier

periods. Mr. Chalmers, I may take the opportunity
of noting, was for many years an officer of the Board
of Trade. His book is an admirable essay in every
way. Mr. Gregory King himself was by profession
a surveyor, and, therefore, well acquainted with the
data he uses, chiefly those showing the income and
value of land, for which, as already hinted, in the 4s.
tax and other official records which have either
perished or are buried in the Record Office, there
were probably more official data available to people
like Gregory King, disposed to use them, than we
should now be apt to imagine.

There are three documents of Gregory King's,
which may be referred to. Only one of these is a
statement of capital, but the other two are useful by
comparison and otherwise for studying it.

The first of these is Gregory King's calculation of
the income and expense of the community according
to the different classes,—a most minute table. The
second is a table exhibiting the author's idea of the
several sorts of land in cultivation, the produce, the
rent, the capital of the cultivation, and the like
particulars. The third is the table to which I shall
have to call particular attention, including, as it does,
a statement of the estimated value of the property
of the nation. The first is, apparently, the most
fanciful, the nature of the data not being apparent;
but if we compare it with the others, it will be
obvious that the author must have had data of some
sort, at any rate, for the totals, however imperfect
his distribution among different classes may be.

The general effect, then, of these tables is as
follows :—1. The income of the country in 1688 is
reckoned as £43,500,000, or nearly £8 per head, of

which about £13,000,000 is the rent of land and
other hereditaments, about £10,000,000 being considered the rent of land alone, and the remainder is
derived from trade and industry or labour of some
kind, including agricultural labour.

2. The valuation of the country is computed at
£650,000,000, or, deducting a valuation of income
from personal services in which Sir William Petty's
similar computation is followed, at £320,000,000, the
items being as follows :—

| | |
|---|---:|
| 1. Rent at 18 Years' Purchase ... ... ... ... ... | £234,000,000 |
| 2. *Capitalised Value of Remaining Income of the Nation, 11 Years' Purchase ... ... ... ... ...* | *330,000,000* |
| 3. Stock in Money, Plate, Jewels, and Household Goods ... ... ... ... ... ... ... ... ... | 28,000,000 |
| 4. Stock in Shipping, Forts, Stores, Goods, Instruments, and Materials ... ... ... ... ... ... ... | 33,000,000 |
| 5. Live Stock, Cattle, Beasts, Fowls, &c. ... ... .. | 25,000,000 |
| Total ... ... ... ... ... ... ... | £650,000,000 |
| *Deduct—* | |
| Item No. 2 as on a different basis from modern Estimates ... ... ... ... ... .. ... ... ... | £330,000,000 |
| Net Total ... ... ... ... ... ... | £320,000,000 |

3. The annual accumulation of the country, the
excess of the income over the expense, is put at no
more than £1,800,000, which would be in round
figures about £20,000,000 every ten years.

In many respects, therefore, Gregory King, like Sir
William Petty, supplies figures in a form which can
be compared with those of the present time. The
methods followed are, in fact, much the same, and I
am disposed to think that Sir William Davenant and
Gregory King have simply bettered Sir William
Petty's instruction, going through the data more
fully, and discussing some points—such as the probable excess of actual over assessed rental—with
perhaps greater knowledge.

Before comparing the two statements, let me only just notice, as regards Gregory King's, how real the computation for the most part is. Thus, as regards rent, the second statement referred to shows that he was fully alive to the difficulties in the way of arriving at an exact figure. He expressly points out that his estimate is larger than the rental of the country which had been got hold of in the assessments for the 4s. tax, now known as the land tax, and he points out in detail where the difference arises. Farther, his statement shows that he has compared the value of the produce with the rent per acre, and the yield of the different crops required for the consumption of the community valued at current prices. He may err on points, but his figures are not pure guesses; they are built up on data which he must have had some means of checking. Comparing his figures with those of our modern agricultural returns, we find that he has hit the mark pretty nearly. His estimated area is 39,000,000 acres, as compared with 37,000,000 acres ascertained in modern times. His cultivated area, again, is only 21,000,000 acres, as compared with 24,000,000, or thereabouts, in modern times, from which we may infer that his estimate was somewhat in excess, allowing for commons and waste land since brought into cultivation, but not more, perhaps, than 10 per cent. in excess. Considering the data which must have been in his possession, his work is thus, in my opinion, wonderfully good. At any rate, allowing for the great distance of time, and the wide difference in values, we may at least use Gregory King's estimate of capital, like that of Sir William Petty, for comparison with the present time *quantum valeat.*

The estimate altogether comes to about £120 per head on an estimated total population of 5½ millions as compared with the present average of £270 per head for the United Kingdom and £415 for England only. As already seen, too, the question of changes in the purchasing power of money does not affect the comparison. Whether we take this estimate or that of Sir William Petty already noticed for comparison with the present time, the differences are plainly immense.

The differences between the two statements are brought out in the following comparison in which I omit any capitalisation of personal services :—

*Capital Valuation in 17th Century.*

| Sir William Petty, (1679) | mlns. £ | Gregory King & Davenant, (1688). | mlns. £ |
|---|---|---|---|
| Land ... ... ... ... ... | 144 | Rental ... ... ... ... ... | 234 |
| Houses ... ... ... ... ... | 30 | Live Stock, &c. ... ... ... | 25 |
| Stock of Cattle, &c. ... ... | 36 | Money, Plate, Jewels, and | |
| Shipping ... ... ... ... | 3 | Household Goods ... ... | 28 |
| Coined Gold and Silver ... | 6 | Shipping, Forts, Stores, | |
| Wares, Merchandise, Plate, | | Goods, Instruments, and | |
| and Furniture... ... ... | 31 | Materials ... ... ... ... | 33 |
| Total ... ... ... ... | 250 | Total ... ... ... ... | 320 |

Thus, the main cause of Sir William Davenant's estimate being higher than Sir William Petty's is the higher value put upon the rental by the latter than the former in two ways. It is first taken to be 13½ millions instead of 12½ millions, which is Sir William Petty's figure, owing to the special allowance made by Gregory King for the reasons stated on account of the under assessment for the 4s. tax. Next, Gregory King capitalises the whole rental, land and houses together, at 18 years' purchase, while Sir William Petty only capitalises house rent at 12 years' purchase. The extra rent allowed for, capital-

ised at 18 years' purchase, makes a difference of
£18,000,000 ; and the different rate of capitalisation
for the house rent, viz., 6 years' purchase, on $2\frac{1}{2}$
millions, makes a difference of £15 millions—total 43
millions. In proportion, the difference is very considerable, but it may be partly accounted for by
Gregory King's estimate being made at the later
date, as well as by greater care in allowing for under-
estimate in the tax assessments. The additional
number of years' purchase on the average seems also
to be justified by the fall in the rate of interest in
the interval between the two statements, so that if
Gregory King had valued land and houses separately
as Sir William Petty had done, he must have taken
land at more than 18 years' purchase, although 12
years' purchase might still have been about sufficient
for houses.

With regard to the other items, constituting what
was at that time called the stock of the country, the
circulating as distinguished from the fixed capital, a
close comparison is not easy owing to the cross
divisions. The general effect is that this stock is
valued by Sir William Petty at £76,000,000, and by
Gregory King at £86,000,000, the latter, it will thus
be seen, being again in excess. The difference, on the
whole, might not be considered serious, but there is a
curious difference in detail. Sir William Petty, it
will be observed, is in excess of Gregory King in one
item, that of live stock, where his estimate is
£36,000,000 against Gregory King's £25,000,000.
The consequence is, that the remainder of the stock
is valued by Sir William Petty at £40,000,000, by
Gregory King at £60,000,000, a difference of 50 per
cent. between them, which is all the more serious

as the difference is in the opposite direction to that which arises in regard to the live stock, and there are no circumstances which make it likely that live stock would diminish in value between the two dates, while other descriptions of stock in the same period would increase in value. I find on examination, however, that a large part of the difference would be accounted for by Sir William Petty's exceedingly low estimate for coinage. The difference between the coinage estimates of Sir William Petty and Sir William Davenant amounts to about £12,000,000 ; the former arriving at a sum of £6,000,000, according to a method explained in his *Quantulumcumque,* and the latter arriving at a sum of about £18,000,000 by a different method. Into the details it is unnecessary to enter here, as the question was brought to the test of experiment shortly after, at the great recoinage of 1696, when a coinage of £7,000,000 in silver was required to renew the silver coinage alone, and the whole circumstances were such that the gold coinage in use and hoarded must have been considerably more. Gregory King's estimate on this head, then, seems to be the more correct ; but we must recollect that he estimates for a date later than Sir William Petty, and this may always account for a small part of the increase.

On the whole, we cannot conclude that the capital of England increased between Sir William Petty and Gregory King's estimates to the amount of the difference between them, though some increase must have taken place, and I am disposed to accept Gregory King's figure as, on the whole, the more carefully and thoroughly done, and the one most properly comparable with the estimates made in this essay for the present time. Practically, the advance is so great since two centuries ago that, great as are the differences between some of Sir William Petty's and Gregory King's figures, if we look at them strictly, the impression of the comparison with the present time is the same, whichever estimate we take.

I have noticed that these estimates can be used to form a third estimate, going back to 1600, but I shall only refer to this briefly. The authority is a writer in the *British Merchant,* a publication of the early part of the last century, in which the Treaty of Commerce with France of that period was discussed from a Protectionist, or perhaps we might say even more accurately, a Fair Trade point of view, and the principal articles of which publication were afterwards collected in three volumes under the same title of a " British Merchant."*  The writer referred to, who is described as the Inspector-General of Customs, requires for his argument to estimate the proportion of foreign commerce to the income and wealth of England, for which purpose he accordingly falls back on what are evidently the estimates already referred to, though there are minor discrepancies, discussing therewith other estimates which had been made. From this paper it appears that at the beginning of the seventeenth century the rental of England was about £6,000,000, giving a capital of £72,000,000 only at twelve years' purchase. As the "stock," according to the above proportions, would not be much more than a third, the total valuation of England at the beginning of the seventeenth century could not be more than £100,000,000, or about £20 per head.  The Inspector-General's figure is only

---

* The British Merchant : or, Commerce Preserved.  London, 1721.

£17,000,000 for the stock, making with other capital only £89,000,000 in all. These figures, it may be added, are *prima facie* probable, assuming a rental of about £14,000,000 at the end of the century, because there was a great fall in the purchasing power of money in the early part of the century. Of course, in comparisons with the present time, this change in the purchasing power of money would have to be allowed for, though we need make no such change as we have seen in comparisons with the latter part of the seventeenth century.

The same British Merchant practically also gives a figure for the time he writes—viz., between 1713 and 1721, since he estimates the population of England as then 7,000,000,* the annual expense £49,000,000, and the rental at least £14,000,000, equal at eighteen years' purchase to £252,000,000. The stock at the same time he estimates at £88,000,000, — total, £340,000,000. There is a little want of precision, however, in the data, so that in one way this is little better than a fresh estimate on the basis of Sir William Petty and Gregory King's figures, and for a period which at this distance is practically the ·same. It is probable enough that with the defective data of those days, the liability to difference, owing to the changes caused by lapse of time, was not sufficiently allowed for by those who were making the estimates, and who had not even in view the expediency of making comparisons for the statistical object alone, the figures being always employed for some other argument. The "British Merchant" recognises progress during the seventeenth century, but, curiously enough, does not explicitly

---

* An over-estimate apparently.

make an estimate of the capital and stock of England for his own time, as distinguished from the latter part of the seventeenth century. We may be sure, however, that as the best estimate of the population of England about 1696 does not carry it higher than $5\frac{1}{2}$ to 6 millions, then, allowing for the probable increase down to 1713 or thereabouts, the estimate of 7 millions for the time, though a little in excess of the true figure, with the corresponding estimates of income and capital, could not be far off the mark. At the most I think the figure of 340 millions should be increased by no more than a tenth to make it properly comparable with Gregory King's estimate of 320 millions for the latter part of the seventeenth century.

Passing from the seventeenth century and the beginning of the eighteenth century, I find no good estimates of income and capital properly comparable with those already described until we come to the close of the last and beginning of the present century, when the great wars arising after the French Revolution seem to have given fresh and practical interest to the question of the resources of the country. There are one or two publications, however, which I should like to notice before passing on.

The first is Sir Matthew Decker's essay on the " Causes of the Decline of Foreign Trade," written in 1740, in which there are several notices of the rental and income of the people of England at that time, although there is no attempt to capitalise them. His estimate of the income is based on that of the British Merchant already referred to, with the two differences that the population which the British merchant estimated at 7,000,000 is now reckoned at

8,000,000,* and that the expense per head is reckoned
at £8, instead of £7 per head, on account of the
increase of the average expense, owing to taxes, &c.,
in the interval.† As regards the question of the
expense per head, the calculation is perhaps open to
some criticism ; at any rate we should have liked a
fuller contemporary investigation on the point.   But
it is also to be observed that a statement of the kind
by a writer like Sir Matthew Decker, who was altogether wideawake, is not without its value.  It would
not have been made without some reference to what
was actually probable on various grounds, as well as
on the grounds stated, at the time.   The result then
is that the income of the people of England is valued
in 1740 at £64,000,000, as compared with Sir
William Petty's and Gregory King's estimate of
£40 to £45,000,000 at the end of the previous
century, and the British Merchants' estimate of
£49,000,000 at the beginning of the 18th century.
The amount of this income considered to be rental
(land and houses together) is also estimated in the
same essay at £20,000,000   a great advance, it will
be observed, on the £6,000,000 at the beginning of
the 17th century, and the £12,500,000 to £14,000,000
at the end, although at the time Sir Matthew Decker
wrote rents are spoken of as having lately been
falling, or at least the net income of the landlord
diminishing, owing to poor rates and taxes.  Sir
Matthew Decker's object was in fact to improve the
condition of the landlord by removing restraints and
taxes upon trade and especially upon foreign trade,

* An excessive estimate apparently.   The true figure could hardly
have been much more than 7,000,000.

† Sir Matthew Decker, p. 28.

and it is probable enough, for many reasons, that rents before 1740 had not been rapidly increasing.

Using these figures of Sir Matthew Decker as the basis, and applying Sir William Petty's and Gregory King's methods, the valuation of England about 1740 would be something like the following :—

|  | Mlns. |
|---|---|
| Rental (18 years' purchase of 20 millions) ... ... ... | 360 |
| Stock—one-third of ditto... ... ... ... ... ... ... | 120 |
| Total ... ... ... ... ... ... ... ... ... | 480 |

(In round figures about £500 millions.)

—a figure which, at any rate, would compare not unfairly with the preceding estimates, there having been no material change of prices in the interval to be allowed for.

The next publication to notice is a curiosity in its way, and I should almost have passed it over altogether if it had not been a curiosity, and if it had not also been noticed in a third publication, which will be referred to presently, and which is one of the most interesting I have come across in the series. This second and curious publication is called "The Essay on the National Debt," &c., by Andrew Hooke, who ventures very dogmatically to supersede Sir William Petty and Davenant, and to substitute what he calls an improved method for valuing a country's wealth, which is to multiply the cash, or assumed cash, of the country by 20 to find the amount of the personal stock, and then, after ascertaining the capital value of the land directly, to add together the values of the cash, the personal stock, and the lands. In this way Mr. Hooke arrived at a net valuation for

England in 1749 of exactly 1,000 millions, as follows :—

|  | Mlns. |
|---|---|
| Cash Stock ... ... ... ... ... ... ... ... ... ... | 30 |
| Personal Stock ... ... ... ... ... ... ... ... ... | 600 |
| Land Stock ... ... ... ... ... ... ... ... ... ... | 370 |
| Total ... ... ... ... ... ... ... ... ... | 1,000 |

Moreover, correcting Sir William Petty and Davenant, he gives the following estimates for 1600, 1660, 1688:—

|  | 1600. | 1660. | 1688. |
|---|---|---|---|
|  | Mlns. | Mlns. | Mlns. |
| Cash Stock ... ... ... ... ... ... ... ... | $6\frac{1}{2}$ | 14 | $18\frac{1}{2}$ |
| Personal Stock ... ... ... ... ... ... ... | 130 | 280 | 370 |
| Land Stock ... ... ... ... ... ... ... ... | 80 | 173 | 228 |
|  | $216\frac{1}{2}$ | 467 | $616\frac{1}{2}$ |

Finally, warming with his subject, and working on an assumed cash stock, which is a hypothesis based upon a hypothesis, he winds up with a valuation of England under the three heads stated for each year from 1600 down to 1748, ending with the round figure of 1,000 millions!

This is a most curious essay altogether, and of a kind to bring all such essays into disrepute.

The obvious criticism is that no exact proportion between cash and personal property can be stated; that the proportion must have been constantly varying; and that the method by which the proportion of 20 is arrived at is the loosest observation of individual habits in the matter. What is just as fatal is that the amount of cash which the writer confidently puts at £30,000,000, could never be known with the exactness necessary to base such a calculation upon, while the method which he follows, that of an assumed annual increment based upon Davenant's examination of the Mint reports, import and export statistics, &c., was most fallacious. The essay is altogether most curious.

It need hardly be added that the slightest attempt to give the items of the £600,000,000 of personal stock, which, Mr. Hooke states, would have exhibited the fallacy of the whole proceeding. The value of cattle with the numbers and current prices ; the value of shipping ; the value of furniture ; the value of goods in trade which can hardly exceed the annual produce of the country—must always constitute the main items in such a valuation ; and even when so good a plan as the metod of the Income Tax returns is available, these main items must be thought of, much more in the case of such a guess upon a guess as that of the present writer. It is interesting to find that the mode of valuing national capital in the air, as it were, and without reference to data which is not altogether unknown at the present day, was introduced so long ago in a way to demonstrate its folly.

Almost the only solid piece of fact I can find in this pretentious pamphlet is the statement that the rental of England was then 20 millions sterling, based on the computation that the Land Tax yield of two millions was only a tenth of the actual rental, though nominally assessed at 4s. per £, which is very much the same statement as that of Sir Matthew Decker. This rental, Mr. Hooke suggests, should be capitalised at 18½ years' purchase. He makes no suggestion as to the difference between houses and lands.

The third publication I have to notice is called "A

General View of England from the Year 1600 to
1762, in a letter to A.M.L.C.D. by M.V.D.M. ; " and
is the translation published in 1766 of a French
book published in 1762.  The translator states in his
preface that the author "is (upon pretty sure grounds)
supposed to be a French gentleman, who, several
years ago, resided for some time in England, and
who, within these last ten years, was at the head of
the finances of France.  During his residence here
he was extremely assiduous in obtaining all the information he could procure with regard to the constitution, laws, finances, tillage, manners, and commerce of
this kingdom." The translator then speaks in the
highest terms of the judiciousness and accuracy of
the writer, which must be obvious, I think, to all
who read him.  It is enough to show that the estimate of 20 millions as about the rental of England
in the middle of last century was based upon a real
study of data, and was not a guess ; and that the
best writers who gave their minds to these subjects
were well aware what they were doing.  Every statement is here examined and questioned, and compared
with similar facts in France.

What we find as most important for the present
purpose is the criticism of Sir Matthew Decker's and
Hooke's estimate of a rental of 20 millions sterling.
The writer, for the purpose he had in view, required to
make a distinction between land and houses, which
compelled him to recognise that houses were assessed
less in proportion to the actual rental than lands,
although not so much less in proportion to their selling value, which was less in proportion to income
than that of land*.   Altogether his general view is

* " A General View of England," p. 36.

that the land rental of England is 385 million livres, or £15,500,000, and of houses 95 million livres, or about $4\frac{1}{2}$ millions. He states incidentally, however, that the capital value of land is about 22 years' purchase, against 12 years' purchase for houses only, at which rate lands would come out as worth about 340 millions and houses about 45 millions—total 385 millions ; as compared with the above estimate of 360 millions, taking the rental at 18 years' purchase only, and Mr. Hooke's estimate of 370 millions, taking the rental at $18\frac{1}{2}$ years' purchase. On this basis, and following the same mode of dealing with the stock as that followed by Sir William Petty and Gregory King, it would still be impossible to place the valuation of England alone at the middle of last century on any basis which can properly compare with those we have been making for the present time at much more than £500 millions.

There is one point noticed by the latter writer,[*] and I think by other writers in their books which I have been reading, which deserves a passing notice. This is that a considerable part of the National Debt of England was at that time held by foreigners. The estimates are that a third of the debt was so held. Whether any other foreign capital was lent to England does not appear, but not impossibly, looking at the amount of English debt held abroad, some was so lent. England as an indebted country, then, if an exact statement could have been made, should have had something deducted from the valuations above made to show its exact position, which is the very opposite of what must be done now. But the amounts are too small, and the whole estimates too rough, to

---

* See p. 160.

make it worth while to attempt any rectification beyond calling attention to the fact.

Another point for which the present writer may be used is his references to the resources of Scotland and Ireland. Of Scotland he does not think much ; but Ireland he speaks of as a serious quantity, its general position, he thinks, being much like that of England before the Revolution. This last statement, however, is based mainly upon the national expenditure of Ireland, which is stated to be £2,000,000, and there are no details such as would enable us to give a contemporary valuation of Scotland and Ireland for comparison with the present time.

The next statement to be noticed is that of Mr. Pulteney, in a pamphlet written in 1779, about the time of the American war, entitled, " Considerations on the Present State of Public Affairs and the Means of Raising the Necessary Supplies." Mr. Pulteney is referred to frequently as having made a valuation of the aggregate national wealth, but it is evident that whatever value attaches to Mr. Pulteney's remarks he made no valuation in the nature of the valuations already referred to, or of a kind which can properly be compared with those of the present day. His main plan is to state the rental of land in Great Britain at 20 millions, to assume that the farmers have an equal net income out of it, and then to multiply the net produce of land thus arrived at by 25, assumed to be the number of years' purchase applicable. In this way a sum of one thousand millions is arrived at for land alone, " without taking in other property to an immense amount which equally constitutes national wealth." Another plan suggested by Mr Pulteney is to take the average income per head of

the people of Great Britain, which is estimated at
£7 10s. for a total population of 7,000,000 (apparently
a very low estimate of population) by which he
arrives at a total of 52½ millions as the income of the
people, and thence reckoning the stock or fund
from which this revenue is derived to produce 5 per
cent. he calculates the fund itself at 1,050 millions.
It is evident from these statements that they are not
calculations of national wealth properly comparable
with those already used for the 17th century or with
those of the present time. By such methods the
rental of land in the United Kingdom in 1885 would
be capitalised at no less a sum than 3,250 millions,
and the income of the people of the United Kingdom,
at about 1,300 millions, would indicate a capital of
26 thousand millions!

Mr. Pulteney's distinct statement, however, as to
the land rental of Great Britain at the time he wrote
being about 20 millions, appears to be consistent
with the statements of Petty, Davenant, Decker, and
others already noticed, and gives an intermediate
figure between their estimates of rental and the
much larger figures twenty or thirty years later,
with which we shall presently have to deal. His
estimate of population, however, is altogether too
low, as already glanced at, and there are not sufficient data in what he states from which to make up
a contemporary estimate of wealth at the time he
writes, viz.: 1779. It seems tolerably certain that
there must have been considerable advance between
1750 and 1780, population increasing, commerce increasing, and more than one contemporary writer,
speaking of a great rise of rents in many parts of
the country owing to continued enclosures and con-

tinued progress in the art of agriculture. There is, however, no contemporary estimate of national wealth, such as is supposed to have been made, but was not, in fact, made by Mr. Pulteney.

We come, then, to the time of the great wars at the end of last and the beginning of the present century, when the pressure of a great struggle for existence compelled a discussion of the national resources as a practical question, and the instrument of the Income Tax at once supplied the means, and was in part the result, of such estimates.

Here we find a writer, Mr. Beeke, *apropos* of Mr. Pitt's scheme of an Income Tax, discussing fully both national income and national capital, and giving detailed estimates which there is no difficulty in comparing with previous estimates, and with those of the present time.* Mr. Beeke deals ostensibly with income mainly, but the examination involves questions as to capital as well, and finally the author states, in a postscript, that he had made notes specially as to capital, which he completes and reproduces. This postscript I have extracted, and put in the appendix (see Appendix IV.)

It will be apparent at a glance from this postscript that the author's work is very nearly on all fours with the method which I have used at the present time, the principal differences being that he includes the amount of the debt as part of the capital of the country, which I have consistently excluded, and that he capitalises that part of the income of the country permanently applied to the annual expenditure of the Government and the payment of interest on the

* Observations on the Produce of the Income Tax, &c. By the Rev. H. Beeke, B.D. A New and Corrected Edition. London: J. Wright, Piccadilly. 1800.

National Debt. His estimate of 2,300 millions, therefore, as the national capital would fall to be reduced by the item of 300 millions for the debt, and 250 millions for the capitalisation of the income of the nation applied to Government expenditure and debt interest, leaving a sum of 1,750 millions as an estimate of national capital for Great Britain in 1800 approximately on all fours with the estimates which I have lately made. The items of this sum are as follows, and, for convenience' sake, I have taken the liberty of picking out from Mr. Beeke's text corresponding estimates of income from capital, and the approximate number of years purchase he must have reckoned* :—

Summary of Mr. Beeke's Estimates of Income and Capital, 1800.

|  | Income. | Years Purch'se (about) | Capital. |
|---|---|---|---|
|  | Mlns. | Years. | Mlns. |
| Lands ... ... ... ... ... ... ... | £24.0 | 30 | £720 |
| Tithes ... ... ... ... ... ... ... | 2.5 | 30 | 75 |
| Houses ... ... ... ... ... ... ... | 11.5 | 18 | 200 |
| Mines, Canals, Timber, Tolls, &c. ... | 5 | 20 | 100 |
| Farming Capital ... ... ... ... ... | 17½ | 7 | 125 |
| Home Trade ... ... ... ... ... ... | 18 | 6½ | 120 |
| Foreign Trade and Shipping ... ... | 10 | 8 | 80 |
| Foreign Possessions ... ... ... ... | 4† | ... | ... |
|  | 92½ | ... | 1,420 |
| Waste Lands ... ... ... ... ... ... | ... | ... | 30 |
| Household Furniture ... ... ... ... | ... | ... | 160 |
| Plate, Jewels, &c. ... ... ... ... ... | ... | ... | 50 |
| Specie ... ... ... ... ... ... ... | ... | ... | 40 |
|  | | | 1,700 |
| Shipping, Arsenals, &c. ... ... ... ... | | | 15 |
| Provincial and Municipal Buildings, &c. ... ... ... ... | | | 25 |
| Grand Total ... ... ... ... ... ... | | | 1,740 |

* It will be seen that I have not taken the precise figures in Mr. Beeke's Table on p. 136 of his pamphlet, but that various corrections are made, which I have done after carefully perusing his text.

† I have been unable to identify this item, which appears in Mr. Beeke's Income Table, p. 136, with any item in the Capital Table in his postscript.

The figures in this summary as to income and number of years' purchase must of course be taken subject to the observation that they are not placed by Mr. Beeke himself alongside his capital figures, while to some extent I have been obliged to estimate them because the first four items are not given at all by Mr. Beeke for Great Britain but are given by him for England and Wales only, with an addition in the gross for Scotland. As regards land, however, the remarks of Mr. Beeke fully justify what is done, and I think in other cases there is also sufficient warrant. The most tantalising item of all is that of Foreign Possessions which appears in the income table, but not explicitly in that of capital ; but it may perhaps be considered as properly belonging to foreign trade and shipping.

So far as I can judge, Mr. Beeke's figures are not extravagant. His figure of 30 years' purchase for land might be thought so, but the income he deals with, it is found on examination, is a net income, and the gross rental of land in Great Britain was considered by him to be nearly 30 millions. This mode of dealing with the income may have been partly his justification for capitalising that part of the income of the nation applied to national expenditure—the land tax, for instance, being in this way treated as a rent charge belonging to the State, which might properly be capitalised. This, however, would raise the question whether all the income is not capitalised at too high a rate by Mr. Beeke's method, 30 years' purchase being apparently too high for land in his time if taken upon the gross rental. There is no need, however, to go into minute criticism on such points. The principal objection I would make to the figures would be that furniture, plate, &c., and specie, are, together, taken rather too high. The value of houses comes out as 200 millions only, but furniture alone is 160 millions, with plate, &c., 50 millions, and specie 40 millions more. The furniture and contents of houses, altogether, I have not ventured to put at more than half the capital value. I am making these remarks, however, in the absence of all details on this head, which do not come into Mr. Beeke's paper on income, although it is evident from his postscript that he probably had notes on this subject. In all other respects, however, Mr. Beeke is moderate. There is no reason that I can see why his estimates should not be made use of as good contemporary estimates, properly comparable with earlier and later estimates, at least after the qualifications above introduced.

Comparing them with earlier estimates, they show an enormous advance. Deducting about an eighth on account of Scotland being included, a sum of 1,500 millions is left, as compared with a little over 300 millions at the time of Gregory King, and between 500 and 600 millions half-a-century later. Per head of population, the rise is from about £60 per head in Gregory King's time to about £140 in the year 1800 ; and the greater part of this advance both in amount and per head must have been in the latter half of the 18th century.

Astonishing as the increase is, all the evidence seems to show that while part of the improvement may have been owing to that remarkable rise of prices which commenced between 1780 and 1790, yet a very large part indeed must have been an increase of things

and not of money values merely. Mr. Beeke himself
contends that up to the date he wrote, notwithstanding the war, the capital of the country in things had
been increasing rapidly ; that shipping had been increasing rapidly ; and imports and exports, measured
by things, had also been increasing in the same way
as the shipping ; and that increase in well-being and
population in a most striking degree had been going
on simultaneously. The book of Mr. Chalmers to
which I have already referred, may also be noticed in
the same connection, besides not a few other authors
to the same effect. The matter is put by Mr. Vansittart in a very striking way in one of the war pam-
phlets, written in 1794,* in a passage which I venture
to quote :—

"It is clear that whatever sums any Government may levy upon
its subjects, if the income of the nation, after defraying those sums,
furnishes a surplus to be added to its productive capital, unless its
expenses are increased in proportion to the new income furnished by
this additional capital, a still larger surplus will remain at the next
period of computation; this will again be added to the capital, and
as long as these accumulations continue the wealth of the nation will
increase in a proportion perpetually accelerated. It is impossible to
estimate with precision the progress of national riches, as they arise
from the aggregate savings of all the individuals in the State; but
it is not difficult, by many obvious circumstances, to discern in
which of any two periods of time it has been most rapid. If there
have been extraordinary sums expended upon works of public
utility; if harbours, bridges, high roads, and inland navigations have
been improved, and multiplied ; if numerous buildings have suddenly
arisen; if cultivation has extended over wastes; if shipping has
increased in a manner more remarkable at one period than the other.
—no one can hesitate in deciding in which the national capital, and
consequently the public power and prosperity, has most rapidly aug-
mented. It will hardly be denied that all these signs of eminent felicity
exist in the nation beyond all former example, but some other circumstances must be taken into consideration to give an adequate idea of
the magnitude of its advancement. If, in addition to the vast sums
which have been employed in the improvements I have mentioned, a

* Reflections, &c. by N. Vansittart. A New Edition. London : Stock-
dale, 1794

great capital has been absorbed into the vortex of the National Debt, it will show the extent of these resources of public industry and economy which have at once supplied the one and provided for the other. In this point of view they cannot fail to excite our astonishment. Between the years 1776 and 1786 £115,190,000 were added to the National Debt, yet so completely has the general wealth kept pace with so vast an increase that the share possessed by foreigners in our funds is understood to be much less than in former times, when their extent was comparatively trifling. An addition of £4,864,000 was, in consequence, made in the same time to the annual interest and charge of the debt, and during the late peace many occasional expenses of a large amount were discharged,* while the peace establishment was more considerable than at any former period. Yet the taxes necessary to furnish such extraordinary payments have not diminished the comforts of the people, or injured any branch of their industry. On the contrary, it is certain that in both these respects a great improvement has taken place."—*Extract from Vansittart's "Reflections on the Propriety of an Immediate Conclusion of Peace." London, 1794, pp. 122-7.*

Such was the contemporary belief in 1800 as to the recent progress. Whatever numbers and whatever classes failed to benefit by the growth of income and wealth in the latter part of the 18th century, a vast increase of aggregate income and wealth did undoubtedly take place, of which one proof among others is furnished by comparing the estimates of wealth on similar bases made at the beginning and end of the period, and allowing for a mere rise of prices. I should doubt whether the additions for the rise of prices, comparing 1700 with 1800, ought to be more than 50 per cent. upon the figures of the former period, so that the comparison would be between about 500 millions in the former and 1,500 millions in the later period, or from about £90 to £170 per head, still leaving an enormous advance to

---

* In addition to the increased charges of the National Debt, many large sums were raised during the late peace for purposes of a temporary nature, particularly Debentures granted to the American Loyalists, £1,991,000.

be marked. Whatever may be the exact corrections necessary, the broad result is undeniable.

Before passing from Mr. Beeke's figures I should like to mention that many of his calculations were fully justified by the results of the Income Tax. The total of all the schedules in 1803 for Great Britain was £115,351,000, which compares with Mr. Beeke's estimate of about £90,000,000 net, excluding certain trade items. Owing to the Income Tax Returns sometimes only dealing with net income instead of the gross as well, and the like causes, exact comparisons all the way through between Mr. Beeke and the first Income Tax Schedule are difficult ; but I am satisfied that Mr. Beeke's calculations were so good that we may practically accept his valuation of national wealth as upon an Income Tax basis. His work in all is extremely good. As regards Schedule A in particular, the gross assessments in the Income Tax were in 1803 for Great Britain £38,691,000, which would include lands, houses, tithes, mines, and other items, while the total of Schedule B was £24,279,000, not far short of Mr. Beeke's figure for lands only. The total of £35,000,000 for trades and professions agrees fairly well with Mr. Beeke's estimate of income from home and foreign trade, allowing for differences in arrangement and classification between his method and that of the Income Tax Schedules.

I need not compare Mr. Beeke's figures in detail with the more recent valuations which have been made. It will be sufficient to say that the increase apparently shown from his time to the present would be added to and not diminished by bringing in the question of prices. In any case it may be expedient to look first at one or two valuations for the earlier part of the present century.

One of these is a valuation for about the year 1812,
the height of the war, by Mr. Colquhoun, who, like
Mr. Chalmers, was, I believe an officer of the Board
of Trade, and who at any rate speaks of himself as an
official person. Mr. Colquhoun who gives a valuation
of income, or, as he speaks of it, production, as well
as of capital, is most elaborate and detailed, while he
gives figures for every British dependency as well as
for the United Kingdom itself. His work is spoken
of with a good deal of disapproval by Mr. McCulloch,
as has already been noticed, and many of his details
are no doubt somewhat fanciful, while the work is
also open to further criticism as not recognising
sufficiently the special objects of such investigations
and the necessary unsuitability of the figures for
general purposes owing to the inherent difficulty of
the data. For the present purpose, however, and
comparing Mr. Colquhoun's results with those of Mr.
Beeke, allowing for the growth of population and
income tax in the interval, Mr. Colquhoun's estimate
is obviously not so wide of the mark for the time
of which he wrote that it cannot be utilised for
comparison with earlier and later figures. This is
especially the case as regards the valuations of capital
with which we are more immediately concerned.

The following is a summary of Mr. Colquhoun's
valuations of capital. (See p. 103) :—

| | £ |
|---|---|
| England | 1,846,900,000 |
| Scotland | 281,080,000 |
| Total Great Britain | 2,127,980,000 |
| Ireland | 563,600,000 |
| Total | 2,691,580,000* |

* Add dockyards, ships, &c., £45 millions, making a total of £2,736
millions, as on p. 103.

And these figures compare with the above totals of 1,500 millions for England and 1,750 for Great Britain, which are Mr. Beeke's figures, when certain corrections are made as to the debt and other matters. Mr. Colquhoun, in fact, leaves out the debt in his totals, and otherwise so deals with the subject as to place his calculations, as far as the omission and inclusion of items are concerned, very much on all fours with the more recent valuations. It cannot be said, I think, that an increase from 1,500 to 1,846 millions for England between 1800 to 1812, an increase of about 23 per cent., is at all out of the question or extravagant ; nor the similar increase for Great Britain from 1,750 to 2,127 millions. Looking at the great growth of business and the rise of prices in the interval, these changes are not out of the question. If Mr. Beeke is near the mark, Mr. Colquhoun cannot be far wrong.

I am disposed to think Mr. Colquhoun's figures for Ireland are too high, but not much, Ireland, however, not coming into Mr. Beeke's valuation. Still, it has to be remembered that Ireland was a much more important part of the United Kingdom, in proportion, at the beginning of the century than it is now, while its agriculture was specially stimulated at the expense of the people of Great Britain by the Corn Laws.

It may be convenient to state here for the sake of comparison the following principal items of Mr. Colquhoun's valuation, altering his arrangement a little so as to make them more easily comparable with other figures.

*Mr. Colquhoun's Estimates of Property*, 1812.

[In Millions.]

| | England. | Great Britain. | United Kingdom. |
|---|---|---|---|
| Lands ... ... ... ... ... ... | 750 | 900 | 1,200 |
| Tithes ... ... ... ... ... ... | 80 | 80 | 80 |
| Agricultural Property and Live Stock ... ... ... ... ... ... | 143 | 168 | 228 |
| Dwelling Houses ... ... ... ... | 300 | 330 | 400 |
| Mines and Minerals ... ... ... | 68 | 73 | 75 |
| Canals, Tolls, and Timber ... ... | 46 | 48 | 50 |
| Manufactured Goods — Home Trade ... ... ... ... ... ... | 100 | 116 | 140 |
| Foreign Merchandise ... ... ... | 33 | 37 | 40 |
| British Shipping ... ... ... ... | 20 | 24 | 27 |
| Fisheries ... ... ... ... ... ... | 3 | 6½ | 10 |
| Total ... ... ... ... ... | 1,543 | 1,782½ | 2,250 |
| Waste Lands, &c. ... ... ... ... | 82½ | 99 | 132 |
| Household Furniture ... ... ... | 130 | 145 | 185 |
| Wearing Apparel ... ... ... ... | 16 | 17½ | 21 |
| Plate, Jewels, &c. ... ... ... ... | 34 | 37½ | 44 |
| Specie ... ... ... ... ... ... | 9 | 11 | 15 |
| | 1,814½ | 2,092½ | 2,647 |
| Public Property, as Buildings, &c. | 32 | 35 | 44 |
| Dockyards, Ships, &c. ... ... ... | ... | ... | 45 |
| Total ... ... ... ... ... | 1,846½ | 2,127½ | 2,736 |

Mr. Colquhoun's estimate of income is given in such a way that details cannot be separately stated for England or Great Britain. The general result is as follows :—

*Property Created in Great Britain and Ireland in the Year 1812-13*

[In millions.]

| | |
|---|---|
| Agriculture in all its branches ... ... ... ... ... ... ... | £217 |
| Mines and Minerals, &c. ... ... ... ... ... ... ... ... | 9 |
| Manufactures ... ... ... ... ... ... ... ... ... ... | 114 |
| Inland Trade ... ... ... ... ... ... ... ... ... ... | 31½ |
| Foreign Commerce and Shipping ... ... ... ... ... ... | 46 |
| Coasting Trade ... ... ... ... ... ... ... ... ... | 2 |
| Fisheries, exclusive of Newfoundland ... ... ... ... ... | 2 |
| Chartered and Private Bankers ... ... ... ... ... ... | 3½ |
| Foreign Income Remitted ... ... ... ... ... ... ... | 5 |
| Total ... ... ... ... ... ... ... ... ... | £431 |

At first sight this seems too high, the figure of agricultural production being especially very large. The error, however, cannot be such as to throw us out much when comparisons are made with distant periods. The Income Tax income of Great Britain about 1812 was 130 millions sterling, and adding about a fourth for Ireland, which seems to have been the calculation of the relative resources of Ireland to those of Great Britain at that time, we get a total of 165 millions. This figure, according to modern experience of the relation of Income Tax income to total income would justify an estimate of such total income at about 350 millions ; and assuming, what seems to be the case, according to Mr. Beeke's estimate and other estimates at the time, that the Income Tax income bore a less proportion to the total than it now does, a figure of about 400 millions at least as the national income in 1812, at the high prices then ruling, would not appear to be far off the mark. This would also appear from a comparison with Mr. Beeke's estimate of income, which amounts to 218 millions for Great Britain in 1800. Allowing for the increase of population to 1812, and for rise of prices, &c., in the interval, this total in the latter year would not be far short of 320, and an addition of one-fourth for Ireland would bring the sum up to 400 millions. I think, however, judging by various signs, that Mr. Colquhoun's estimates of income are not, perhaps, so well supported by data as his estimates of capital, and at any rate they are not required for our present purpose. I have only called attention to these points to show that the figures are at least near enough the mark to be available for some distant comparisons.

Shortly after he wrote—viz., about 1820—Mr. Colquhoun's work was considered and discussed by Mr. Joseph Lowe, to whom I have already referred, whose corrected figures I now propose to add to those of Mr Colquhoun. There is the more reason for this, as values were, no doubt, somewhat inflated in 1812, when Mr Colquhoun wrote, and the inflation had died out in 1823, when Mr Lowe wrote.

I extract, then, from Mr. Lowe's work* a statement as to the capital of the country at the time he wrote. (See Appendix v.)

The principal items of this 1822 estimate are :—

|  | Mlns. |
|---|---|
|  | £ |
| Land under cultivation | 1,200 |
| Farming Capital | 200 |
| Dwelling Houses, Warehouses, and Manufactories (Houses) | 400 |
| Manufactured Goods | 140 |
| British Shipping | 20 |
| Other Mercantile and Manufacturing Capital | 130 |
| Mines and Minerals | 65 |
| Canals, Tolls, and Timber | 45 |
| Total | 2,200 |

Mr. Lowe's figures it will be seen are substantially those of Mr. Colquhoun with a few modifications in detail, and with the omission of those items of unproductive private property, such as furniture, plate, &c., and certain items of public property which I believe Mr. Colquhoun very properly includes. The effect then of Mr. Lowe's corrections generally is that

* See "The Present State of England." By Joseph Lowe. London 1823.

he believes the increase of population between 1812 and 1822, and the increase of things, nearly made up for whatever excess in Mr. Colquhoun's estimates was due to the inflation of prices in 1812. It will be seen, indeed, from the Table in the Appendix that Mr. Lowe himself gives the corrected figure of Mr. Colquhoun for 1812, for comparison with his own in 1822, as 2,350 millions. Substantially Mr. Lowe's figures are thus Mr. Colquhoun's figures, but they imply, it should be understood, real and considerable progress between the two dates—apparently, amounting to about 6½ per cent., or equal to the corrections which Mr. Lowe suggests for the fall in prices in the interval. It is Mr. Lowe's explicit opinion that there was this progress.

About sixteen years after Mr. Lowe, we come upon another valuation by Mr. Pablo de Pebrer, who is described as having written in English, and as being a member of several scientific societies, but of whose book I have only seen a French translation, published in 1839. This book is called "Histoire Financière de l'Empire Britannique," and it contains an elaborate calculation of capital and income based upon Mr. Colquhoun's valuations, on the general plan of adding one-third to them, being less than the increase of population in the interval, which was about 41 per cent. The writer, however, though he follows this general plan, is careful to justify its moderation by reference to many details, while he points out that Mr. Colquhoun was generally moderate according to the prices of the time. The result is not so satisfactory as if the writer had made a wholly independent and new valuation, but *quantum valeat* it may be referred to.

The principal items are :—

*Summary of Valuation of the United Kingdom for about the year 1833.*
[*Pablo de Pebrer's, based on Mr. Colquhoun's*].

| | England | Great Britain. | U. K. |
|---|---|---|---|
| | £ | £ | £ |
| Lands | 1,000 | 1,200 | 1,600 |
| Tithes | 106 | 106 | 106 |
| Agricultural Property | 190 | 223 | 302 |
| Houses | 400 | 440 | 533 |
| Mines and Minerals | 91 | 97 | 110 |
| Canals, Timber, Railways, &c. | 61 | 63 | 66 |
| Manufactured Goods | 133 | 154 | 186 |
| Foreign Merchandise | 44 | 49 | 53 |
| Shipping | 26 | 31 | 35 |
| Fisheries | 4 | 9 | 13 |
| Total | 2,055 | 2,372 | 2.995* |
| Waste Land | 110 | 132 | 176 |
| Household Furniture | 173 | 193 | 246 |
| Wearing Apparel | 21 | 23 | 27 |
| Plate, Jewellery, &c. | 45 | 49½ | 58½ |
| Coin, &c. | 12 | 14½ | 20 |
| Savings Banks | 13 | 13 | 14½ |
| Chancery Money, &c. | ... | ... | 40 |
| | 2,429 | 2,797 | 3,576* |
| Public Property, Buildings, &c. | 26 | 29 | 35 |
| Dockyards, Arsenals | 16 | 17 | 23 |
| War Ships, &c. | ... | ... | 46 |
| Total | 2,471 | 2,843 | 3,690* |

Such is a valuation about 1833, believed to be about the mark by an author who has taken some pains, though unfortunately for us he has only in form applied a somewhat mechanical method to a former valuation without making up an entirely new valuation from original materials. The weakest point in the whole is, perhaps, the new figures which the author gives for Savings Banks and Chancery money

* These figures, according to the addition, should be 3,004, 3,586 and 3,680; but the exact figures are copied.

as if these items were on the same footing as coin in
circulation, not observing that these moneys being
invested must appear under some other head in the
general valuation.  The amount is too small to make
any material difference in the general total, while the
item of coin itself to which these items are intended
to be supplementary is itself too small, as the reintro-
duction of specie payments must have caused, I should
say, a much greater addition than one-third before
1833, to the coin in circulation in 1812.  With all
defects, however, M. Pablo de Pebrer's valuation may,
perhaps, pass as a contemporary valuation for the
period between 1830 and 1840.

Subsequently to the latter date there are Income
Tax returns once more to be made use of, and as I
have now practically made three valuations based on
these returns, viz., for 1865, 1875, and 1885, I may,
perhaps, be allowed to leave the history at this
point.  I shall only point out that the first returns
to the renewed Income Tax for 1843 exhibit such
an increase as on the whole to confirm M. Pablo de
Pebrer for 1833.  The assessments to the Income
Tax for Great Britain, which were 130 millions in
1812, amounted to 240 millions in 1843—an increase
of about 80 per cent. as compared with the increase
of 30 per cent., which M. Pablo de Pebrer allows for
up to 1833.  Adding 80 per cent. to Mr. Colquhoun's
estimate of 2,700 millions as the property of 1812,
we should get a total of over 4,800 millions as the
property of 1843.  This figure would be, perhaps,
excessive, and it allows for an increase in Ireland
equal to what had gone on in Great Britain, which
is not likely to have occurred, but a figure of 4,000

millions for the United Kingdom about 1845 would
certainly not be over the mark. Some difference
might be made in the items, the increase in lands
being less, and the increase in other items, such as
houses, being more than M. Pablo de Pebrer shows;
but all the figures tend to show an enormous advance
between the two dates notwithstanding the fall of
prices.

None of these figures show much advance in the
amount per head as compared with Mr. Beeke's
valuation for Great Britain in 1800. This indicates,
however, a real advance in wealth, a fall in prices
being in progress the whole time from 1812 downwards. The infusion of the population of Ireland,
which is convenient for the sake of having a computation for the United Kingdom, also brings down
the average a little.

We may attach the more importance, therefore, to
the advance shown by the subsequent figures, especially as there is no doubt regarding the very latest,
that they are not inflated in any way by prices—that
prices generally in 1885 were about as low as at any
previous time in the century. If property has increased from about 2,000 millions and £140 per head
at the beginning of the century, and from about 4,000
millions, and the same amount per head towards the
middle of the century, to no less a figure than 10,000
millions and £270 per head at the present time, then
the latest experience is quite unprecedented. On a
very much larger scale the experience of the 17th
century, when the rental of England increased from
6 to 14 millions; and of the 18th century, in which
the capital of England increased from a little over
300 to about 1,500 millions; has been repeated in
the 19th century. The increase of capital in the

present century has again been nearly five times, and there is no suspicion, such as attaches to the increase in the 18th century, that it is partly due to a mere rise of prices.

A short Table, putting the leading results together, and introducing a comparison per head all through, may be interesting :—

*Growth of Capital and Population in England and the United Kingdom since 1600.* [*In round figures.*]

| Year. | Population. | Property. | Property per Head. |
|---|---|---|---|
| | Mlns. | Mlns. Stg. | £ |
| 1600 ... ... ... ... ... ... ... (British Merchant, &c.) | 4½ | 100 | 22 |
| 1680 ... ... ... ... ... ... ... (Petty.) | 5½ | 250 | 46 |
| 1690 ... ... ... ... ... ... ... (Gregory King-Davenant.) | 5½ | 320 | 58 |
| 1720 ... ... ... ... ... ... ... (British Merchant.) | 6¼ | 370 | 57 |
| 1750 ... ... ... ... ... ... ... (Various.) | 7 | 500 | 71 |
| 1800 ... ... ... ... ... ... ... (Beeke.) | 9 | 1,500 | 167 |
| **GREAT BRITAIN.** | | | |
| Beeke ... ... ... ... ... ... ... | 11 | 1,750 | 160 |
| **UNITED KINGDOM.** | | | |
| 1812 ... ... ... ... ... ... ... (Colquhoun.) | 17 | 2,700 | 160 |
| 1822 ... ... ... ... ... ... ... (Colquhoun-Lowe.) | 21 | 2,500 | 120 |
| 1833 ... ... ... ... ... ... ... (Colquhoun-Pablo de Pabrer.) | 25 | 3,600 | 144 |
| 1845 ... ... ... ... ... ... ... (Income Tax.) | 28 | 4,000 | 143 |
| 1865 ... ... ... ... ... ... ... | 30 | 6,000 | 200 |
| 1875 ... ... ... ... ... ... ... | 33 | 8,500 | 260 |
| Present time ... ... ... ... ... | 37 | 10,000 | 270 |

The changes are thus constantly in an upward direction, with the exception of the short period between 1812 and 1822, when allowance had to be made for the fall in prices. No doubt part of the rise, with the exception of that in the present century, may be ascribed to the rise in prices which undoubtedly took place in the first half of the 17th and the latter part of the 18th century, but on the whole there is a vast real advance as well as nominal advance all through. As already remarked, as far as the increase in the present century is concerned, comparing the latest with the earliest date, no part can be ascribed to the rise of prices, since prices are now at the lowest level on which they have been since the beginning of the century. There may have been some such rise affecting the valuations of 1865 and 1875, but that rise has since been lost, and comparing the present time with a date like 1812, and perhaps 1800, there is undoubtedly a fall of prices.

It is interesting to observe also the variations in the amounts of some of the principal items of property and their proportions to the total. I need only show the two items, land and houses, and at one or two of the dates only :—

*Summary Showing the Growth of Lands and Houses and their Proportion to Total Property.*

| | LAND. | | HOUSES. | |
|---|---|---|---|---|
| | Amount. (In mlns. stg.) | Proportion Per Cent. of Total. | Amount. (In mlns. stg.) | Proportion Per Cent. of Total. |
| ENGLAND. | | | | |
| 1690 ... ... ... ... (Gregory King.) | 180 | 60 | 45 | 15 |
| 1800 ... ... ... ... (Beeke.) | 600 | 40 | 180 | 15 |
| UNITED KINGDOM. | | | | |
| 1812 ... ... ... ... (Colquhoun.) | 1,200 | 44 | 400 | 15 |
| 1865 ... ... ... ... | 1,864 | 30 | 1,031 | 17 |
| 1875 ... ... ... ... | 2,007 | 24 | 1,420 | 17 |
| 1885 ... ... ... ... | 1,691 | 17 | 1,927 | 19 |

Thus, lands, from constituting at the beginning of the period 60 per cent. of the property of the country, and while forming as late as 1865 about 30 per cent. of the property, do not now constitute 20 per cent. of the total, there having also been in the most recent years an absolute decrease in amount, while other capital is increasing. Houses, on the other hand, maintain a rather increasing proportion of a total property, which is itself constantly increasing in amount; and in the last period of all this tendency has been accentuated till houses—buildings—have come to constitute a fifth part of the total property of the country. Changes like this have undoubtedly been in progress. The proportion of individual property held in land has been steadily diminishing, other property increasing by leaps and bounds, while land, though participating in the unearned increment, has improved more slowly, and of late years has diminished absolutely in value, owing to the unearned increment having for the moment disappeared under the influence of foreign competition. At the same time the progress of civilisation is steadily marked by the growth and improvement of buildings, which increase not only with population and the increase of property generally, but in even a greater ratio.

This is hardly the place to introduce general economic remarks, or deduce special lessons from the figures, especially as I reserve a chapter for the discussion of the uses to which such figures may be put. I should like, however, just to say a word in passing, on a question which will perhaps occur to many.— How do these figures bear on the problem of the improvement or detoriation of the masses from period to period? I think it has been sufficiently demonstrated, that in the last fifty years there has been progress all round; in recent years, as I need not remind you, not so much at the top as lower down ; but it is alleged that just fifty years ago the masses had sustained a special deterioration. Sometime ago on the strength of mortality and other statistics I put in a *caveat* against this conclusion, and on the strength of the figures here given I am disposed to strengthen this *caveat*. All through it seems to me there must have been improvement all round. The necessary effect of a continuous increase of capital is dispersal. If the land monopoly had been constantly absorbing more and more of the national earnings through unearned increment, the conclusion might have been different, but the unearned increment is plainly *un peu de chose.* What all the figures point to is that there has been a steady levelling up among the masses for several centuries ; that this improvement largely takes the shape of constant additions to the lower middle class and the upper artisan class ; and that there is a residuum which does not improve much, and hardly, by comparison, seems to improve at all, but this residuum certainly diminishes in proportion, and probably diminishes in absolute amount, from century to century and from period to period. It would be impossible to set out fully here the facts supporting this view ; but as the question may arise on the general figures here exhibited, I desire to anticipate a natural and hasty, but what I believe a most erroneous conclusion inconsistent with many other facts.

Of course other communities throughout the world have progressed in a like manner—the United States even more remarkably. The statement made is not intended to be of a Chauvinist or spread-eagle kind. It is merely to state scientifically in a line how immensely greater in reality are the resources of modern communities than those of their predecessors in a very recent period—to render a little clearer, in fact, the degree of material improvement in modern times.

# CHAPTER VI.

---

## ACCUMULATIONS OF CAPITAL IN FOREIGN COUNTRIES.

I PROPOSE now to consider for a little the question of the accumulations of capital in other countries. What estimates on the subject have been made by our principal neighbours? and how far are the results arrived at comparable with our own ?

The United States is above all the foreign country, if it is correct to speak of it as a foreign country at all, in which we are most interested, while it is also a country in which for a considerable period, attempts at a national valuation have been made. Let us look, then, first at what is done in the United States.

There is first of all in the United States an official valuation. The principal source of revenue in the States and localities is a tax upon property, which must by the terms of the constitution itself be equal upon all property. Hence every State has an official valuation. But, like attempts to tax property elsewhere, this provision has failed. Either property escapes taxation by being greatly undervalued, or it escapes assessment altogether, the property called personal, as distinguished from real, it need hardly be said, being the kind which escapes. In consequence, at every census since 1850, the officers entrusted with the duty have endeavoured to arrive at a true valuation, as well as to bring together the figures of the assessment. The method and details of this true valuation are not, as far as I have observed, fully explained in the census reports, but the nature of the attempt is at any rate partially indicated. That there is a great difference between the assessment and the " true valuation " goes without saying. The differences since 1850 have been as follows :—

| | Assessment. Mln. Dollars. | True Valuation. Mln. Dollars. | Proportion of Assessment to True Valuation % |
|---|---|---|---|
| | $ | $ | |
| 1860 ... ... ... ... | 12,083 | 16,159 | 75.50 |
| 1870 ... ... ... ... | 14.187 | 30,068 | 47.23 |
| 1880 ... ... ... ... | 16,902 | 43,642 | 38.73 |

—showing an increasing discrepancy between the assessment and the true valuation, which may be largely ascribed, there is no doubt, to the vast growth of personal property in recent years.

Practically also for the present purpose we must discard the official assessment and look at the true valuation only, as being at any rate an attempt to arrive at a figure resembling the valuations which we have been using as a means of computing the accumulations of capital.

The true valuation of 1880, then, is given in the census of that year (see vol. 7, pp. 11, *et seq*) as follows :—

"*True*" *Valuation of the United States according to the Census of 1880.*

| | Miln Dollars. | Milns Stlg. |
|---|---|---|
| | $ | £ |
| Farms | 10,197 | 2,039'4 |
| Residence and business real estate | 9,881 | 1,976'2 |
| Railroad and equipment | 5,536 | 1,107'2 |
| Telegraphs, shipping, and canals | 419 | 83'8 |
| Live stock, farming tools, and machinery | 2,406 | 481'2 |
| Household furniture, painting, books,clothing, jewellery, household supplies, and food, fuel, &c. | 5,000 | 1,000'0 |
| Mines, petroleum wells, and quarries, with one-half the annual product estimated as amount on hand | 781 | 156'2 |
| Three fourths of the annual products of agriculture and manufactures, and of the imports of foreign goods estimated as the average supply on hand | 6,160 | 1,232'0 |
| All real estate exempt from taxation | 2,000 | 400'0 |
| Specie | 612 | 122'4 |
| Miscellaneous—including tools of mechanics | 650 | 130'0 |
| Total | 43,642 | 8.728'4 |

And comparing this broadly with the similar valuation for the United Kingdom above given, which is for five years later, or the similar valuation for the United Kingdom for 1875, which is for five years earlier, it is easy to see that the United States' figures are at least within sight of the mark. In 1880 the United States had a population of 51 millions, as compared with 37 millions in the United Kingdom in 1885, and although the United States might be assumed not to have the manufacturing capital or the large investments of the people of the United Kingdom, yet their agricultural and general wealth could not but be enormous, and might easily reach in 1880 the total of the United Kingdom in 1875.

In detail also there is nothing improbable in the particular items. Thus the valuation of "farms" corresponds very closely with the item of lands in the statement for the United Kingdom, which seems by no means unreasonable considering that the cultivated area of the United States in 1880 amounted to over 160,000,000 acres, or more than three times the cultivated area of the United Kingdom. The relation of capital value to income is not explained in the United States returns, but making all allowance for the inferiority of the cultivation and the smaller saleable value of the same net income in the United States compared with the United Kingdom, the value of farms in the United States must be enormous.

The next item of "residence and business real estate" appears to come into comparison with the item of Houses, &c., in the Income Tax returns, and is more than the similar English valuation for 1875, and just about the English total for 1885. Always remembering, however, the enormously greater population of the United States compared with that of the United Kingdom, the figure cannot but be considered as at least an approximate one.

The next item of "railroads and equipment" is supported fairly by the railway returns of the United States, though the figure seems a little too high as compared with what a valuation by net income capitalised at so many years' purchase would have produced. The net income of the United States railways in 1880, according to the United States Statistical Abstract, was about £42,000,000, and to justify a valuation of £1,100,000 this sum would have to be capitalised at 26 years' purchase, which seems above the rate at which railway income sells for, or rather sold for in 1880, in the United States. Still the figure cannot be said to be excessive or unreasonable.

The next item, that of "live stock, farming tools, and machinery," amounting to £480,000,000, seems very large. It does not include the whole farming capital, much less the whole capital corresponding to Schedule B in England, and it points to a much larger figure for agricultural capital in the United States than anything I have ventured to assign for England. But we should look for some such result. The agricultural business of the United States is enormous compared with that of England, and even at much smaller values for every kind of stock and produce, the valuation runs into very big figures.

The next item, that of "household furniture," is expressly defended by Mr. Gannett, of the United States Census, who is responsible for it, as having been very carefully made, though the process by which it is built up, as is the case with the other items, is not shown in detail. It is interesting to note that, however it may be arrived at, it corresponds very closely to half the valuation of the item of "houses," which we have assumed it would be a safe rule to follow in the United Kingdom.

The item of mines, &c., like the same item in the United Kingdom, is comparatively small, notwithstanding the importance attached to mines.

The next large item, that of "Three-fourths of annual products of agriculture and manufactures and of the imports of foreign goods estimated at the average supply on hand," has nothing exactly corresponding in the English method, but with the addition of two other items, "specie" and "miscellaneous," may be assumed to correspond fairly well with the items of Other Public Companies, Trades and Professions, Trades and Professions Omitted, and Income of Non-Income Tax classes derived from capital in the United Kingdom valuations, with this difference only, that perhaps a fifth of the American valuation under this head is really agricultural capital. American figures on this head for 1880 would thus compare with similar figures for the United Kingdom in 1885 :—

| AMERICAN FIGURES. | Mlns Stg. |
|---|---|
| Three-fourths of Annual Products, &c. ... ... ... ... | £1,232 |
| Specie ... ... ... ... ... ... ... ... ... ... ... ... | 123 |
| Miscellaneous ... ... ... ... ... ... ... ... ... ... | 130 |
| | £1,485 |
| Deduct— | |
| One-fifth assumed to be Agricultural Capital ... ... ... | 297 |
| Total ... ... ... ... ... ... ... ... | £1,188 |
| ENGLISH FIGURES. | |
| Other Public Companies ... ... ... ... ... ... ... ... | £696 |
| Trades and Professions in Income Tax ... ... ... ... | 541 |
| Do. do. omitted ... ... ... ... ... | 123 |
| Capital of Income and Non-Income Tax Classes derived from Capital ... ... ... ... ... ... ... ... ... ... | 335 |
| Total ... ... ... ... ... ... ... | £1,694 |

Perhaps one or two other items ought to go into the valuation of the United Kingdom for comparison, but I doubt if anything very considerable. I cannot help thinking, then, that on this head there is either some under-valuation in the English returns, or some over-valuation in the United States. A large part of the special wealth of England is in its stocks of goods—the circulating capital of its shops and warehouses. The population engaged in these branches must be much larger than the similar population in the United States. It is hardly possible that the corresponding capital can be so little more. I am disposed to think that the English valuation is rather under the mark, but the point is not very material.

The items in which the English valuation differs most from the American is in the amount of capital invested abroad. To this there is, of course, nothing corresponding in the American return, although it amounts to £1,300 millions in the English valuation. There is, also, no valuation of national property in the United States returns.

On the whole, then, there seems nothing unreasonable in the American valuation so as to make it unsuitable for comparison with the English valuation, the object of both being to state a figure representing the exchangeable value of property belonging to the people at current rates. The process by which the American figures are built up is not shown in detail as the similar process is in England ; but there are other modes of checking the main items, as we have seen. So long, therefore, as there is no attempt at reasoning too finely, and the comparisons are limited to such objects as showing the comparative growth of capital proportionately to former amounts, the United States figures may be taken to be as sufficiently on all fours with those of the United Kingdom for the purpose.

There is only one important qualification to be made, I think. This is, that the United States being a country where a large part of the capital in use is owned abroad, a deduction from the capital brought out by the above method of calculation ought to be made so as to exhibit the net capital of the community of the United States. Not only should the valuation of the United Kingdom differ from that of the United States, by including an item for capital invested abroad, but there should be the further difference that the valuation of the United States should exhibit a deduction in respect of foreign capital invested in the United States.

How much should that deduction be ? If there were no borrowing or lending transactions going on, and no remittances from the United States to other countries to pay the expenses of Americans travelling or residing abroad, the interest of the indebtedness ought to be shown by the excess of exports over imports ; but corrections must, of course, be made. I am inclined to submit the following account as for about the year 1880 :—

*Statement showing the sum approximately due Annually by the Community of the United States in respect of Foreign Capital invested in the United States:—*

| | Mlns. | | Mlns. |
|---|---|---|---|
| **Dr.** | £ | **Cr.** | £ |
| Imports—Average 1879-81 | 122 | Exports—Average 1879-81 | 170 |
| Under valuation of ditto in official returns ... ... | 20 | | |
| Amount annually due for Americans travelling or residing abroad ... ... | 20 | | |
| Balance ... ... ... ... | 8 | | |
| | 170 | | 170 |
| | | Balance brought down ... | 8 |
| | | Add estimated annual borrowing or sales of securities in Europe on American account ... | 42 |
| | | Total ... ... ... | 50 |

Of course an account like this is only a rough guess at the reality, and everything it will be

observed turns upon the point as to the amount of
the annual borrowing in Europe on American account,
which must be very large, and but for which the
excess of exports now shown in the American returns
would be even larger than it is. At twenty years'
purchase the 50 millions of estimated annual indebtedness of the American community on account of foreign
capital invested would come to 1,000 millions sterling,
which is a serious deduction from the valuation
of capital above stated. Instead of having been
£8,700,000,000 in 1880 according to the above statement, it must have been under £8,000,000,000.
Some deduction must be made.

It need hardly be added, however, that the valuation being for 1880, and the growth of population
in the United States being enormously rapid, the
capital figures for 1885, if we had been able to get
them, so as to show a figure properly comparable
with the valuation of the United Kingdom, would
have been nearly as much as, if not more than, those
of the United Kingdom, even making a deduction,
as above suggested, for foreign capital invested in
the United States.

The growth of capital in the United States may
now be shown. For this purpose I extract from my
former essay, with the addition of the above figures
for 1880, a statement of the comparative growth of
capital in the United States according to the " true
valuation" since 1850, and with an estimate on a
similar basis for the census periods before that made
by the United States census authorities. The figures
before 1870, it should be explained, include the
valuation of slaves in the Southern States ; and there
are, of course, other minor discrepancies, in conse-

quence of changes, of which there is no record, in the method of valuation, but the real growth must evidently have been so large that minor discrepancies are lost. As explained in a note, also, the figures for 1870 are subject to a deduction of 15 per cent., or thereabouts, so as to reduce them to a gold valuation; and it will, of course, be understood that all the figures are subject to further deduction on account of foreign capital invested in the United States. (See p. 125.)

Deducting for foreign capital invested in the United States the figures would still be very large.

This statement may be compared with the similar statement for the United Kingdom (*supra* p. 110). The growth in the United States absolutely is greater than in the United Kingdom, but the wealth of the latter community per head is still the larger.

It must be kept in mind, of course, that the comparison is here of capital and not of income. Nothing would, in fact, be more interesting than to show the different relation of income to capital in different countries. It does not follow that because one community is inferior to another in the exchangeable value of its property either in total amount or per head, therefore everything has been said as to their relative resources. The differences in the stage of economic development they have reached, the potentialities as well as the actualities of their condition, the earning power as distinguished from the exchangeable value of the property, are all matters to be considered. The property test is useful as far as it goes, but it is not the only test. And we can all see that these points must be specially kept in mind with regard to the United States. A new country so full of un-

[CONTINUED ON P. 126.]

*Statement showing the Population and Wealth of the United States by
decades from 1790 to 1880; Decennial percentage Increase of
Population; Decennial percentage of Increase of National Wealth;
and Average Property to each person. (See table, p. 186 of " Essays
in Finance," 1st series):—*

| Year. | Popula-tion. | Wealth. | Decennial Percentage Increase. | | Average Property to each person. |
|---|---|---|---|---|---|
| | Mlns. | Miln. dollars. | Popula-tion. | Wealth. | $ |
| 1790 ... | 3·9 | $750 (estimated) | ... | ... | 187·00 |
| 1800 ... | 5·3 | 1,072 ,, | 35·02 | 43·0 | 202·13 |
| 1810 ... | 7·2 | 1,500 ,, | 36·43 | 39·0 | 207·20 |
| 1820 ... | 9·6 | 1,882 ,, | 33·13 | 25·4 | 195·00 |
| 1830 ... | 12·8 | 2,653 ,, | 33·49 | 41·0 | 206·00 |
| 1840 ... | 17·0 | 3,764 (official) | 32·67 | 41·7 | 220·00 |
| 1850 ... | 23·2 | 7,136 ,, | 35·87 | 89·6 | 307·67 |
| 1860 ... | 31·5 | 16,159 ,, | 35·59 | 126·42 | 510·00 |
| 1870 ... | 38·5 | 30,069 ,, | 22·00 | 86·13 | 776·96* |
| 1880 ... | 50·1 | 43,642 ,, | 30·13 | 45·47 | 870·00 |

\* Allowance ought to be made here for the depreciation of the dollar
between 1860 and 1870. In the introduction to Vol. VII. of the Tenth
Census of the United States, p. 8, it is also stated that between 1860 and
1870, allowance ought also to be made for the fact that slave property
is included in the former census and had disappeared in the latter. Mr.
Gannett suggests that, including slave property in 1860, as well as in
1870, and allowing for the depreciation of the dollar in 1870, *i.e.,* reducing the values at that date to gold values, the more approximately correct
figures of the true valuation for 1860 and 1870 would be :—

    1860 ... ... ... ... ... ... ... 9,253,000,000 dollars
    1870 ... ... ... ... ... ... ... 23,973,000,000 „

I have thought it more convenient, however, to retain the official
figures in the text. It brings up to a point, what is said elsewhere, as
to the importance of price in these valuations.

developed resources may develope much quicker than another. The comparison one day shows it to be inferior in capital or property to another community; but the next time we look the whole position may be changed.

Let us next turn to France, which, for historical reasons, as well as reasons of neighbourhood, is by far the most interesting country to us,—next, at any rate, to the United States.

Here, we find, computations of national wealth have been made, especially in recent years, as to which we may put the question how far they are comparable with our own.

M. de Foville, whose name is so well known in this country, and whom every statistician must honour greatly for the good work he has done, has investigated the subject so thoroughly as regards France, summing up what has been done by others as well as himself, that one is necessarily spared a great deal of labour in the discussion. If there is any imperfection in our reference, it will be easy for those interested to refer to the various writings of M. de Foville.

It is obvious, then, at the outset, that it would not do to accept any valuation of property for another country, and compare it with the figures above set out for the United Kingdom, and we must now add the United States figures, without looking into the details, and understanding the process by which the account is made up. M. de Foville gives the following list of different estimates in recent years, and although the first is, perhaps, of too old a date to be comparable, yet the others are obviously recent

enough, regard being had to the slow growth of
population in France, to justify the expectation that
they would approximate closer than they do if they
were all made on the same basis :—

*Estimates of Property in France* [*mlns. stg.*] \*

| Authors. | Date. | Real Property. | Personal Property. | Total. |
|---|---|---|---|---|
|  |  | £ | £ | £ |
| M. de Girardin ... ... | 1853 | 3,680 | 1,320 | 5,000 |
| M. Wolowski ... ... ... | 1871 | 4,800 | 2,200 | 7,000 |
| M. C. Duc d'Ayen ... ... | 1872 | 4,000 | 3,800 | 7,800 |
| M. C. D. Vacher ... ... | 1878 | 8,640 | 1,760 | 10,400 |
| M. Amelin ... ... ... | 1878 | 5,400 | 4,200 | 9,600 |
| M. S. Mony ... ... ... | 1881 | 4,600 | 4,040 | 8,640 |

I need not weary the reader with the details of
these estimates, though to the students who wish to
understand what statistical method is, I can recom-
mend M. de Foville's criticism and comparison. It
is quite plain that, however useful even widely dif-
fering estimates may be, if each set of estimates for
different years is made up in the same way, for showing the progressive accumulation of capital and the
variations in the rate of accumulation, and for similar
purposes, yet that such estimates themselves cannot
even be compared with each other properly, or with
those of other countries, without an understanding
as to details and method. I need only mention that
in some no distinction is made between incomes from
property and incomes from personal exertion, but all
are capitalised alike ; whereas in others, agreeing with
the plan we have ourselves followed in the United
Kingdom, and which appears to be followed in the
United States, the idea of property, which is really
exchangeable, is steadily kept in mind, and there is
no capitalising of income, except there is property to

* M. de Foville : "La France Economique," p. 438.

answer to it. M. de Foville refers to even larger
estimates that have been made in France than some
of the above, but there is, of course, no need to refer
to them.

For all practical purposes I need only use for comparison with our own valuations M. de Foville's own
estimates, because they are obviously devised with
the same end in view, and have the confirmation to a
large extent, as he points out, of partial estimates by
M. Maurice Block, another name we must mention
with honour in this country, as regards real and
personal property at different times in France.

M. de Foville then made the following estimate in
1878, which he supplements by a less detailed estimate for the present time in his recent book, "La
France Economique":—

*M. de Foville's Estimates of French Property.*

| 1878.* | £ | 1886.† | £ |
|---|---|---|---|
| Real Property, exclusive of Houses ... ... ... | 4,000 | Real Property, exclusive of Houses ... ... ... | 3,200 |
| Houses, &c. ... ... ... | 1,000 | Houses, &c. ... ... ... | 1,600 |
| French Property Abroad | 600 | French Funds & Foreign Securities ... ... ... | 1,200 |
| Gold and Silver ... ... | 320 | Other moveable Property | 2,000 |
| Furniture, Personal Pro-perty, Works of Art ... | 400 | | |
| Agricultural "Material" | 160 | | |
| Farm Animals and others | 200 | | |
| Agricultural "Appro-visionnement" ... ... | 200 | | |
| Other Commercial Capital | 200 | | |
| Other Industrial Capital | 800 | | |
| Marine, Arsenals, &c. ... | 120 | | |
| Total ... ... ... ... | £8,000 | Total ... ... ... .. | 8,000 |

The estimate for the present time is much the
same in total as for 1878, but the details are generally
not comparable. In reality, the 1886 estimate is less
than the 1878 estimate, as it includes the amount of
the French National Debt not included in the 1878

* *Economiste Francaise,* Jan. 18, 1879.    † *La France Economique,* p. 442.

estimate, but that there is ground for a reduction of some sort, or, at any rate, for little or no increase, is justified by M. de Foville on the score of the fall in prices and the consequent fall in value of much real and other property in the interval.

In two respects, it will be observed, the above figures for the present time differ from those employed for the United Kingdom. They include in the valuation of property the amount of the home debt, which is not included in the above valuation for the United Kingdom, and which in France is a larger sum than it is in the United Kingdom, and they do not include the amount of Government and local property, which items are included in the valuation of the United Kingdom. M. de Foville discusses this point ; and, making an addition to his figures for the present time, so as to include the property of Government and local authorities, and then deducting the aggregate amount of their debts, he arrives at a sum of about 7,200 millions sterling, which would be properly comparable, as far as I can judge, with the valuation of the United Kingdom.

An examination of the details confirms the *vrai-semblance* of these figures for France. By far the most important item, it will be observed, is that of " real property not built upon," answering to the lands in our own returns, and for this figure there are undoubtedly abundant data, the net income and selling value, (the latter through the registration duties on the transfer of property,) being matters of official record. In point of fact, the selling value of real property not built upon in France was officially reckoned by the French Financial Administration in 1882 at 3,663 millions sterling, so that M. de Foville's figure in the above estimate shows a considerable falling off. There are similar means of dealing with the next great item—the house property, which seems to me rather more highly valued than similar property in the valuation of the United Kingdom, if we assume, as I suppose we may, that farm-houses are valued with the land, but still not so highly valued as to make the comparison wholly out of place. As regards others, M. de Foville shows that he is quite alive to all the points to be considered, and it would be out of place to follow him minutely. That the moveable property of the United Kingdom must be enormously greater than in France goes without saying, though perhaps some may think not so great as represented by the figure of about 6,000 millions sterling for the United Kingdom, and less than 3,000 millions for France.

If the valuations of the United Kingdom and of France, in any case, are not properly comparable, the data as regards France are very fully supplied by M. de Foville, and there need be no mystery on the point.

M. de Foville has discussed, with no small ingenuity, a method of ascertaining the amount of property in France from the amounts annually passing by succession, a process to which he has resorted in the absence of income tax figures corresponding to those which we have for England. The conclusion at which he arrives is that the average annual amount of the successions, *plus* about a fourth for successions *inter vivos*, may be multiplied by 36 so as to show the amount of property held in the country—the assumption being that 1-36th part is succeeded to annually either by death or gift, about 1-45th part by death alone. The speculation is a most interesting one, and is based largely upon data of a kind in the possession of the Ministry of Finance, which are either not in the possession of our own Inland Revenue department or are not published by them. Mr. Porter in this country, as I pointed out in my former essay, seemed to arrive at a similar proportion of 1-45th annually passing by death. I should like to see the question followed up more carefully both in this country and in France. Meanwhile it may be observed that if the proportion can be assumed not to vary for considerable periods, as I think may be the case : there is every antecedent probability, looking at the slow change in the rates of mortality or the customs of people regarding inheritance, that it will not vary greatly : then the growth of property passing by succession should indicate the growth of property itself. Succession figures are most useful for our discussion. We can compare the rate of growth of property which we arrive at by successive valuations with the rate of growth indicated by the amounts passing at death.

Looked at in this way there is no doubt that the growth of property in France has been very rapid, as rapid during the present century as in the United Kingdom. The following are the French succession duty figures at ten years' intervals since 1826 :—

*Successions and Donations* inter vivos *annually taxed in France at the undermentioned dates.**

|  | Successions. | Donations. | Total. |
|---|---|---|---|
|  | £ Stg. Mlns. | £ Stg. Mlns. | £ Stg. Mlns. |
| 1826 ... ... ... ... ... | 53·5 | 18·0 | 71·5 |
| 1835 ... ... ... ... ... | 61·6 | 20·8 | 82·4 |
| 1845 ... .. ... ... ... | 69·7 | 28·1 | 97·8 |
| 1855 ... ... ... ... ... | 96·3 | 29·0 | 125·3 |
| 1865 ... ... ... ... ... | 121·2 | 34·0 | 155·2 |
| 1875 ... ... ... ... ... | 170·2 | 42·7 | 212·9 |
| 1885 ... ... ... ... ... | 216·3 | 40·1 | 256·4 |

* *La France Economique*, p. 440.

Allowing for a change in the method of valuing rural property in 1875, these figures show comparatively little progress since that time, apparently confirming M. de Foville's disposition not to swell the totals, but rather to diminish them since he made his estimate in 1878. In the United Kingdom there would equally have been little progress, as far as we can judge, apart from the increase of population. Thus in France, as in the United Kingdom, the progress in money values has not been so great since 1875 as before.

I do not propose to go into the subject of estimates of property in other countries. Students who desire to follow this subject will find references in M. de Foville's papers. The only other countries for which verifiable computation seems to have been made are Belgium and Italy. In the former case the estimate is that of M. Massalski, whose work I have not seen, but who has followed, apparently, the method of M. de Foville—the preferable method in a country which has data like those of France or Belgium or Italy—and who thus arrives at a total of about £1,200 millions (29½ milliards of francs)—a calculation so far supported by an estimate of £440 millions alone for the value of the real property, land, and houses, which is stated to have the authority of M. Malou, who valued in 1880 lands at £300 millions and houses at £136 millions.* The total of £1,200 millions seems to compare closely with that above given for Scotland, which has a smaller population, but which is probably somewhat richer per

---

* See De Foville: "La France Economique," p. 446. I have not seen this calculation of M. Malou, but it is not improbable, as M. Malou has made a valuation of £320 millions for the year 1865 or thereabouts.

head. With regard to Italy, we have the advantage
of a very elaborate study by M. Pantaleoni, a most
able Italian economist, who discusses fully the whole
question of valuations of property in different
countries in his work, entitled, *Dell 'Ammontare
Probabile della Richezza privata in Italia*, published
at Rome in 1884. Finally, M. Pantaleoni adopts
the method of M. de Foville in calculating from the
figures of the succession duty by means of a co-effi-
cient, though he supports the results by direct calculations as to the value of lands and houses. In this
way he arrives at a total of £1,920 millions for Italy
composed approximately as follows :—*

|  | Mlns. stg. |
| --- | --- |
|  | £ |
| Land ... ... ... ... ... ... ... ... ... | 1,160 |
| Houses ... ... ... ... ... ... ... ... ... | 360 |
| Other property ... ... ... ... ... ... ... | 400 |
| Total... ... ... ... ... ... ... ... | 1,920 |

I should have thought, at first sight, that such
figures were too small for Italy, whose population is
three-fourths that of France, but whose wealth,
according to this account, is something like 2-7ths
only. It is not essential, however, for our present
purpose to criticise minutely ; M. Pantaleoni has certainly discussed the subject in a proper manner, and
I could not go behind his data. That he considers it
not improbable that the private wealth of Italians is
much less than that of Frenchmen is a fact of itself
to be taken note of. The figures may not be very
exact, but some such difference, we may be sure,
exists, much else that is known of the economic condition of Italy agreeing with the estimates.

* Pp. 221 et seq.

Still, neither as to Belgium, nor Italy, do I wish to critise in detail, especially in the absence of any figures as to the accumulation of capital which is our special topic. What I wish to point out is that, for those who care to follow up the subject, certain data are accessible in many countries, which would assist in the compilation of useful figures, although the limit of error would necessarily be somewhat wide. The chief items everywhere must be land and houses, and in most cases now railways, the first being relatively more important in almost every other country than it is in England. Limits of the valuation in gross of other items, if land, houses, and railways can be valued, are always capable of being ascertained, even if no exact figure can be stated. But it is absolutely necessary for comparison that the process should be set out in full; that a valuation of capital, as much as possible, should be made on some calulation of income; and that such points as whether a community is a creditor or indebted in respect to other nations should be allowed for.

# CHAPTER VII.

## THE USE OF NATIONAL VALUATIONS.

In my former essay, and in the introduction to the present essay, the uses to which general valuations of the property of a community, and of the estimates of accumulation of capital derived from them, may be put are briefly indicated. After this long inquiry it may be useful to return to the topic, and explain in some measure how the statistics may be applied.

But first let it be understood, as it cannot be too frequently repeated, that the figures, which can be arrived at by any method, are necessarily not exact. A detailed valuation of each description of property is hardly possible, and would present many difficulties of its own, while it would be subject in any case to the observation that only by a violent hypothesis can the property of a community be valued like that of an indidvidual member of it, seeing that it is not conceivable that it can all be the subject of a sale at a given moment. In actual fact, however, we have to be content with something that falls very far short of such a detailed valuation, and to apply average rates of value to gross quantities either of property or income which are themselves imperfectly ascertained. For certain purposes the results may be good enough, and I believe are good enough ; but they are certainly not to be treated as sums in an account definitely ascertained, and compared one with another, without attention to the nature of the data themselves, and the similarity or dissimilarity of the processes by which the results are arrived at.

The uses to which the figures can properly be put, regard being always had to the fact that the data and methods employed are sufficiently alike for the special purpose in hand, appear to be the following :—

1. To measure the accumulation of capital in communities at intervals of some length—not less, perhaps, than ten years—this having been the main object in view in my essay in 1878 on the accumulation of capital, and being perhaps the most important use to which such figures can be put.

2. To compare the income of a community, where estimates of income exist, with its property.

3. To measure the burden of national debts upon different communities.

4. To measure, in conjunction with other factors, such as aggregate income, revenue, and population, the relative strength and resources of different communities.

5. To indicate generally the proportions of the different descriptions of property in a country to the total—how the wealth of a community is composed.

6. To measure the progress of a community from period to period, or the relative progress of two or

more communities, in conjunction with the facts as to progress in income, population, and the like ; to apply, in fact, historically and in conjunction with No. 1, the measures used under the above heads 2, 3, 4, and 5 for a comparison at a given moment.

7. To compare the aggregate accumulation in a community with that portion of the accumulation which can be described as free savings, and which is gradually invested through the agency of the Stock Exchange.

8. To throw light on the question of changes in the value of money, which are themselves among the facts to be investigated and allowed for in comparing the valuations of different countries, or the valuations of the same country at different times.

There are, no doubt, other uses to which the figures of national valuations, when judiciously used, can properly be put ; but the above, it may be allowed, form a good enough list if it can be shown, as I think it can, that with all their inexactness the figures still supply useful materials for discussion. There is, of course, no reason why such figures should not be used if they are exact enough for the purpose, and if they are the best obtainable.

To take the various heads of comparison in their order, there can be no doubt, to begin with, that it is with reference to the accumulation of capital, and especially for the comparison of such accumulations over different periods, that valuations of property are, perhaps, most useful, and it was for this purpose mainly that the present study has been entered upon. Here, from the nature of the case, whatever roughness there may be in the property valuations themselves, the results arrived at become trustworthy for comparison, provided the same method is followed in the valuations. Of course, the figure of accumulation is itself mainly useful as a comparative figure for comparison with other figures, as we shall notice presently ; but accumulation is so obviously important a matter that it may be given a separate head. The problem whether a community is adding to its possessions or not is of manifest interest.

That the calculation is rough is also no serious drawback to its utility. It is even important to know whether there is progress or not ; and not only can progress or retrogression be shown, but the limit of error is reducible to a narrow percentage. According to a well known rule of statistics, also, the movement may be even more exactly appreciated than the amount of the accumulation at a given period. Suppose the accumulation at two dates to be inexactly stated, owing to the necessary imperfection of the figures by 10 per cent., the intermediate accumulation will also be inexactly stated by an equal percentage. But the proportion of this intermediate accumulation to the total property at a given date, as it is itself only a fraction of the total, need not be inexact by more than a small percentage of that total property. When the figures of valuations of property, therefore, are spoken of as inexact, it should be remembered that the real utility of the figures is not thereby brought into question. The proportion of the accumulation to the property may be shown more exactly than the valuation of the property itself at a given date.

We come next to the use of such valuations for the purpose of comparison with estimates of the income of the communities concerned. Here, again, minute

accuracy must be unnecessary, while the utility of
the proposed comparison is obvious.  The relation
between property and income, roughly as the figures
may be done, must disclose something as to the
economic condition of the communities, and help to
render clearer the true idea of that economic condition
which might be best derived from other sources.  It
is obvious, for instance, that the income of the community of the United States is probably much larger
in proportion to the property than it is in an older
country.  The fact that it is a community indebted
to other communities instead of being a creditor
community is, and is caused by, a material difference
in their circumstances.  It is because their income is
so large, because their natural resources undeveloped
or in process of development are so large, that they
can afford so well to borrow.  Potential is quickly
converted into actual capital, and individual members
of the community have less need of capital.  But the
circumstances are likely enough to change rapidly,
and even now the different conditions of geographical
groups within the greater community of a nation
like the United States must present great variety.

Of course, for any such purpose the figures of
property valuation can only be used with great
discretion, and by avoiding any attempt to reason
finely, especially as approximate figures of income
are as difficult as approximate figures of property.
The conclusions which the figures may point to are
illustrative and suggestive ; but it is wise, of course,
to use them only with a due consideration on independent data of what their real meaning may be.

The next special and obvious use of a property
valuation which has been mentioned is to make a

comparison between it and the amount of national
and local indebtedness. Here, again, there is no
question of the appositeness and sufficient accuracy
of the figures. We need give only a few illustrations.

Our own National Debt looks enormous, but, after
all, it is only about 7½ per cent. of the property of
the country, a mere bagatelle, especially taking into
account the fact of its being held at home. Reducing
the national valuation itself by any conceivable
amount, it must still be a bagatelle. It is mostly, in
fact, as well as appearance, a charge upon the income
of property as distinguished from the income from
personal exertion, and it has to be viewed as really a
mode of distributing the wealth of the community
among individuals, and not as a burden upon taxpayers, who are separate in fact, as well as in name,
from the fundholders ; but, apart from such views as
to the burden of National Debts, the proportion of the
debt to the whole wealth of the country in our own
case is plainly a small one, and would still be a small
one, however much the valuation of the property
might conceivably be modified. Even adding the
debts of local authorities—about 200 millions in
all—the indebtedness of the community to the fund-
holder is under 10 per cent.

The value of these comparisons is even more clearly
seen if we look abroad. In France, it is plain, the
national indebtedness is a much more serious affair
than it is in England. The national and local debts
together in France cannot be put at less than about
1,200 millions sterling—about a sixth part of the
property of the community as compared with a
proportion of less than a tenth in the United

Kingdom. No doubt in France, as in the United Kingdom, the debt is only a mode of distributing the property of the propertied classes. What they pay as taxpayers they get back as fundholders ; but the difference in the two proportions must be felt in France as regards that portion of the debt burden which must be borne by the income from personal exertions as distinguished from the income of property.

In the United States, again, the debt is obviously a bagatelle. It is 300 millions only, or less, as compared with a property of, probably, at the present time, 8,000 or 9,000 millions, deducting what the community owes to foreign countries. Even if we add the indebtedness of State and local authorities, the United States, as a community, is singularly free from the burden of Government debt.

Illustrations could be multiplied without difficulty, but it is easy enough to see that the question of National Debts could hardly be properly treated at all except in the terms of property, and that however widely property may be estimated useful comparisons between its amount and that of the debt may be made.

We have next to deal with the use of such valuations as a rough measure of the relative strength of different communities, along with comparisons of other factors, such as territorial area, population, revenue, principal sources of revenue, and the like. Here there can surely be no doubt of the appositeness and sufficient accuracy of the figures. The comparison of the property of the respective communities in a line, as it were, even if it is somewhat roughly done, shows markedly how two communities may differ in wealth, and, as far as wealth is a measure of strength, qualifies any inferences that might be drawn from a comparison of population alone, or of one or two items of wealth only, or of actual as distinguished from potential revenue. Where the differences are great the value and necessity of the comparison are obvious. If they can be supplemented by comparisons of national income so much the better, and nothing else can supply their place.

We have only to look at the estimates of property for the two chief countries mentioned in the preceding chapter and compare them with similar results for the United Kingdom to perceive how any conclusions as to relative strength from numbers of population and actual revenue alone must be modified.

In population France exceeds the United Kingdom a little; in Imperial revenue a great deal, though in Imperial and local revenue together, not so much. In population, the United States exceeds the United Kingdom enormously; in actual Imperial revenue it falls short a little, though, perhaps, not so as regards Imperial, State, and local revenues all put together. A superficial examination of population and revenue alone would tempt to the conclusion that France has larger resources than the United Kingdom, because it has more population and more revenue; and that the United States has more resources than either because it has larger population, and does not fall short in revenue when Imperial, State, and local revenues are put together.

These conclusions themselves may also be true, apart from the data; there may be other data to support

them ; but at least the data we have been dealing
with as to property show that it would be unsafe to
rest in the conclusions without farther examination
and discussion.

Taking population alone, the figures for the three
countries are about :—

|  | Mlns. |
|---|---|
| United Kingdom ... ... ... ... ... ... ... ... ... ... | 37 |
| France ... ... ... ... ... ... ... ... ... ... ... ... | 38 |
| United States (part estimate) ... ... ... ... ... ... ... | 56 |

Taking actual revenue alone, the figures are :—

|  | Imperial. | Local (includ'g State). | Total. |
|---|---|---|---|
| United Kingdom (mlns.) ... ... ... | 90 | 60 | 150 |
| France „ ... ... ... | 140 | 40 | 180 |
| United States „ ... ... ... | 70 | 65 | 135 |

The amounts per head being :—

|  | £ s. |
|---|---|
| United Kingdom ... ... ... ... ... ... ... ... ... ... | 4 0 |
| France ... ... ... ... ... ... ... ... ... ... ... ... | 4 10 |
| United States ... ... ... ... ... ... ... ... ... ... ... | 2 10 |

In property, however, the figures would work out :—

|  | Total. | Per head. |
|---|---|---|
| United Kingdom ... ... ... ... ... ... ... | 10,000 | 270 |
| France ... ... ... ... ... ... ... ... ... | 7,200 | 190 |
| United States ... ... ... ... ... ... ... ... | 8,000* | 160 |

—showing that if the United Kingdom has fewer
numbers than its great neighbours, and a smaller, or
not greater, actual revenue, yet its property as

* Not deducting for indebtedness to foreign countries.

actually developed is greater, and especially greater per head, which must surely qualify very much the conclusion from numbers and revenue alone. That this must be the case can be seen by the simplest comparison between the property and the actual revenue. In France the Imperial taxation is nearly 2 per cent. of the property; Imperial and local revenue together, $2\frac{1}{2}$ per cent. of the property. In the United Kingdom the proportion is for Imperial revenue about 0 9 per cent only; for Imperial and local together, less than $1\frac{1}{2}$ per cent. Whatever the income from property may be, these differences in what is taken by the Government must be serious. Similarly, in the United States, although the taxation per head is less than in the United Kingdom, the annual revenue of the central government in proportion to the capital of the community mounts up to about 1 per cent. of the property; and the annual revenues of the central state and local governments together to about $1\frac{1}{2}$ per cent. of the property. The notion that taxation in the United States is low compared with the figure in the United Kingdom is thus shown to be unfounded, while we get a notion of the burden of taxation in France, which alters altogether the superficial impression conveyed by the amount of the national revenue itself. If we were to go farther, and compare taxation with income and taxable income as well as with property, the aspect of the facts would be still further altered, I believe, to the advantage of the United Kingdom in the comparison; but it would clearly be useful also to compare the property.

The broad facts are also such, it will be observed, that any possible variation from the true facts as to property would modify the conclusions very little.

The greater wealth of the United Kingdom per head, as compared with either France or the United States, would still remain undoubted, however the figures may be modifiable ; though we must now conclude that in absolute amount at the present moment the wealth of the United States is probably much greater than that of the United Kingdom, and almost certainly as great.

Comparing the wealth of the United Kingdom, or of France and the United States, with other States, such as Italy and Belgium, there is room of course for a still wider margin of error without affecting the broad conclusion of their immense preponderance in resources.

The preponderance of England by itself in the United Kingdom as compared with either Scotland or Ireland, especially Ireland, is equally apparent, and no possible modification of the figures would alter the conclusion. It is infinitely greater than the preponderance shown by population alone.

A special point on this head may also be referred to. We hear a good deal of the vast expenditure on military armaments, and the burden they impose on certain communities. Heavy as the burdens are, does not the vast amount of property relatively indicate that the point of exhaustion may be more remote than is commonly supposed ? To treat this topic suitably would require a paper by itself, which I hope to write some day ; but it may be useful now to hint at the conclusions I am disposed to arrive at. The relativity of the burden of military armaments has been too little considered, I fear, by economists who have denounced them in the abstract, and whose denunciations have, in fact, been falsified by the continued prosperity of the countries which ought to have been ruined but were not.

The next suggested use of the figures is that of indicating generally the proportions of the different descriptions of property in a community—how the wealth of a community is composed. Here we find that the relative bulk of the main descriptions of property comes out clearly enough, while the utility of being able to answer, however roughly, how much of the property is land, how much houses, how much is invested in industry, and so on, is manifest. These are obviously all matters which may become of practical interest in connection with problems of taxation, as they were, in fact, of interest at the beginning of the century, when Dr. Beeke made one of the studies on the subject to which reference has been made in the course of the present essay. The fact of exact figures being impossible hardly affects the value of the result. It is important, for instance, to know whether land represents about three-fourths, or a-half, or a-third, or a less proportion of the whole wealth of a community, although it may not be possible to state to a fraction whether the proportion, instead of being exactly three-fourths, is perhaps 70 per cent. only, or perhaps 80 per cent. Within a very wide limit of error the figures may obviously be of some use.

The value of the results is increased when historical comparisons are attempted, or comparisons between different countries. If in a country like England we find land at one historical period to constitute 60 per cent. or upwards of the total wealth, and then by a gradual descent to be less than 20 per cent., the value of the land itself almost all the while steadily increasing, then, in spite of inexactness in the figures, the broad fact is in many ways instructive. Whether the change, if more exactly described, would be from, say, 65 or 55 to 25 or 15 per cent., the nature of the change would hardly be affected, while it is obvious that the limit of possible error is not nearly so wide. In comparing England with France, again, or with the United States, it is at once obvious that economic conditions are entirely different, seeing that England has less than a fifth of its wealth in land, while France has half, or more than half, and the United States more than a third. Minute accuracy is here unnecessary, while the proportions, if fractionally changed, would still justify the broad conclusions which they now appear to justify.

We come next to the question of applying the figures in the comparisons above stated in the illustration of historical problems, either in the history of a particular country or in the comparative history of one or more countries. Here, again, minute accuracy is less necessary than ever, while the appositeness of the figures is more than ever palpable. This has already been seen incidentally in various ways, as, for instance, with reference to the last head of the comparison where attention has been drawn to the changing proportion of land to other property in England. But many other illustrations could be given. To begin with,—The concrete instances already given in Chapters III. and VI., have only to be mentioned to show how practically useful these comparisons may become. The conspicuous difference between the proportions of the National Debt to our resources at the end of the great wars

at the beginning of the century, and at the present
time, shows, perhaps, most strikingly the value of the
comparison.   The whole debt, allowing especially for
the recent increase of the debt incurred for the
purpose of making loans to local authorities, has not
diminished much in the interval ; but seventy years
ago this debt amounted to a third of the property of
the community.   The accumulations of the community in the interval, from about 2,200 to 10,000
millions, or, in round figures, $7\frac{1}{2}$ thousand millions of
accumulations, are about ten times the National
Debt proper, and about eight times the debt of the
Imperial Government and the localities put together.
Comparing the progress of the accumulation with
revenue, what appears is that, whereas the revenue of
the State seventy years ago was equal to a tax of
about 3 per cent. on the property of the community,
it is now, as we have seen, about 0·9 per cent. only of
the property, and, even adding local revenues, the
whole is less than $1\frac{1}{2}$ per cent. of the property.   The
burden of Government is thus greatly less than it
was.

When the respective amounts per head are compared, the facts are exhibited even more strikingly.
Whatever doubts, it may again be repeated, exist as
to the valuations themselves, yet the limit of error
is such, when we compare such distant intervals, as
to leave no doubt that, when all possible corrections
are made, the comparisons of the accumulations with
the growth of population, revenue, and debt would
be substantially unaffected.   That there has been an
immense reduction of burdens compared with resources is clear.

Even comparing the last two or three decades only,

where we have not the advantage of distant intervals
to take away the effect of unavoidable error in somewhat rough computations, the figures are found to
be so large as to justify our affirming with certainty
a great reduction of burdens.  Between 1865 and
1875 the increase of property, amounting to 2,400
millions, was about three times the debt; between
1875 and 1885 the increase, amounting to 1,500
millions, was nearly twice the debt.  The valuations
at each date may be rough, but being made on the
same basis on each date, the figures as to the accumulations can hardly be exaggerated.  Suppose the
mode of valuation to exaggerate the property at a
given date 10 per cent., the effect would be to exaggerate the accumulation between two dates by an
equal percentage.  In the first period, therefore, the
correction would be to substitute about 2,160 for 2,400
millions, and in the second period to substitute 1,350
for 1,500 millions, which would for all practical purposes show so enormous a growth of property in comparison with debt as to make the difference between
them and the larger figures immaterial.

The figures, of course, are only to be used in conjunction with other facts, and such a fact, for instance,
as the fall of prices qualifies them materially for some
comparisons.  In the present case, however, the comparison is of one money value with another, and the
relation of property to debt has changed in the way
described.  It is quite conceivable, however, that
along with changes in a community as regards real
wealth, wealth in things as distinguished from money
values, in the direction of greater prosperity, or the
reverse, there might be changes in money values in
the opposite direction.  All that is noticed here is the

actual change as between property and debt, which is not affected by this consideration.

The comparisons are even more interesting when we pass to France and the United States. In France, it may be doubted whether property has been increasing for several years, but debt has been increasing. Between 1865 and 1875, again, came the Franco-German war, which added several hundred millions to the debt. If we go back fifty years ago or so, it might appear that French resources have increased to an enormously greater amount than the debt ; but it may be doubted whether the proportion of debt to resources is not higher than it was—at least, if a comparison is made for the last ten years or so.

In any case, if there is improvement in France as regards resources in relation to debt, and a similar improvement as regards property and revenue, it is not so great an improvement as there has been in the United Kingdom in the same period.

The same facts could be shown by a comparison of the growth of expenditure only, which has been much greater in amount and proportion in the last fifty years than it has been in the United Kingdom; but the relation between resources and burden makes the comparison far more complete.

The history of the United States on this head is quite the opposite. As lately as 1865 the United States had a debt of 600 millions sterling, with an annual charge of 30 millions sterling, bearing a considerable proportion, there is no doubt, to the property and resources of the country at the time. The sum of 600 millions, as compared with the true valuation of 1860 above given, is about 20 per cent. Now the debt is only half what it was, and the property is three times what it was. The debt, from being a fifth of the property, has, in the short period of twenty years, become one-thirtieth only.

In no other way could the difference in financial progress between France and the United States be so vividly shown as by introducing this factor of property in dealing with the financial history. The difference between the United States and the United Kingdom, though not so marked, is also very great. Our accumulations in the same period are about five times our debt, which has not much changed in the interval. The accumulations in the United States are ten times what the debt was at the commencement of the period, and twenty times what it is now.

Of course the results thus arrived at are only materials for the critical economist or historian who has to discuss causes and consequences. The United States may have acted unwisely and might have been able to exhibit even better results if it had acted differently. Either France or the United Kingdom, on the other hand, may have done the best that could be done with the means at their command. Communities have their good and bad fortune. The criticism and discussion should be all the clearer, however, the better the facts are brought out.

We come next to the use of the statistics for comparing the growth of the capital in a given period with the amount annually available for investment through the mechanism of the Stock Exchange. On this head the figures appear to be most instructive as regards an economic fact of exceeding importance and difficulty. It is most difficult to realise, until one thinks of it, that savings in the modern industrial world can only be made by a community as a

whole *as they are invested;* saving and investment
go on *pari passu.* But the appreciation of this fact
is necessary to the comprehension of our monetary
system. If the two things were not to go on *pari
passu,* and the saving community in all directions
endeavoured to heap up its savings in hard cash even
for a month, certainly if it did so for a year, the
Money Market would collapse. The accumulations of
a single year, even taking them at 150 millions only,
according to the figures of 1875-85, instead of the
higher figures of the preceding decade, would absorb
more than the entire metallic currency of the country.
They cannot, therefore, be made in cash. An individual may save by depositing what he calls cash
with his banker; but the banker must either invest
directly or indirectly through a borrower, and there
must be new investments for the new money, or the
investments could not be made in the aggregate, for
although the banker or his borrower may purchase
old investments, the seller has immediately the same
money to re-invest. Hence the importance of the
question of what has been described as free savings
coming on the Stock Exchange for investment, as
compared with accumulation generally. Savings, in
fact, are made as a rule individually. A shopkeeper,
or merchant, or manufacturer making profit adds to
his stock, or improves his premises, or buys a new
house. In this or some similar way profits and
savings are invested directly as they are made, and
they have no visible effect on the Money Market.
The industrial world could not, in fact, go on unless
by a fixed arrangement for saving,—a portion of the
community being constantly employed by the savings
directly to create the investments in which the

savings may be put. It is only a certain part of
the whole savings which goes to the Stock Exchange,
and seeks new securities of the kind dealt with there.
Even a portion of this part is comparatively steady ;
but there is a varying surplus, and the changes in
this surplus, or final margin, are most significant of
the general state of trade. When the surplus is at
a maximum it is a sign of inflation, of great and
unusual profits in trade ; when it is at a minimum it
is a sign of losses and discredit. It is probable that
even the final margin never varies so much as it
seems to vary; difficulties arising through people,
when prosperous, engaging to invest more than they
afterwards find they can save, but the real savings
not even then being changed. But there are undoubtedly variations in the final margin which it
would be interesting to trace. Whatever it is, let it
be understood that the margin is one which, like all
other savings, is accruing constantly, and is constantly
being invested. If it were not so, there would be a
great accumulation of cash in the banks, and this we
never see.

How much is the free saving in proportion to the
total, how much is the margin, and how much does
the margin vary ? No complete answer can be given
to these questions; but from calculations I have made
at different times I should say that about 80 millions
annually represents this free saving, or about a third
of the annual accumulations between 1865 and 1875,
and about a half of the annual accumulations between 1875 and 1885. This means, however, that
the amount as a rule is about a third, because the
fall of prices has to be allowed for in the latter
period. But for this fall the money value of property

at the present time would be more than it is, and we may assume that the new accumulations, in things, have been more than the difference of the valuations in 1875 and 1885. In any case the figure must be a large one. The saving in the form of new houses and furniture, the largest items in the above list, is not free savings; and the same may be said of many of the investments in mines and other property, especially in trades and professions. The savings are invested as they are accumulated, directly by the owners, and are not free. As to the final and varying margin it is impossible to give exact figures, but even a small sum, such as 20 millions, coming on the Stock Exchange in a fat year compared with a lean year probably makes an enormous difference. Any greater apparent difference probably implies much inflation and paper profit which swells Stock Exchange prices for a time, but disappears as it began. The free margin, whatever it is, goes very largely into foreign and colonial securities, but the exact amount invested in this manner cannot easily be traced in consequence of the continual sales and purchases of old securities as distinguished from new issues which are being made. It is quite easy for the Stock Exchange of London to purchase and bring over from New York batches of existing American securities, the money which is paid for them being invested by Americans in new securities. The rule that there cannot be a new saving in the aggregate without a new investment is thus complied with; but the aggregate in the case supposed must include the whole field of investment—the new investment need not be at home, and it may be made abroad in an indirect manner. *Qua* the English investor the transaction is the purchase of an old security, but *qua* the general field of saving and investment, there is in the whole transactions a new investment.

The final question to be treated is the use of these general figures in discussions as to changes of prices and in the purchasing power of money. Illustrations have already been given on this head in connection with the question of the comparative rate of progress of accumulation in different periods during the last fifty years and longer (see Chapter III. *supra*); but it may be useful to point out even more generally how the figures may be used.

It is plain, then, that the results of the valuations of the property of the community at different dates unavoidably suggest that changes of prices may have to be allowed for. The increase of the valuation, it is plain, may either be in exact proportion to the increase of population, or in proportion to that increase multiplied by an assumed increase of the productive capacity of the people in the period under review. If two periods are compared in which the increase of population is known to be at much the same rate throughout, and the increase of productive capacity may be assumed to be at the same rate or not less in one of the periods than in the other, then if the apparent accumulation of capital in the one period proved to be less than in the other, it must be ascribed to some change in the money values. All other factors are equal, but the money expression of wealth has not increased as it would have done if prices had also been equal. This has been fully shown in the illustration already referred to from recent periods in English history. The utility of the figures, therefore, to illustrate changes of prices is apparent.

That the phenomena are quite general is obvious, moreover, from a comparison with the French returns of successions already referred to. Whatever may be the causes of these changes of prices, their visible effect on the periodic valuations of property leaves no doubt that they can only be described as significant of changes in the purchasing power of money—in the ratio of exchanges between money and other things. If the valuations were to be corrected by the ratio of exchange of a group of staple articles, a more steady rate of growth would be apparent.

Farther, there is no doubt that in future such valuations may even be more useful in connection with questions of changes in prices than they have been in the past. As valuations are made more frequently from time to time, and the method and data improve, while other data, showing the progress of population and of industrial power, also improve, the varying rates of the accumulation of property as expressed in money cannot but attract attention. The failure of a money accumulation to come up to a normal rate, or its excess over that rate, or its correspondence to that rate, will all be matter for observation and discussion, and will serve to correct and qualify the notions as to changes in the standard itself which may be otherwise arrived at. It is already permissible to anticipate that the next valuation of the United Kingdom may show about as slow a progress as that of the last decade, and not the rapid advance of the years 1855-75. The same in other countries. The reason being not that real wealth—the wealth in things—is not progressing at

as great a rate as ever it did before, but that the
material of which money is made, notwithstanding
the constantly new appliances for the efficiency of
money, does not alter in such a way as to maintain
prices at their former level.

Valuation of property, therefore, and studies of the
accumulation of capital, though the figures are necessarily rough, have their uses in various investigations.
They make a little clear what would otherwise be
most dark, and they suggest problems for inquiry
which would not otherwise be thought of.   The
figures, though rough, can be reasoned on safely with
care.   Better figures would be desirable, but in the
absence of better figures it would be folly not to
use what we have, and set our wits to work to use
them properly.

I should be disappointed, however, if the discussions of the last few years do not lead in time to the
production of better figures.   As the practice of
periodic valuations continues, light should be thrown
on the value of the method and the way in which it
can be used properly, while investigations could be
made by means of the various property taxes and
otherwise which would throw light on some of the
more difficult parts of the problem.   If the Inland
Revenue Department, for instance, were to inquire
into the proportions of different kinds of property
passing at death, and to publish the results, these
proportions might become a check upon general
valuations of property.   The resemblances or differences in the proportions might suggest points for
inquiry, and by arguing from the known to the
unknown, useful corrections, at least, in minor details,

could probably be obtained. The census might also
be made use of, as it is in the United States, in order
to obtain data for an independent valuation apart
from the Income Tax returns. Were all this trouble
taken, results would be arrived at which would be of
the utmost value to the Government practically, as
well as to economists in their discussions. The
progress of revenue is intimately connected with the
progress of national resources, and the progress of
money revenue with the progress of the money
expression of these resources. The resources themselves and the money values must be studied by
Chancellors of the Exchequer with almost equal
anxiety, and they should both, at any rate, be studied
together. Periodical complete valuations of property
are in this view as indispensable as the census of
population itself.

# APPENDIX.

I.—Estimate of Annual Interest on English Capital Invested
Abroad in Public Loans or Shares of Companies.

*(Compiled from "Investor's Monthly Manual," 31st May, 1886, and Banking
Supplement to "Economist" for 22nd May, 1886.)*

[000's omitted.]

| | £ | £ |
|---|---|---|
| 1. *Public Loans* in "Manual" List, exclusive of United States, French, Austrian, and Italian, only partially held here, and of Prussian, Dutch, and certain (recent) Russian loans, almost wholly held abroad. | 38,470 | |
| Add estimate for proportion of United States, French 4½ per cents, Austrian, and Italian held here. Total interest = £37,267,000, say 1/10th.* | 3,726 | |
| | | 42,196 |
| 2. *Railways.*— | | |
| (a) United States, excepting shares and bonds of lines in default | 13,906 | |
| (b) Indian and Colonial | 6,264 | |
| (c) Foreign, £7,042, less £1,168, half of Lombardo-Venetian interest | 5,874 | |
| (d) Add—French railways £17,990, say 1/10th held in England | 1,799 | |
| | | 27,843 |
| 3. Dividends of Anglo-Foreign and Colonial | | |
| (a) Banks | | 3,656 |
| (b) Canal companies† | 314 | |
| (c) City loans | 964 | |
| (d) Gas and waterworks | 1,093 | |
| (e) Coal, iron, and steel companies | 120 | |
| (f) Land, financial, and investment companies | 1,328 | |
| (g) Tea Companies | 71 | |
| (h) Other companies | 1,293 | |
| (i) Mines | 500 | |
| | | 5,683 |
| 4. Capital investment of English insurance companies doing business abroad, say £11,000,000 at 6 per cent | | 660 |
| 5. Deposits of Anglo-Foreign and Colonial banks,= £176,000,000 (*Economist*), at say 3 per cent | | 5,280 |
| Total | | 85,318 |

* In 1878 this item was estimated at ⅛th, but apparently since that time the English holding of these particular securities would seem to have been diminished in proportion.

† Exclusive of Suez Canal Shares.

II. - *Summary of List of Public Issues of Loans and undertakings on account of Foreign Countries in the years 1876-85 inclusive, as published in " Statistical Society's Journal," March, 1882, pp. 91 et seq and to be continued in the " Statistical Society's Journal" for 1890.*

[In thousands of pounds, 000's omitted.]

| | 1876. | 1877. | 1878. | 1879. | 1880. | 1881. | 1882. | 1883. | 1884. | 1885. |
|---|---|---|---|---|---|---|---|---|---|---|
| | £ | £ | £ | £ | £ | £ | £ | £ | £ | £ |
| Colonial Government Loans...................... | 16,240 | 7,370 | 11,451 | 18,934 | 12,982 | 11,168 | 9,177 | 24,097 | 23,937 | 23,530 |
| Municipal Loans ...... | 681 | 974 | 792 | 1,538 | 1,368 | 100 | 641 | 1,512 | 1,832 | 2,295 |
| Foreign Government Loans...................... | 3,479 | 6,272 | 10,730 | ... | 859 | 6,471 | 10,088 | 7,601 | 10,029 | 7,265 |
| Railway Issues ......... | 5,242 | 4,164 | 2,931 | 2,626 | 14,671 | 26,302 | 25,260 | 15,554 | 12,754 | 18,584 |
| | 25,642 | 18,780 | 25,904 | 23,098 | 29,880 | 44,041 | 45,166 | 48,764 | 48,852 | 51,674 |
| Miscellaneous Companies ................. | ... | 1,700 | 755 | 4,040 | 3,990 | 13,542 | 17,122 | 15,028 | 12,267 | 3,582 |
| Mining Companies .. | ... | ... | ... | ... | 7,051 | 11,082 | 2,643 | 2,500 | 3,852 | 2,252 |

III.—Valuation of England, Scotland, and Ireland, separately,
according to Income Tax Returns.—Year 1885.

## ENGLAND.

*Amount of Income in Income Tax Returns, derived from Capital ; Number
of Years' Purchase at which the same may be Capitalised ; and Approximate Amount of Capital, together with Estimate of remaining Income
and Capital in the Country.*

[000's omitted in amount columns.]

| | Income. | Years' P'rchase | Capital. |
|---|---|---|---|
| | £ | | £ |
| Under Schedule A— | | | |
| Lands | 47,594, | 28 | 1,332,632, |
| Houses | 112,792, | 15* | 1,700,741, |
| Other Profits | 732, | 30 | 21,960, |
| Schedule B— | | | |
| (Farmers' profits) | 47,788, | 8 | 382,304, |
| Schedule C— | | | |
| (Public funds less home funds) | 18,641, | 25 | 466,025, |
| Under Schedule D— | | | |
| Quarries | 821, | 4 | 3,284, |
| Mines | 6,609, | 4 | 26,436, |
| Ironworks | 1,924, | 4 | 7,696, |
| Gasworks | 4,463, | 25 | 111,575, |
| Waterworks | 2,945, | 20 | 58,900, |
| Canals | 3,012, | 20 | 60,240, |
| Fishings | 194, | 20 | 3,880. |
| Market Tolls, &c. | 520, | 20 | 10,400, |
| Other public companies | 29,692, | 20 | 593,840, |
| Foreign and colonial securities, &c. | 9,328, | 20 | 186,560, |
| Railways in United Kingdom | 28,190, | 28 | 789,320, |
| ,, out of United Kingdom | 3,681, | 20 | 73,620, |
| Interest paid out of rates, &c. | 4,567, | 25 | 114,175, |
| Other profits | 1,046, | 20 | 20,920, |
| Trades and professions—one-fifth of total income of £154,360,000 | 30,872, | 15 | 463,080, |
| Total under Income Tax | 355,411, | ... | 6,427,588, |
| Trades and professions omitted, 20 per cent. of amount assessed, or £30,872,000, of which one-fifth is | 6,174, 840,† | 15 15 | 92,610, 12,600, |
| Income of non-income-tax paying classes derived from capital | 57,000, | 5 | 285,000, |
| Foreign investments not in Schedules C or D | 50,000, | 10 | 500,000, |
| Movable property not yielding income, e.g., furniture of houses, &c., works of art, &c. | ... | ... | 850,000, |
| Government and local property, say | ... | ... | 450,000, |
| | 469,425, | ... | 8,617,793, |

* The number of years' purchase here is a small fraction over 15.
† Estimate of income escaping assessment by raising limit of exemption in 1876

## SCOTLAND.

*Amount of Income in Income Tax Returns, derived from Capital; Number
of Years' Purchase at which the same may be Capitalised; and Approximate Amount of Capital; together with Estimate of remaining Income
and Capital in the Country.*

[000's omitted in amount columns.]

|  | Income. | Years' P'rchase | Capital. |
|---|---|---|---|
| Under Schedule A— | £ |  | £ |
| Lands | 7,462, | 28 | 208,936, |
| Houses | 12,280, | 15* | 185,500, |
| Other Profits | 48, | 30 | 1,446, |
| Schedule B— (Farmers' profits) | 7,462, | 8 | 59,696, |
| Schedule C— (Public funds less home funds) | 1,400, | 25 | 35,000, |
| Under Schedule D— |  |  |  |
| Quarries | 99, | 4 | 396, |
| Mines | 982. | 4 | 3,928, |
| Ironworks | 341, | 4 | 1,364, |
| Gasworks | 372, | 25 | 9,300, |
| Waterworks | 265, | 20 | 5,300, |
| Canals | 409, | 20 | 8,180, |
| Fishings | 363, | 20 | 7,260, |
| Market Tolls, &c. | 24, | 20 | 480, |
| Other public companies | 3,813, | 20 | 76,260, |
| Foreign and colonial securities, &c. | 442, | 20 | 8,840, |
| Railways in United Kingdom | 3,792, | 28 | 106,176, |
| „ out of United Kingdom | 109, | 20 | 2,180, |
| Interest paid out of rates, &c. | 283, | 25 | 7,075, |
| Other profits. | 369, | 20 | 7,380, |
| Trades and professions—one-fifth of total income of £19,215,000 | 3,843, | 15 | 57,645, |
| Total under Income Tax | 44,158, | ... | 792,336, |
| Trades and professions omitted, 20 per cent. of amount assessed, or £3,843,000, of which one-fifth is | 769, 100,† | 15 15 | 11,535, 1,500, |
| Income of non-income-tax paying classes derived from capital | 7,500, | 5 | 37,500 |
| Foreign investments not in Schedules C or D | ... | ... | ... |
| Movable property not yielding income, e.g., furniture of houses, &c., works of art, &c. | ... | ... | 90,000, |
| Government and local property, say | ... | ... | 40,000, |
|  | 52,527, | ... | 972,871, |

* The number of years' purchase here is a small fraction over 15.
† Estimate of income escaping assessment by raising limit of exemption in 1876

## IRELAND.

*Amount of Income in Income Tax Returns, derived from Capital; Number of Years' Purchase at which the same may be Capitalised; and Approximate Amount of Capital; together with Estimate of remaining Income and Capital in the Country.*

[000's omitted in amount columns.]

| | Income. | Years' P'rchase | Capital. |
|---|---|---|---|
| | £ | | £ |
| **Under Schedule A—** | | | |
| Lands | 9,983, | 15 | 149,745, |
| Houses | 3,387, | 12* | 40,644, |
| Other Profits | 97, | 30 | 2,910, |
| **Schedule B—** | | | |
| (Farmers' Profits) | 9,983, | 8 | 79,864, |
| **Schedule C—** | | | |
| (Public funds less home funds) | 1,055, | 25 | 26,375, |
| **Under Schedule D—** | | | |
| Quarries | 13, | 4 | 52, |
| Mines | 12, | 4 | 48, |
| Ironworks | ... | 4 | ... |
| Gasworks | 191, | 25 | 4,775, |
| Waterworks | 50, | 20 | 1,000, |
| Canals, &c. | 125, | 20 | 2,500, |
| Fishings | 61, | 20 | 1,220, |
| Market Tolls, &c. | 46, | 20 | 920, |
| Other public companies | 1,284, | 20 | 25,680, |
| Foreign and colonial securities, &c. | 89, | 20 | 1,780. |
| Railways in United Kingdom | 1,288, | 28 | 36,064, |
| „ out of United Kingdom | 18, | 20 | 360, |
| Interest paid out of rates, &c. | 191, | 25 | 4,775, |
| Other profits | 20, | 20 | 400, |
| Trades and professions—one-fifth of } total income of £6,904,000 | 1,381, | 15 | 20,715, |
| **Total under Income Tax** | 29,274, | ... | 399,827, |
| Trades and professions omitted, 20 per cent. of } amount assessed, or £1,381,000, of which one- } fifth is | 276, 20,† | 15 15 | 4,140, 300, |
| Income of non-income-tax paying classes derived } from capital | 2,500, | 5 | 12,500, |
| Foreign investments not in Schedules C or D | ... | ... | ... |
| Movable property not yielding income, *e.g.*, furni- } ture of houses, &c., works of art, &c. | ... | ... | 20,000, |
| Government and local property, say | ... | ... | 10,000, |
| | 32,070, | ... | 446,767, |

\* This is less than the average for the United Kingdom.
† Estimate of income escaping assessment by raising limit of exemption in 1876.

IV.—Mr. Beeke's Valuation of Great Britain *circa* 1800.

*Extract from Mr. Beeke's Observations on the Produce of the Income Tax*
*&c. (pp, 182-5.)*

POSTSCRIPT.

I subjoin a short statement of the present value of the capital of Great Britain, abstracted from one which I drew up with some attention a few years ago, and which was calculated on grounds similar to those of the preceding estimate of income. It will not be expected that I should here enter into the particulars of my calculations, but this summary sketch may have its utility in pointing out the amount to which human industry has raised the value of this country beyond that of its natural produce, and in giving some idea of the immensity of the losses which might be occasioned by an overthrow of the principles of order and a disregard of the security of property. For this reason I have included a very moderate estimate of many articles of public property not convertible into money (at least, to any considerable amount), but which are necessary to the enjoyment of civil society in its present form, and which were originally provided, and must be replaced if destroyed, at an expense vastly exceeding what I have allowed for them.

PRIVATE PROPERTY.
PRODUCTIVE OF INCOME.

| | £ |
|---|---:|
| 1. Cultivated lands, South Britain, £600,000,000 ; North Britain, £120,000,000.* | 720,000,000 |
| 2. Tithes, in South Britain only after deductions for the personal service required on account of the part possessed by the clergy.† | 75,000,000 |
| 3. Houses not included in the rent of lands.‡ | 200,000,000 |
| 4. Mines, canals, timber, tolls, &c., &c.§ | 100,000,000 |
| 5. Present value of income from the public debt | 300,000,000 |
| 6. Farming capital, equal at present to not less, on an average, than 5 clear rents, viz., pasture, 2 to 3; arable, 5 to 7 rents | 125,000,000 |
| 7. Home trade.‖ | 120,000,000 |
| 8. Foreign trade and shipping** | 80,000,000 |
| | 1,720,000,000 |

| UNPRODUCTIVE OF INCOME. | £ |
|---|---:|
| 9. Waste lands, after excluding all such as are incapable of any improvement adequate to the expense, and also allowing for incidental diminution of the value of adjacent lands in case of their loss of the benefit of pasture, &c., about 10,000,000 acres | 30,000,000 |
| 10. Household furniture | 160,000,000 |
| 11. Plate, jewels, and all other useful and ornamental articles not considered as household furniture | 50,000,000 |
| 12. Specie, about | 40,000,000 |
| Unproductive private property | 280,000,000 |
| Productive private property | 1,720,000,000 |
| Total | 2,000,000,000 |

* See p. 19, &c.   † See p. 23, &c.   ‡ See p. 38.   § See p. 36, &c.   ‖ See p. 112. &c.   ** See p. 44, &c., and 111.   [These references are to the pages in Mr. Beeke's pamphlet.]

## PUBLIC PROPERTY.

| | £ |
|---|---|
| The value of that part of the permanent income * of the nation which is applicable to the annual expenditure, about | 160,000,000 |
| The value of that part which is appropriated to extinguish the public debt, about | 90,000,000 |
| Value of shipping, arsenals, national buildings, stores, credits, and all other assets, after deducting all unfunded debt | 15,000,000 |
| Value of all provincial and municipal buildings, &c., &c., as churches, hospitals, bridges, prisons, &c., &c., with the effects belonging to them | 25,000,000 |

* This calculation is founded on the produce of the national income in 1798, exclusive of the aid and assessment, or any other temporary articles. In 1799 that produce was much more considerable.

N.B.—A good deal of public has been already estimated jointly with private property, such as the crown lands, corporate incomes, &c., &c. But in so general a statement as this a more accurate analysis appears to be unnecessary.

The above statements must certainly, in many parts of them, depend on circumstances which allow a considerable latitude of conjecture; but they are not made in any instance without some attention to the general, civil, and political economy of the country, and probably do not vary more than one-tenth, at most, from the real value of the whole capital of Great Britain, which appears to be about £2,300,000,000 or between two thousand and two thousand five hundred millions sterling, exclusive of any value which might be assumed for personal labour; and also exclusive of foreign possessions to the value of at least £100,000,000 sterling, which belong to settled inhabitants of this country, and which, therefore, if sold, and if the produce of their sale were remitted to Great Britain, would obviously be considered as a part of the national capital, and perhaps ought now to have been included as such in the preceding estimate of productive private property.

## V.—Mr. Lowe's Valuation of the United Kingdom *circa* 1822.

*Extract from Mr. Joseph Lowe's " Present State of England"*
*(Appendix, pp. 82-3).*

### CALCULATION OF NATIONAL PROPERY.

| Great Britain and Ireland. | Computation for 1812, nearly in the form adopted by Mr. Colquhoun. | A similar Computation for 1823. |
|---|---|---|
| | £ | £ |
| Land under cultivation, whether in pasture, tillage, or gardens ............ | 1,280,000,000 | 1,200,000,000 |
| Farming capital, whether vested in implements of husbandry and farming stock, or in corn and other produce ...................................... | 228,000,000 | 200,000,000 |
| Dwelling - houses, warehouses, and manufactories ............................. | 400,000,000 | 400,000,000 |
| Manufactured goods in progress or ready for sale, whether in manufactories, warehouses, or shops; also foreign merchandise on hand ......... | 160,000,000 | 140,000,000 |
| British shipping of every description... | 27,000,000 | 20,000,000 |
| Here it seems fit to make an addition to Mr. Colquhoun's statements on account of— | | |
| Mercantile and manufacturing capital not specified by him, viz., money in hand, advances to correspondents abroad, manufacturing machinery, tools and implements of mechanics... | 130,000,000 | 130,000,000 |
| This carries to nearly £300,000,000 our mercantile and manufacturing capital employed in current business, and exclusive of whatever capital our merchants may have in fixed property, such as the funds, land, or houses. | | |
| Such are the great heads of our national property—the lesser, as given by Mr Colquhoun, are— | | |
| Mines and minerals ...................... | 75,000,000 | 65,000,000 |
| Canals, tolls, and timber ................ | 50,000,000 | 45,000,000 |
| Total ............................. | 2,350,000.000 | 2,200,000,000 |

This table is to be understood as representing private property, and exclusive of—

1. All public property, such as military stores, churches, hospitals; also of

2. Such private property as is unproductive—viz., waste lands, furniture, or wearing apparel; and, finally, of

3. Whatever is expressive of a debt from one part of the community to another, such as the stocks, mortgages, or mercantile acceptances.

How, it may now be asked, does it happen that the decrease of our national property, since the peace is so much less than is commonly supposed? The reasons are—

Land, as a property, is worth, in peace, from thirty-two to thirty - five years' purchase; in war, only twenty-seven or twenty-eight years' purchase; so that, though on our rental we reckon a fall of fully 30 per cent., the principal has not sunk above 15 or 20 per cent.

Farming capital experiences at present a depression of value far beyond the reduction in our table, but its amount in 1812 was, we believe, underrated by Mr Colquhoun, while, in point of quantity, whether of implements, cattle, or corn on hand, it has increased, probably, 20 per cent. since that year.

As to buildings, whether warehouses, manufactories, or dwellings, the surprising increase in the number appears fully to have balanced the decrease of rent, particularly as such decrease appears to have been much smaller in this kind of property than in land.

In our manufactured and foreign goods on hand the fall of price, great as it has been, is nearly equalled by the increase of quantity. In our shipping the case is otherwise, and we have accordingly made a large deduction.

Such is the comparative amount of our national property in 1812 and 1822 when represented in money of the respective years. But were the calculation for both made in money of equal value, the balance would be in favour of the present year; we mean, that the valuations for the present year, if made in the money of 1812, would not be short of £2,500,000,000.

Were we to take a retrospective view of the value of our national property since 1792, we should, in the absence of satisfactory returns for the earlier years, estimate it at two-thirds of the present amount.

individuals' calls for privacy. On July 15th 2010, Governor Jan Brewer of Arizona let state contracts expire for thirty-six fixed cameras and forty vans installed with cameras. The dismantling of the cameras and vans began the next day. Brewer's predecessor and the current Secretary of Homeland Security, Janet Napolitano, instituted these devices in September 2008. Behind the guise of advocating road safety, then Governor Napolitano believed the fixed and mobile cameras could generate up to $90 million in revenues to the state in the first year. In order to achieve such revenues, the cameras snapped photos of individuals traveling more than eleven miles per hour over the speed limit and then issued tickets for $181.[2] However, $90 million of revenue was never reached because the payment rate on the tickets was only 26 percent.[3] The refusal of folks in Arizona to pay the tickets issued by the government, and the subsequent dismantling and removal of the cameras and vans, is a testament to the power of individuals standing up for their rights—specifically, the right to privacy.

## Constitutional Guarantees

The United States Constitution does not expressly state a right to privacy. While numerous historians speculate and propose reasons as to why the Founders did not articulate this right in the text, the most telling reason may be the use of the word *privacy* in eighteenth-century America. In fact, a search of Thomas Jefferson's sixteen thousand writings and letters produces not a single usage of the word *privacy*,[4] because in the eighteenth century *privacy* referred to the bathroom or outhouse. Rather, the Founders used the term *security*, which meant to them essentially the same thing as our contemporary understanding of privacy. For example, the Fourth Amendment states, "The right of the people to be *secure* in their persons, houses, papers, and effects, against unreasonable searches and seizures, shall not be violated, and no Warrants shall issue, but upon probable cause."[5]

Moreover, additional amendments in the Bill of Rights address the issue of what we call privacy. The Third Amendment, which holds, "No Soldier shall . . . be quartered in any house, without the consent of the Owner," was directed at the British quartering of troops in the colonists' homes; an egregious violation of security for an eighteenth-century mind and privacy to a twenty-first-century mind. The Founders were determined not to repeat history. They assured the colonists their homes would no longer be invaded on a whim by the agents of the government, and their privacy there would be secure.

The Ninth Amendment then clearly states, "The enumeration in the Constitution of certain rights shall not be construed to deny or disparage others retained by the people."[6] The rights retained by the people are the unalienable natural rights, with which you are born. Natural rights can be compared to a sphere within which "individuals must remain free from [government] interference."[7] Privacy is essential to this sphere, and relates to the right or the ability of individuals to determine how much and what information about themselves is to be revealed to others. Additionally, privacy relates to the idea of autonomy, the freedom of individuals to perform or not perform certain acts, or subject themselves to certain experiences.[8]

For example, the German physicist Werner Heisenberg discovered the principle of uncertainty, or the Heisenberg Effect. The Heisenberg Effect stands for the principle that no individual can repeat the same performance unobserved as he can while being observed. In other words, we change or conform our behaviors when we know we are being watched. Take, for example, your daily job. When the boss is known to be in the office, most individuals are much more diligent than when they know no one is watching their daily actions. The same can be said for cameras on every street corner. If you know you are being filmed and want to whisper "sweet nothings" into your partner's ears, you may refrain from doing so because you know a uniformed policeman may be watching and listening on the other end. Thus, observation alone changes individuals' actions and strips them of their natural right to be left alone.

## You're Safe Nowhere: From Polaroids to Street Cameras

While today the natural right of privacy is widely recognized (and widely ignored), the right to be left alone was not always easily conceptualized. While our forefathers inherently valued their privacy, it was not until 1890 that the right to privacy entered the United States as a rational legal theory. In 1890, Justice Louis Brandeis recognized individuals' desire to remain anonymous.[9] In his now famous *Harvard Law Review* article, "The Right to Privacy," Justice Brandeis introduced the concept of a right to privacy when he stated, "The right to life has come to mean the right to enjoy life,—*the right to be le[f]t alone.*"[10] Moreover, the article reveals that Justice Brandeis was influenced to write on the right to be left alone in large measure by the then growing trend in technological advances.

Justice Brandeis would be horrified today if he observed the erosion of our right to privacy. In 1890, Brandeis expressed concern over the growing trend in technological advances because he worried that "instantaneous photographs and newspaper enterprise have invaded the sacred precincts of private and domestic life; and numerous mechanical devices threaten to make good the prediction that 'what is whispered in the closet shall be proclaimed from the house-tops.'"[11] This was in 1890! One can only imagine what Justice Brandeis would think of the countless cameras, license-plate readers, Web sites with personal profiles and picture-sharing applications, digital cameras, cell phones with cameras and recording devices, wiretapping, face-recognition technology, fingerprinting devices, Google maps displaying aerial views of your home, and similar technologies ripe for government abuse today.

Yet, it would be thirty-eight years before Brandeis advanced this theory in the Supreme Court. In the famous case of *Olmstead v. United States* (1928), the majority of the Supreme Court held the government's wiretapping of private telephone conversations to be constitutional under the Fourth and Fifth Amendments. Justice Brandeis's dissenting opinion, which set the precedent for future cases, gave us the phrase, "the right to be left alone." Justice Brandeis wrote,

The makers of our Constitution undertook to secure conditions favorable to the pursuit of happiness. They recognized the significance of man's spiritual nature, of his feelings and of his intellect. They knew that only a part of the pain, pleasure and satisfactions of life are to be found in material things. They sought to protect Americans in their beliefs, their thoughts, their emotions and their sensations. They conferred, as against the Government, *the right to be le[f]t alone*—the most comprehensive of rights and the right most valued by civilized men.[12] (Emphases added)

Brandeis was correct in his analysis of the Constitution. Nowhere in the Constitution is the government granted the power to monitor or regulate our daily conduct. Remember, the Constitution grants power to the federal government and retains for the states and people that which is not granted. It keeps the government off our backs. (Well, it is intended to do that.) We retain all unalienable rights, and the right of privacy—the right to be left alone—is certainly one of them. By simply being human, all persons have a right to privacy existing far before the founding of the United States. As the majority of the Supreme Court wrote in the case of *Griswold v. Connecticut* (1965), "We deal with a right to privacy older than the Bill of Rights [and] older than our political parties." That sentence alone acknowledges privacy as a natural, or if you prefer the secular term, fundamental, right, which cannot be taken away without due process of the law.

For example, suppose you have a collection of rare coins. You've spent years acquiring these coins and have searched all over the world for them. In doing so, you've catalogued each and every detail of the individual coins and placed them in a special cabinet. Does the government have the right to observe and copy your catalogue and publish its own catalogue of your coins? Most certainly not! This is your *private* collection of coins, which you choose to keep for yourself. The government cannot view these coins without violating your natural right to privacy.

## The Government's Intrusion on This Right: Marriage

The design of the law must be to protect those persons with whose affairs the community has no legitimate concern, from being dragged into an undesirable and undesired publicity and to protect all persons, whatsoever; their position or station, from having matters which they may properly prefer to keep private, made public against their will. It is the unwarranted invasion of individual privacy which is reprehended, and to be, so far as possible, prevented.

—Justice Louis D. Brandeis

Why must we seek the approval of the government to enter into marriages? For centuries, governments never interfered with marriages, but rather they were based on religion, parental choice, culture, tradition, and the mutual love of two persons. It certainly is not the government's role to meddle in your most personal of affairs. If the decision-making process that leads to the free choice to marry another person is not considered private, then what can be considered private? Again, our right to privacy stems from our desire to keep certain matters out of the public eye and between another and ourselves. There are few decisions more personal than deciding with whom you want to spend the rest of your life.

Why is the government involved at all with the institution of marriage? The government should not be in the business of determining who receives the contractual benefits of marriage, such as medical visitation and decision-making rights, inheritance rights, property co-ownership, and so on. You and your soon-to-be partner should determine who shares in the benefits of that marriage. Marriage should not be an institution of the state, but rather a contract recognized by the contracting parties and solemnized by either a cultural or a religious procedure or no procedure at all. When you buy a house, who solemnizes the contract?

Despite the relatively simple concept of excluding the government from your most personal affairs, our government's history includes frequent meddling with this tradition. Before the Founders signed the Constitution, before colonial leaders signed the Declaration of Independence, they sought to prohibit interracial marriages. The first documented interracial marriage in our nation's history was that of Pocahontas to John Rolfe. The story of these two individuals was passed down for ages and culminated in a Disney movie dramatizing the love between these two. While they were fortunate enough to marry almost forty-five years before the first anti-miscegenation law passed in 1661, the fairy tale was not happy for many other individuals. The anti-miscegenation laws prohibited mixed-race marriages in Virginia and numerous other states for more than three hundred years until the U.S. Supreme Court heard the case of *Loving v. Virginia* in 1967.[13] Unfortunately, the period between 1661 and 1967 was fraught with additional government intrusions on the natural right to privacy.

At first, the laws were not so restrictive. For example, in the early years, the colonial governments required colonists formally to register their marriages, but it soon became common practice to accept cohabitation as a form of registration. Yet, by the late nineteenth century, state governments began to nullify common-law marriages and exert more control over who could marry whom.[14] By the early 1920s, thirty-eight states prohibited whites from marrying blacks, "mulattos," Japanese, Chinese, Indians, "Mongolians" "Malays," or Filipinos.[15] And, as if things couldn't get worse, in 1924, Virginia passed a law prohibiting whites from marrying any individual with a "single drop of Negro Blood."[16] The Virginia legislature went as far as to prohibit marriages between a white individual and another individual who was 99-plus percent "white" and one drop "Negro." Perhaps even more astounding is that this occurred *within the last century*. The government clearly felt no shame in meddling in the most intimate of affairs.

Congress, which has the power under the Fourteenth Amendment to nullify state laws that take life, liberty, or property away without due process, did nothing about these horrific laws. Congress allowed one law after another to pass without exerting any effort to protect natural rights. Fortunately, the Founders were wise beyond their years and created a government of checks and balances. In this case, the Supreme Court provided the "check."

In the case of *Loving v. Virginia* (1967), the Supreme Court found Virginia's anti-miscegenation laws unconstitutional and recognized our natural right of privacy. The case involved Perry Loving, a white man, who married his African American and Native American wife, Mildred Jeter. The couple married in Washington, D.C., which had no racial restrictions on marriage. After their ceremony, they returned to Virginia in the hopes of living in matrimonial bliss; yet, the bliss quickly faded. One morning, police officers broke into their home and barged into their bedroom to ask them what they were doing in bed together. Mr. Loving pointed to the marriage certificate on the wall, which the officers informed him Virginia did not recognize. The two were then arrested and jailed. And the case only gets worse.

At trial, the judge gave the Lovings two options: Either move out of Virginia for twenty-five years or spend one to three years in jail. The Lovings chose the former. Subsequently, the judge delivered an opinion, which can only be characterized as profound fundamentalist ignorance. He stated,

> Almighty God created the races, white, black, yellow, malay and red, and he placed them on separate continents. And but for the interference with his arrangement there would be no cause for such marriages. The fact that he separated the races shows that he did not intend for the races to mix.[17]

It is unfathomable that a judge entrusted with the protection of our constitutional rights could write such a statement. Fortunately, on appeal the Supreme Court displayed far superior intellect and respect for natural rights and formally recognized the natural right to privacy in regards to marriage. Chief Justice Earl Warren stated, "The freedom to marry has long been recognized as one of the vital personal rights essential to the orderly pursuit of happiness by free men."[18] In other words, a natural right.

While decades ago the Supreme Court formally settled the issue of interracial marriages, the nation is currently engulfed in the battle over same-sex marriages. For the same reasons the government should not interfere with marriages between individuals of various races, the government should not interfere with marriages between individuals of the same sex. What effect do same-sex marriages have on other individuals? As Jefferson might have said, they neither pick your pocket nor break your leg. They do not harm anyone or violate your natural rights.

## To Love and to Cherish, Till the State Do Us Part

In 1996, Congress enacted and President Clinton signed the Defense of Marriage Act (DOMA), defining marriage as "a legal union between one man and one woman as husband and wife," and providing that states need not recognize same-sex marriages from other states.[19] Currently, thirty-seven states have their own acts similar to DOMA, and two states have stronger language defining marriage as only between one man and one woman.[20] Additionally, Section 3 of DOMA relates to the unconstitutional federal benefits married couples receive. In fact, in January 1997 the General Accountability Office issued a report clarifying the impact DOMA has on federal laws. The report concluded that 1,049 federal laws are affected. These laws include those relating to welfare programs such as Social Security, health benefits, and taxation.[21] A subsequent study in 2004 found 1,138 federal laws "tied benefits, protections, rights, or responsibilities to marital status."[22] How has the institution of marriage, which governments traditionally never regulated, become an institution tied to more than 1,138 federal laws?

In 2010, a federal district court judge in Massachusetts found the section of DOMA that permitted states to grant or withhold benefits based on the sexual orientation of one's marital partner to be unconstitutional because it violated the Equal Protection Clause embodied in the Due Process Clause of the Fifth Amendment.[23] In *Gill v. Office of Personnel Management* (2010), Judge Joseph L. Tauro embraced the view that the states historically were in charge of requirements for marriage, and it is not a constitutional concern of the federal government; rather, the individual states are to make this determination. Judge Tauro held that DOMA encroaches on "a historically entrenched tradition of federal reliance on state marital status determination." Moreover, in dismissing the government's justifications for the Act, Judge Tauro concluded only "irrational prejudice" motivated the classification of same-sex couples as separate from heterosexual couples. Thus, DOMA violates the Fifth Amendment's mandate of equal protection.

In the companion case to *Gill*, called *Commonwealth of Massachusetts v. United States Department of Health and Human Services* (2010), Judge Tauro concluded DOMA was also unconstitutional under the Tenth Amendment. The Tenth Amendment states in relevant part, "The powers not delegated to the United States by the Constitution, nor prohibited by it to the States, are reserved to the States respectively."[24] As noted previously, historically the states determine the necessary conditions for marriage within their boundaries because nowhere in the Constitution is there a granting of congressional power to make these determinations. Thus, a disparity exists when Congress enacts laws, such as DOMA, regulating behaviors that the states previously regulated.

This case was brought by the State of Massachusetts because in 2004, the State decided to recognize same-sex marriages. In fact, as of February 12th 2010, Massachusetts issued marriage licenses to at least 15,214 same-sex couples.[25] Unfortunately, because of DOMA, these couples' marriages are not recognized in all states, and individuals are unable to receive the unconstitutional, but federally provided, benefits granted to heterosexual couples. Despite the government's attempt to regulate local matters and interfere with your personal decision to marry whom you choose, Judge Tauro correctly decided the case. He first acknowledged that "family law, including 'declarations of status, e.g. marriage, annulment, divorce, custody and paternity,' is often held out as the archetypal area of local concern."[26] Judge Tauro then concluded that by enacting DOMA, the federal government "encroaches upon the firmly entrenched province of the state, and, in doing so, offends the Tenth Amendment."[27]

While these decisions are a great step forward for marriage equality and respect for the natural right of privacy in choosing a life partner, Judge Tauro errs in relying on the historical approach of recognizing state marital status determinations. The history of our nation does include state determinations of who may marry whom; however, just because a power is entrenched in history does not make it correct. Neither the federal government nor the state governments should interfere with private decisions to marry because those decisions are unique to individuals—they are made, figuratively and literally, in the heart of privacy. They are the essence of personal behavior immune from government—state or federal—intrusion or regulation. Without any interference from the federal or state government, you choose what college to attend, what career to pursue, where you want to reside; likewise, you should be free to choose whom you want to marry.

Another step forward has come with a recent federal district court's ruling that Proposition 8 in California is unconstitutional. California's Proposition 8, passed by voters in 2008, mandates that marriage can only be between a man and a woman. Judge Vaughn Walker struck it down on the basis that it violated the right to marry, or stated otherwise, that the right to choose a marital partner does not require the permission of your neighbors or the voters or the government. He enforced the right to be left alone.

Judge Walker stated that

the right to marry has been historically and remains the right to choose a spouse and, with mutual consent, join together and form a household . . . same-sex couples are situated identically to opposite-sex couples in terms of their ability to perform the rights and obligations of marriage under California law.

Thus, there can be no legitimate reason for differential treatment. And as to the claim that such marriages were not procreative in function, Judge Walker noted that the state has never inquired into mixed-sex couples' capacity to reproduce in deciding whether to grant a marriage license. Such a world would be no less despotic or terrifying than the Third Reich, with its policies of eugenics and forced sterilization! This judicial giant reminds us that if it were not for an independent judiciary, which is committed to the Constitution, nothing would prevent a runaway majority from taking the liberty or the property of the minority. Government can't be trusted. And every once in a while, judges will stop the beast in its tracks.

## The Government's Intrusion on This Right: Sexual Freedom

While Americans readily accept the government's intrusion on the institution of marriage, there is greater push back on private matters concerning our bodies. Take, for example, the contentious issue of contraception. Imagine meeting someone and falling madly in love. You decide to take the big "leap" and invite all of your family and friends to help you celebrate. Inevitably, your mother and father begin to ask when they can expect grandkids, but you refrain from giving a precise date because you and your spouse have decided to pursue your respective careers. While this response sounds practical, it was not always feasible.

As recently as 1965, Connecticut law prohibited the possession, sale, and distribution of contraceptives to married couples. While the Supreme Court concluded the law was unconstitutional, the reasoning behind this conclusion was far from unanimous. Justice Douglas wrote of the famous "penumbras" and "emanations" of various Bill of Rights guarantees creating a zone of privacy, while Justice Goldberg relied on the Ninth Amendment's language of "other rights retained by the people," and Justice Harlan argued the Fourteenth Amendment's Liberty Clause forbids government conduct which is inconsistent with "the concept of ordered liberty."[28] Despite the convoluted reasoning, the Court correctly decided the case and recognized the Constitution's protection of a "zone of privacy"—an area of human behavior immune from government intrusion or regulation. The Court illustrated this point when it wrote, "Would we allow the police to search the sacred precincts of marital bedrooms for telltale signs of the use of contraceptives? The very idea is repulsive to the notions of privacy."[29]

## What Happens in Vegas Stays in Vegas?

Las Vegas. Sin City. City of Lights. Entertainment Capital of the World. Whatever you want to call it, Las Vegas is perhaps one of the most liberated cities in the country. In fact, if there ever was a time you and your friends wanted to engage in undocumented activities, it would most likely be while you were in Las Vegas. In Las Vegas you can enjoy alcohol on the streets, gamble all night, frequent gentlemen's clubs, and even get married in an hour and divorced the next day. Many ordinary folks want to go to Las Vegas just to blow off a little steam. And what better time to go than the Christmas season and New Year's Eve? Right?

Wrong. If you were one of the millions of individuals traveling to Las Vegas during the Christmas season of 2003, you are most likely in a government database created in an attempt to track terrorists. However, your name is not the only item in the database. Your airline carrier? Check. Hotel where you stayed? Check. Casinos you visited? Check. Rental car company? Check. The locker you rented from a storage company? Check. Yes, government officials legally collected and analyzed data on more than one million people during the 2003 Christmas season. How was this legal?

## The Most Un-patriotic of Acts

You probably did not realize the government had legal authority to track individuals' every move. It does; and this legal authority continuously expands in the effort to fight the War on Terror. In response to monumental invasions of privacy, such as the events in Las Vegas, the government claims it is not invading your natural right to privacy, but rather, is attempting to prevent further terrorist attacks. Do you buy this? I don't. As Benjamin Franklin stated, "Those who would give up essential liberty, to purchase a little temporary safety, deserve neither liberty nor safety."

And give up liberty we have. In the months after the attacks of September 11th 2001, our country was frantic. More than three thousand lives were lost, and our nation was blindsided by the murderous attacks. The government felt a need to respond, and on October 26th 2001, President Bush signed into law the Uniting and Strengthening America by Providing Appropriate Tools Required to Intercept and Obstruct Terrorism Act of 2001 (USA Patriot Act). And despite what many in Congress would like you to believe, the Patriot Act was not just President Bush's doing. No, the Patriot Act passed both houses almost unanimously with only Senator Russ Feingold[30] in the Senate and Congressman Ron Paul and sixty-five others in the House voting against the bill.[31]

Positivists (who think they can write any laws), like President George W. Bush, and Progressives (who think the government can trump the Natural Law), like President Barack Obama, defend the Act as essential to the security of the nation; in reality, it is an all-out assault on the right to privacy. More specifically, it directly violates the Fourth Amendment right against "unreasonable searches and seizures" and facilitates the issuance of warrants without "probable cause."[32] The government now uses what it publicly calls National Security Letters, or self-written search warrants, and "sneak and peek" warrants to invade your privacy.

Self-written search warrants are provided for in Section 505 of the Patriot Act. The Federal Bureau of Investigation (FBI) describes one of these warrants as "a letter request for information from a third party that is issued by the FBI or by other government agencies with authority to conduct national security investigations."[33] And while the FBI claims other government agencies have the authority to issue these letters, it also states that currently only the "most senior FBI officials" possess the authority to approve National Security Letters.[34] Thus, rather than risking a judge denying a search warrant request, the FBI requests National Security Letters, and the FBI approves these requests!

Moreover, Section 505 is not narrowly tailored to limited circumstances. Rather it is limited to personal records from financial institutions, which are broadly interpreted, and the ridiculous list of financial institutions includes pawnbrokers; travel agencies; car, airplane, and boat dealerships; casinos; medical records; supermarket records; legal records; computer keystrokes; and finally, the institution with which we all engage in our most important financial transactions—the post office. Even the *United States Postal Service* is considered a financial institution under Section 505. When did sending a letter to grandma become the financial equivalent of dealing with a broker registered with the Securities and Exchange Commission? The government's designation of different institutions as "financial" is now so vast that it intrudes on our daily rituals. So, if you were wondering how the government obtained all that information in Las Vegas, wonder no more. In fact, on its Web site the FBI lists the following as information obtainable through self-written search warrants: subscriber information, toll billing records, Internet service provider login records, electronic communication transaction records, financial records, money transfers, credit records, and *other consumer identifying information*.[35] However, it does not inform the reader of how much information is included in the "other consumer identifying information" category.

Additionally, with the passage of the Patriot Act, self-written search warrants are permitted on a host of new subjects, and the Act formally rejected the protections against criminal prosecutions by its predecessors. Before the Patriot Act, if the nation's intelligence agencies came upon evidence of a crime and came upon it by unlawful means, they could not turn it over to prosecutors. After the

Patriot Act, they have been required to turn such evidence over to prosecutors. In fact, the Act requires government investigators to turn over to government prosecutors the unconstitutionally obtained evidence. The Act also mandates the evidence obtained from these wildly unconstitutional self-authorized search warrants is "constitutionally competent" in criminal prosecutions.[36] Thus, until this section of the Act is challenged, the obtained evidence is currently "legal" under federal law, but unconstitutional at the same time because it violates the Fourth Amendment. It is bizarre, indeed, for a thing to be both legal and unconstitutional. Since the Constitution is the "supreme Law of the Land" (as it so states in Article VI), that would make it the rule of law, the baseline below which no government entity (that would include votes by Congress and signatures of presidents) may go. Thus, anything that is unconstitutional must also be unlawful.

As we have seen, the Fourth Amendment protects against warrants being issued without probable cause, an oath or affirmation, and the specification of the "place to be searched" and "the persons or things to be seized." Self-written search warrants do not fulfill any of these requirements. Government officials now have the authority to issue blanket self-written search warrants without an oath or affirmation before any judge. These search warrants do not need to describe a particular location, device, or individual for which they are issued, clearly violating the Fourth Amendment and the right to be secure in our "persons, houses, papers, and effects." Moreover, while the government maintains self-written search warrants are "an indispensable tool and building block of an investigation that contributes significantly to the FBI's ability to carry out its national security responsibilities by directly supporting the furtherance of the counterterrorism, counterintelligence and intelligence missions," the statistics paint another portrait.[37]

A 2007 Justice Department Inspector General audit revealed that not only were self-written search warrants being used to prosecute ordinary criminal activity unrelated to national security, but also government officials misused their authority by evading limits on the self-written search warrants and under-reporting the number of warrants issued. Even though these abuses were revealed, the most recent Department of Justice report to Congress shows the use of self-written search warrants is increasing dramatically. For example, in 2008, 24,744 were issued, compared to 16,804 in 2007.[38]

If self-written search warrants were not bad enough, Section 213 concerning "sneak and peek" warrants further invades your natural right to privacy. This section amended the section of the United States Code on the "Effect of Rules of Court," and allows for a "delayed notice" of search warrants, meaning a target, whose home or business is searched, is not immediately notified.[39] Thus, government officials can enter your home, search for evidence, and then use the evidence in a criminal investigation, without telling you until eighteen months later.

If not for the seriousness of the subject matter, it is almost laughable that the government attempts to argue the constitutionality of these actions. Let me correct myself. The government will *sometimes* argue the constitutionality of these actions. Why sometimes? Because the government does not want to take these cases to the Supreme Court for fear that the Court will rule the entire Patriot Act unconstitutional; it instead manipulates the judicial system and leaves it to the lower federal courts to issue holdings on each issue, thus leaving a legal system with opposing precedents relating to your constitutional right of privacy.

## You Were Searching for *What* on the Internet?!

Now you may be saying to yourself, *I want America to be secure and free from terrorists, and I don't have anything to hide, so why should I care if the government is tracking my trips to Las Vegas or illegally enters my home?* Well, you may not have anything to hide *now*, but what if you got caught up with the wrong crowd and because of mere association were charged with a crime? Then would you be okay with the government using this illegally obtained evidence against you? Would you care if the government read your mail before you received it, and requested information on the Web sites you visited or the searches you performed through your Web browser?

Yes, the government is even willing to go so far as to ask private Internet companies for an index of the Web and information on users' searches. For example, in 2006, the government requested this information from a number of companies including Google. Google's chief legal officer, David Drummond, decided to fight against these government requests that blatantly violate the right to privacy while on the Internet. Unfortunately, Google lost in court and ultimately handed over the information. However, despite losing the legal battle, in April 2010, Google launched a "Government Request Tool," detailing the requests of worldwide governments to take down content, or to turn over information, relating to the uses of its search engine, YouTube, and its blogging software.[40] To no surprise, the United States government ranked second in data requests, with 3,580. To gain perspective, this is more than *three times* the next government's requests, which happens to be one of our closest allies, the United Kingdom.[41] As a user of Gmail, YouTube, or the Google search engine, you must stay vigilant and aware of your right to privacy.

## Conclusion

If the government's historical attempts to regulate who you can marry, when you can have kids, and its ability to track your almost every move are not frightening enough, now consider the passage of Obamacare. Your once private communications and medical decisions with your doctor will now be regulated and monitored by the government. The law requires the Department of Health and Human Services to issue forty thousand laptops, one to each primary care physician in the United States, and it requires the physicians to record for federal bureaucrats whatever you tell your physician and whatever your physician tells you. How can one day the Supreme Court declare a "zone of privacy" that includes the right "to care for one's health and person" and the next day the then-Speaker of the House Nancy Pelosi claim Congress's power to regulate health care is "essentially unlimited"?

And the invasion of your natural right to privacy does not end there. Now, because of the individual mandate, on an ongoing basis you will be required to provide personal medical details to an insurance company. What information is more personal than your health? The ACLU describes medical information as "arguably the most personal and private source of data about us"; yet, the ACLU refuses to challenge Obamacare because of its support for the welfare state.

The philosopher Ayn Rand argued that when government destroys your privacy, it destroys your dignity and your uniqueness. And then, by regulating your privacy, it controls you.

Thus, it is up to you to elect officials willing to repeal Obamacare, the Patriot Act, the spy cameras, and numerous other pieces of legislation stripping you of your natural right to privacy. The government bureaucrats will fiercely fight back by claiming they are maintaining national security, providing medical care to impoverished children, and the Constitution grants them the authority to do so. But do not wane in your efforts to fight this political rhetoric, for we never want to fulfill Benjamin Franklin's prediction of losing our essential liberties for temporary safety.

# Chapter 7
# Hands Off:

*You Own Your Body*

As we have seen, your body is yours and yours alone. If you do not have control over your own body, what then *do* you control as an individual? Think about it. If you were financially broke with absolutely no real property or possessions to your name, the only thing over which you have full and complete autonomy is your own body. You have the power to direct what goes into it—what you eat, what you drink, whether you exercise, and whether you take vitamins or drugs. You also own whatever your body produces—the fruits of your labor, the sweat of your brow, the manner of your expression.

Reason and human nature dictate that the legs, arms, muscles, fingers, toes, torso, eyeballs, brain, and feet with which you enter and exit the world belong to you as the sovereign individual, including every action or word that comes from your body. Your body can move, build, work, talk, think, and express. As a result, having control and autonomy over your body is the most fundamental and natural right that you have as a human being. Right?

Not exactly. Contemporary government in the United States has another model in mind. The government believes that *it* has the right to interfere with your free choices and to monitor what you eat, what you drink, who you sleep with, whether you can donate an organ, and whether you can take that experimental drug from Canada. It believes that it knows your body better than you do, and that it can take better care of your body than you can.

## The World's Oldest Profession

Imagine you are at a formal restaurant with your husband, wife, or significant other. You look around at all the classy, well-dressed clientele enjoying their dinners in the dining room. To the left of your table is a younger couple. Wearing a slinky "first-date" dress, the woman must be twenty-seven or twenty-eight. Her date, in his early thirties, is eyeing his beautiful dinner companion. To your right is an older couple. The man is distinguished looking with a full head of hair while the woman is conservatively dressed in a black dress.

To the outside observer, there are no substantial differences between these couples. All parties are enjoying a delicious dinner with pleasant company. All parties are consensually sitting at the restaurant with an individual of their choosing. All parties will pay their bills upon completion of dinner and head on their merry way. Except . . . there is one difference. The young man is paying for dinner in hopes of sexual activity, while the older man is paying for dinner *and* sexual activity. Prior to dinner, money exchanged hands from the distinguished gentleman to his conservatively dressed date.

Now, I know some of you may consider these claims extreme, but look at these men objectively. Is there really any distinction between the men's *motives* that is the legitimate concern of the government? There are none whatsoever. Each man has the intention to sleep with the woman at his table. The young man is posturing as a refined suitor when, in fact, he has an ulterior motive; he paid for dinner with the anticipation of getting something in return. The older man, on the other hand, was transparent about his intentions from the very beginning by paying for the services rendered directly by his dinner companion. Why is one man's behavior considered benign while the other's is the object of government wrath and potential criminal prosecution? Their behavior is nearly identical, so which man's intentions are more harmful?

The discreet and subtle nature of the young man's desire for sex is potentially more harmful than the older gentleman's transparent exchange of money for sex. Tom Knighton, a libertarian commentator, furthers this argument and posits that all men pay for sex in some way or another: "It may be three fancy dinners and a bouquet of flowers. It may be a trip to Hawaii. It may be a wedding ring. No matter the costs, these guys argue, men pay for it [sex] with something. There is probably some truth to that. And yet, this kind of practice is also perfectly legal."[1] Talk about inconsistency.

## The Moral Case for Prostitution

Prohibitions on how we use our bodies violate our most basic rights as human beings. The government is not even giving you the option to participate in the restricted practice. In truly free societies, any type of prohibition must be void because it violates the fundamental liberties of all individuals who wish (or do not wish) to take part in that specific activity.

In the case of prostitution, as long as the transaction is voluntary, there is no justification for governmental intervention. While the government does have an interest in protecting the individual property rights of a person (the prostitute) from violence, rape, and other harms, the government does not have the right to prohibit prostitution outright. The theory is, "prostitution is the *voluntary* sale (or rental) of a labor service. Individuals own their own bodies and their own labor services and have the absolute right to decide how those labor services should be used."[2] We have the personal liberty and freedom to do with our bodies what we please—both as producer and as consumer of the product. I can rent my body to the owner of a coal mine for thirty years, who will use my work to strip the earth of natural resources, but a woman cannot rent her body to the same coal mine owner for a few hours of private time? Why? Because the government says so, that's why.

Like it or not, prostitution is a victimless crime. Both parties are agreeing to a financial transaction where money is offered in exchange for a service. Both parties are receiving something they want. There is no "evil" inherent in this barter. A "vice," perhaps, may be involved, but vices are not harms *to another*. Vices are harms *to you*, and you have the right to make poor decisions, and the government has no authority to stop you from making these poor decisions because your body is *your* body.

While we will never accurately know how many men and women make a living by full-time or part-time prostitution, the consensus is the numbers are substantial. And despite the government's prohibition of prostitution in the United States, research suggests that its "prohibition" is not working . . . at all. Gee, I wonder why? Moral prohibitions throughout history have never succeeded. Look at alcohol prohibition from 1920 to 1933, for example. See how far that form of prohibition got the government. Albert Einstein once stated, "The definition of insanity is doing the same thing over and over again and expecting different results." Clearly, we have an insane government because it thinks prohibiting prostitution will actually accomplish something of substance. Think again, government.

### The Nanny State Strikes Again: Bigger Government Does Not Equal Smaller Waistlines

New York City's mayor, Michael Bloomberg, is a health fanatic, so much so that he maintains a monthly weight-loss competition with one of his buddies in order to stay slim.[3] He has taken this obsession so far that, with his urging, the New York City Board of Health voted to ban trans fats at restaurants in December 2006. In other words, the government has already decided what you can and cannot eat for dinner at Applebee's tonight. Violating Natural Law, freedom of choice, and the very nature of the Constitution, the government has usurped control over your body yet again. Shortly after New York City passed its ban, the entire State of California followed suit in January 2008 by prohibiting restaurants and bakeries from using cooking oils that contain trans fats. Violators can be fined up to one thousand dollars. And that's just trans fats.

So you want to cool off with a Gatorade, Coke, Sprite, or flavored water on public property in San Francisco? That's too bad; San Francisco's mayor at the time, Gavin Newsom, skipped the whole darn legislative process in *his* personal quest to control your diet and instituted an executive order prohibiting vending machines from carrying artificially sweetened drinks on city property.[4] But don't worry; diet sodas will be allowed in *some* locations in the City by the Bay. Apparently, Mayor Newsom believes it is his duty to force-feed his constituents and San Francisco's visitors water, soy milk, rice milk, or other similar dairy or non-dairy milk in lieu of what they really want to drink on a hot July day.

And from sugar to salt. In March 2010, New York State Assemblyman Felix Ortiz introduced a bill that would prohibit the use of salt in making foods at restaurants.[5] Seriously? You mean salt—the substance that preserves food, regulates body functions including blood pressure and fluid volume, carries nutrients into cells, and regulates muscle contractions? Ortiz's bill states, "No owner or operator of a restaurant in this state shall use salt in any form in the preparation of any food for consumption by customers."[6] Salt in any form is evil and needs to be regulated by the government? I think not!

While trans fats, sugar, and salt—like all things in our diet—should be consumed in moderation, it is not the job or interest of the government to determine what should or should not be consumed by a free individual. These dietary choices are highly personal as they deal with the sustenance of our own bodies—what we eat, what we drink, and how much we eat and drink. It is our natural right as freethinking human beings to make these healthy or unhealthy decisions and live with the consequences. In implementing restrictive food and drink policies, the government is merely treating us like children, deeming us incapable of determining the course of our own health and fitness. This government-knows-best attitude is highly invasive, offensive, and demeaning and will result in more harm than benefit.

When the government makes health decisions on our behalf, we are deprived of the opportunity to learn what is or is not healthy for our own bodies. We thereby become complacent and dependent on the government's (many times incorrect) policies. The government bases its policies only on medical advice it wants to hear and which is often arbitrary, changing from year to year. For example, in the 1980s, the food industry was told to replace saturated fats like coconut oil and butter with oil containing trans fat. Now, science has obviously changed its mind. For this reason, we cannot depend on the government to make these kinds of decisions for us. These decisions are ours, and ours alone.

And one last story of Nanny State absurdity. In April 2010, Santa Clara County, California, passed an ordinance banning restaurants from giving out toys with meals of more than 485 calories! The law bans any "toy, game, trading card, admission ticket or other consumer product, whether physical or digital."[7] A critic of the legislation, Eric Felten, doubted its efficacy, commenting in the *Wall Street Journal*,

> If cheapo trinkets are so seductive, why don't some enterprising health advocates launch a restaurant chain devoted to cauliflower and Brussels sprouts and then package the stuff with fabulous toys? And don't forget the cartoon characters, which surely have the mesmeric power to overcome even the most vegephobic. After all, what kid wouldn't kill for some Sponge Bob-brand seaweed salad?[8]

The government has taken its nannying too far. We are all grown up. Except in the government's eyes.

## Kidney Shortage Is the Fault of Our Self-appointed Protectors

The most reliable and natural way for an individual to acquire something he or she desires is through a system of trade. For example, A has the freedom to trade with B so long as B wishes to trade with A. This voluntary exchange is a natural right and ensures that both parties walk away with something each party wants. This uncomplicated concept goes back to the beginning of time. A man could trade animal skins for meat, gold for tools, or corn for wheat (or today, money for toothpaste). The theory really is as simple as a fifth grader trading her peanut butter sandwich for her friend's two chocolate chip cookies. The desires of both parties are fulfilled, and no rights are violated because the exchange was completely voluntary.

Unfortunately, the federal government thinks it knows what is best for you, your body, and your exchanges. Say you are cutting a piece of plywood at your home. At the sight of a mouse at your feet, you jump, lose control of the circular saw, and consequently cut off a piece of your finger. Ironically enough, the government says you can buy poison to kill that rodent (exchanging money for the toxic substance), but the government says you cannot buy a finger to replace the one lost at the mercy of the saw. The state claims it has outlawed the sale of organs and body parts for your well-being and safety. Unfortunately for your well-being, even if it is available, you cannot acquire that lost finger because the state says so.

By preventing the buying and selling of organs, the government is making it extremely difficult to find sufficient organ donors because there are zero incentives to donate. According to the federal National Organ Transplant Act of 1984, you cannot compensate another person who selflessly donates a kidney (even though the donor has rescued you from fatiguing dialysis and premature death). In fact, this altruistic human being (and violator of the 1984 Act) could be slapped with a fifty-thousand-dollar fine and a felony prison term of up to five years![9] Organ donation is just one more way the government usurps control of decisions—personal and bodily—that are rightfully ours as sovereign individuals.

Because your body is your property, you should have the right to decide to live without one of your kidneys and be compensated accordingly (and conversely, to acquire a kidney through a voluntary trade). It is your body, your decision, your choice. Why does the government even care what you do with your organs, especially when that organ is saving the life of another human being?

Currently, the federal government acts as the *only* authority with the power to buy and allocate kidneys for transplantation. The 1984 Act established the Organ Procurement and Transplantation Network (OPTN), to contract the United Network for Organ Sharing (UNOS), which administers the OPTN under contract from the Department of Health and Human Services.[10] (See how the government did that—taking absolute control through a complicated mess of inefficient networks so that we have no control over the destiny of own organs?)

As you read this, there are more than 85,583 people waiting on the official kidney-transplant list in the United States.[11] With kidney, pancreas, liver, intestine, heart, and lung combined, there are more than a whopping 108,098 people waiting for some kind of organ in homes and hospitals across the nation. In the United States alone, just 16,500 individuals received a kidney transplant in 2008 while almost 7,000 died waiting for one.[12] Thirteen die daily.[13] With a population of more than 300 million, we have a grand total of more than 600 million kidneys (we each have two, but can function with one)—my instinct is that the government is doing something wrong.

## How Did We Get Here?

While people may be repulsed at the discussion of organ trading for compensation, they shouldn't be; we already engage in forms of it. Every day, heart valves are replaced, and amputees receive other people's limbs. People exchange their semen, eggs, and plasma for money. For tens of thousands of dollars, women generously rent out their wombs for those who cannot bear children. We donate blood in exchange for little perks like movie tickets and candy. How can an exchange take place in these situations but not under circumstances including vital organs? The federal government flippantly and arbitrarily makes these rules, but does it have its reasons? Does it have the authority?

In 1984, an "overzealous entrepreneur" testified before Congress of his plans to ship in impoverished people from developing countries, remove their organs to undergird our shortage, and return the "donors" to their homelands with a sum of money to compensate them for their efforts.[14] Appalled, Congress, spearheaded by Al Gore, a Tennessee congressman at the time, enacted the National Organ Transplant Act. While the legislature may have been well intentioned, the consequences have been highly intrusive and purely negative. People are dying, and the need for organs has increased yearly. Although Gore did propose "a voucher system or a tax credit to a donor's estate" if "efforts to improve voluntary donation are unsuccessful,"[15] the United States continues to flounder despite attempts to promote donation after more than twenty-five years. Clearly, the government's efforts have been unsuccessful with more than 80,000 people on kidney-transplant waiting lists. The system is broken, and the time for change is now. It is time to look to compensation, incentives, and market practices to solve the problem. However, under current federal law, we can't. In Pennsylvania, for example, the state legislature proposed an allowance of a mere three hundred dollars to go toward funeral expenses if an individual were to donate organs.[16] The bill, however, failed because government officials feared that it might violate federal law. Whatever happened to federalism?

Sally Satel, M.D., who received a kidney transplant in 2006, tells a story in her article, "The Waiting Game," about a proactive young man on dialysis.[17] Amazingly, Alex Crionas met a man at a party who offered to donate one of his kidneys to Crionas. Unfortunately, Crionas had also created a Web site to help attract potential donors via the Internet, violating parts of the National Organ Transplant Act. As a result, the transplant center refused to perform his surgery, even though Crionas and the donor did not even meet on the Web site (they met at the party). The surgery center's reasoning for denying him the transplant: Brokered transplants "undermine trust in the whole system."[18] It seems to me the system has already been undermined. Fortunately, after seeking out a different transplant center, Crionas was finally able to receive his transplant, which was a success.

## Bad Effects and the Black Market

The organ black market is alive and well. In fact, the black market may account for 5 to 10 percent of transplants worldwide.[19] I do not have to look to faraway places like India or the Philippines to back up my claim; I can look as close as my home State of New Jersey. In July 2009, Rabbi Levy Izhak Rosenbaum was accused of conspiring to broker the sale of a human kidney for a transplant. The recipient would pay $160,000 while the donor received $10,000. According to the complaint filed in federal district court in New Jersey, this was not Mr. Rosenbaum's first dance. He had brokered many deals over the past ten years.[20]

Unfortunately, the effects of criminalizing organ donation are exactly opposite of the government's intent. Dr. Satel states that the strategy of "cracking down" on organ trafficking is doomed because "it ignores the time-tested fact that efforts to stamp out underground markets either drive corruption further underground or cause it to flourish elsewhere."[21] So, instead of allowing people to be compensated for their altruistic act of donation, the government must monitor and build criminal cases against rabbis selling organs in New Jersey. In addition to the danger of black markets, there is the threat of physicians being forced to use organs of lesser quality because of such low supply. The United States' intense shortage has increased the use of these so-called expanded-criteria organs—in other words, organs that are not suitable for transplant.[22] Kidneys are not as "good" when they are donated by people over sixty years old or by people who have a history of medical problems. These organs are more likely to fail in the recipient than organs from younger, healthier donors. Because of the federal government's restrictions, these lesser quality organs are transplanted anyway.

In his *Wall Street Journal* piece, "The Meat Market," Alex Tabarrok described the level of desperation reached by those in need of organs. The situation is so dire, "at the University of Maryland's School of Medicine, five patients received transplants of kidneys that had either cancerous or benign tumors removed from them."[23] These acts of desperation are forced upon these ailing individuals based on rules and regulations passed by the government. Tabarrok goes on to explain that while expanded-criteria organs can be a useful (albeit dangerous) alternative to the shortage, their use also means that the organ shortage is even more drastic than it appears "because as the waiting list lengthens, the quality of transplants is falling."[24] These "alternatives" are not alternatives at all. The fact that people are resorting to these extreme measures to access organs when organ donors could be compensated is unacceptable and immoral. The government must take a second look.

## And the Money?!?

Kidney dialysis is a federal entitlement (no) thanks to the 1972 End Stage Renal Disease (ESRD) component of the Social Security Act. In 2006, Medicare spent almost $23 billion on ESRD, and the total cost per person, per year, was $61,164.[25] The real punch: Only one-third of dialysis patients survive after five years. More specifically, a thirty-five-year-old spending nine years on dialysis will accumulate a total cost of $600,000 while a sixty-four-year-old over four years will cost $300,000. Now compare these extravagant treatment costs with the $75,000 one-time cost of the "surgeries and hospital stays of the donor and recipient, plus the first year of follow-up care (including medicine)."[26] It is more cost-effective to cure than to treat, and we already have the cure. It is called a transplant.

And check out this number crunch. Virginia Postrel of *The Atlantic* magazine suggests transplant centers pay $25,000 or $50,000 to each living kidney donor.[27] As a result, taxpayers would save billions: "Eliminating the waiting list would save taxpayers $8 billion, or $4 billion if each living donor received a lump-sum payment of $50,000."[28] To make an even starker point, Nobel Laureate economist Gary Becker and economist Julio Elías estimated that a mere payment of $15,000 per donor would eliminate the kidney shortage in the United States. These economists suggest the federal government make the payments so as to avoid any inequality in allocation.[29] That, of course, would be unconstitutional.

The bottom line is transplants are cheaper than dialysis, and since dialysis treatment is paid by Medicare's ESRD program, it is in our interest to cut costs. Even more convincing, these monetary calculations completely ignore the benefits enjoyed by the recipient in the form of health, happiness, and quality of life. It seems like a no-brainer, but our government cannot seem to pull it off.

## Success Stories Around the Globe

There is only one country in the world that has eliminated its shortage of transplant organs. Interestingly enough, it is Iran. Iran began its system of organ donation incentives in 1988 and eliminated its shortage by 1999.[30] If Iranian patients are not assigned a kidney from a deceased donor or cannot find a family donor, they apply to a non-profit called Dialysis and Transplant Patients Association (Datpa). Datpa finds donors in its pool of applicants, and an independent third party evaluates them. The government pays the donors $1,200 and provides one year of limited health coverage while those that worked through Datpa receive an additional payment (from Datpa) between $2,300 and $4,500.[31] Although the Iranian donor system is not fully a free market system, it does demonstrate that an organ shortage can be fixed by offering financial incentives. The United States government could learn a thing or two.

Singapore and Israel, on the other hand, use non-monetary methods of incentivizing their people to donate. Alex Tabarrok calls the program, "no give, no take."[32] If an individual "opts out" of Israel's presumed consent system, he or she is assigned a lower priority on the transplant list should one day he or she need an organ.[33] In other words, if you do not give, you do not receive. While this presumed consent program may seem potentially harmful to an individual's autonomy, anyone can "opt out" at any time. Other countries that have adopted presumed consent have had great success in decreasing their waiting lists. Spain, for example, adopted presumed consent in 1989, and within a decade had doubled its donor number.[34] Austria quadrupled its donation numbers when it adopted presumed consent.[35]

## Whatever Happened to Personal Autonomy?

Our government has done it again. The rules of the kidney game are wholly dictated by a governmental monopoly. As a result, you cannot determine what is best for you and your body. However, by attempting to quell organ trafficking, all the government is doing is running the black market further and further underground, making it more and more dangerous for everyone involved.

While opponents of organ trade argue that it is an exploitation of the poor, who am I (or the government) to say that the poor should not be able to make a rational decision to part with an organ—and free themselves from poverty at the same time? That decision is entirely theirs. While outlawing payments to donors is technically a way to keep the system "fair" by giving the rich and the poor equal access, it is only "fair" insofar as both the rich and the poor have an equally rotten chance to receive a healthy kidney. It is simply unfair that people at all economic levels have to succumb to that sad destiny. Why is it that I can purchase poison with which to kill a rodent, but I cannot purchase a finger to replace the one I lost to my saw?

The fact that healthy (and redundant) kidneys are a scarcity makes a compelling case for their economization. We should be using our resources more carefully. If there are thirteen people dying every day because they need a kidney, surely we can incentivize free people in some way. Altruism, apparently, is not enough. The government's plan is not working. We must leave this predicament, like any supply-and-demand scenario, to the markets. While other governments are actually searching for answers to the organ shortage problem, our government is unnecessarily policing—and failing in the process.

## And Lastly, the Drugs . . .

Drug prohibition is a failed public policy that must be abolished in the United States. Drugs continue to be available (whether you are looking for them or not) on street corners and in schools across America. Surveys taken of high school seniors, year after year, reveal that 85 percent say that marijuana is "easy to get."[36] You can smell pot at concert venues in San Francisco. You can witness cocaine residue in bathrooms in New York City restaurants. You can see the explosions of meth labs in small Nebraska towns. It is no secret. Drugs (and their dealers) flourish just fine under the "watchful" eye of the United States government.

No drug in this country was illegal prior to 1914. Hemp is the product from which marijuana is made. In fact, for much of our history, school textbooks were made from hemp! Even many of the Founding Fathers, including Jefferson and Washington, grew hemp. So why then did drugs go from being a major lawful industry to the scourge of society? Early in the twentieth century, a number of business tycoons saw the hemp industry as a major competitor, and thus a barrier to growth (hemp was an alternative to wood in paper production, for example). These tycoons included the DuPonts, Andrew Mellon, and William Randolph Hearst. They began by initiating a smear campaign against marijuana, portraying it as a great social evil, causing everything from insanity to violence (watch the vintage film *Reefer Madness* if you don't believe me). The public bought this nonsense hook, line, and sinker. If this was not enough, congressional hearings on the matter contained deliberately falsified information, such as the following letter from an editor of a newspaper:

Two weeks ago a sex-mad degenerate, named Lee Fernandez, brutally attacked a young Alamosa girl. He was convicted of assault with intent to rape and sentenced to 10 to 14 years in the state penitentiary. Police officers here know definitely that Fernandez was under the influence of marijuana. But this case is one in hundreds of murders, rapes, petty crimes, insanity that has occurred in southern Colorado in recent years.[37]

In reality, Fernandez was drunk, not high.[38] Eventually, in 1937 the Marijuana Tax Law was passed, which made marijuana illegal. Thus, a mainstay of the American criminal law was based off of nothing more than a secretive attempt to destroy business competitors. Put that in your pipe and smoke it!

Since President Nixon's declaration of the "War on Drugs" in 1970, the government has spent over one trillion dollars trying to combat them. Law enforcement agencies have locked up more than 2.3 million people, a higher incarceration rate than any other county.[39] What's more, 60 percent of these incarcerations are for non-violent crimes. What's the point? These people are not invading my body or my rights or my property, or yours. These people are not harming anyone but themselves—and they have the freedom to do that. What's more, the state is spending vast amounts of our nation's resources (tax dollars) attempting to fight an un-winnable fight. When something like drugs (or prostitution) is prohibited, black markets pop up with all the corollary problems that surround them. When free exchange is permitted, a legitimate and workable market develops with supply and demand to act as a check.

## The Lies the Government Tells You 2.0

My Fox News colleague John Stossel recently aired a show on the Drug War and debunked some government-created myths like "some drugs are so addictive that you are hooked the first time you use them." John makes the argument that drugs are not quite as addictive as the government wants us to believe, and the statistics back him up.

According to the National Survey on Drug Use and Health gathered by the Substance Abuse and Mental Health Services Administration, 8.5 million people have tried crack, while only 359,000 are regular users (regular users are defined as those who use it at best once in thirty days); 3.8 million have tried heroin, while only 213,000 are regular users. If these drugs are so addictive, why is there not a greater retention rate? Where are these first-time user addicts of whom the government speaks?

Also, the government wants us to believe that if drugs were to be legalized, there would be far more abuse of them. John Stossel maintains that there is very little evidence to support this assumption. As many know, in the Netherlands, marijuana has been legal for years. The Dutch, however, are far less likely to smoke than Americans. Fully 38 percent of American adolescents have smoked pot, while only 20 percent of Dutch teens have; in other words, marijuana rates in the Netherlands, where pot is legal, are half the rate of those in the United States, where pot gets you jail time![40] The Dutch government's answer to this discrepancy is telling: "We've succeeded in making pot boring."[41] The United States government should follow suit.

## Drug Legalization Would Save the Government Money!

Jeffrey Miron, a professor of economics at Harvard, authored a study on the economics of marijuana legalization. He concluded that marijuana legalization would reduce government spending by $7.7 billion annually.[42] Its legalization would generate $2.4 billion of tax revenue annually if marijuana were taxed like all other goods and $6.2 billion annually if marijuana were taxed at rates comparable to those on alcohol and tobacco.[43]

To put this amount in perspective, Miron takes this calculation and asserts that the $14 billion in combined annual savings and revenues would "cover the securing of all 'loose nukes' in the former Soviet Union in less than three years." "Just one year's savings would cover the full cost of anti-terrorism port security measures required by the Maritime Transportation Security Act of 2002."[44] Talk about putting money to good use! The esteemed Nobel Laureate in Economics, Milton Friedman, and more than five hundred economists called for this drug debate to be brought to light as there is taxpayer money to be saved and government power to be tamed.

## Surprise, Surprise: The State Breaks Its *Own* Laws in Combating the "Drug War"

If the government would profit financially from the legalization of drugs, why won't it concede? Because it likes to waste your tax dollars and assert control over you by violating your privacy and other rights in the process. Don't believe me?

Every day, the government uses unconstitutional means to conduct SWAT raids on homes that may (or may not) have drugs inside. Often, these police tips come from unreliable sources, but the government goes in anyway. According to these police, no judicial due process or search warrant is required, and the government is not obligated to knock at your door. Law enforcement may enter your home, unannounced, in the dead of night.

While SWAT raids are supposed to be used to disperse violent situations, they are increasingly used in non-violent situations to search and seize the premises of homes, thereby violating every civil liberty held by you or me as a human being. There are 100 to 150 SWAT raids *per day* in the U.S. and about 50,000 performed per year.[45] Since the late 1980s, SWAT raids have increased dramatically, almost 1,500 percent.[46] Many of these raids end up at mistaken addresses, causing injury, deaths of dogs, and deaths of humans. The only common thread is the lack of consideration for freedom to live safely and peacefully in one's own home.

Gore Vidal, a playwright and novelist, sees through the government's lies clearly:

> The bureaucratic machine has a vested interest in playing cops and robbers. Both the Bureau of Narcotics and the Mafia want strong laws against the sale and use of drugs because if drugs are sold at cost there would be no money in it for anyone . . . will anything sensible be done? Of course not. The American people are as devoted to the idea of sin and its punishment as they are to making money—and fighting drugs is nearly as big a business as pushing them.

Ironically, the actions our government seeks to control and regulate are the creations of the government itself. The state has perpetuated the dreadful consequences of prostitution—violence and disease—by attempting to prohibit it. The government has lengthened the kidney waiting list by outlawing compensation and incentives to donors. The government has brought on its war on drugs by trying to quash their use. When will it ever learn? It is time the government gets out and stays out of our bodies.

## Conclusion

The government's god-like complex has taken its power trip too far. If you want to consume trans fats, the government should not stop you. If you want to ingest drugs, the government should not stop you. If you find prostitution to be a viable option for employment or enjoyment, the government should not stop you. If you need a new kidney and have the economic resources to purchase one, the government should not stop you. If there are no feasible treatments available for your illness but Switzerland is testing a drug, the government should not stop you from choosing to try it. The moment the government interferes with our right to do with our bodies as we please, the state has unconstitutionally, immorally, and unnaturally overstepped its enumerated powers and has violated our rights as individuals. The purpose of the federal government is to protect our constitutional and natural rights—not to restrict or inhibit them.

When we are children, our parents raise, educate, groom, teach, and lead us to make the important decisions that life will surely demand of us. We will make good decisions. We will make bad decisions. We have the right to make these bad decisions. The poor decisions help us grow and learn to become productive members of American society, and the government must not deprive us of these opportunities. The bottom line is we, as adults, are big boys and girls who can make our own assessments and conclusions. The government should mind its own business, and worry about its own problems (and it has many).

# Chapter 8

# Sticks and Stones Will Break My Bones:

*The Right to Self-Defense*

The Constitution does not allow the government to experiment with your constitutional rights. The Founders did not tell us when we can be baptized, what God we can worship, where to register our religion, when we can speak freely, what books we can read, or where speech free zones exist. Yet, the government today tells us when we can purchase a gun, what guns we can purchase, where we must register the guns, how we can use the guns, and in what areas guns are prohibited.

What the government ignores is that our right to keep and bear arms is a natural or fundamental right. For example, if someone breaks in to your home and attempts to swing his fist at you, it is your natural right to raise your arm and try to defend yourself. You also have the right to use whatever force is necessary to stop the intruder. This is the ancient, and until 1934 in America, universally recognized personal right to self-defense. Today, the use of guns is merely the contemporary exercise of the right. Without the right to defend oneself, individuals would be incapable of protecting themselves against ordinary thugs and tyrannical governments. In fact, the Glorious Revolution of 1688 guaranteed English citizens the right to bear arms, and stripped the power to prohibit guns away from the state. This provided individuals with the necessary force for their own self-defense and removed any reliance on the state to protect them.

In addition, the right to keep and bear arms removes a monopoly of force (i.e., the government) and creates a pluralistic use of force, which is the power of multiple individuals. This in turn creates a respect for Natural Law and other natural rights, such as property. As James A. Donald, a libertarian commentator, explains,

> Similarly a belief in natural rights tends to result in pluralistic use of force, because people obviously have the right to defend their rights, whereas disbelief in natural rights tends to lead to an absolute monopoly of force to ensure that the state will have the necessary power to crush people's rights and to sacrifice individuals, groups, and categories of people for the greater good.[1]

Without this right, we would be unable to defend our property from others and our own government. Fortunately, our Founding Fathers recognized the importance of this natural, or fundamental, right and created the Second Amendment, so as to assure that no government in America could infringe upon it.

Enacted in 1791, the Second Amendment states, "A well regulated Militia, being necessary to the security of a free State, the right of the people to keep and bear Arms, shall not be infringed." While the language of the Second Amendment appears clear, controversy over the true meaning of the language swirls to this day. Yet, controversy did not always surround the idea of protecting the right to self-defense. The 1689 English Bill of Rights explicitly protects a right to keep arms for self-defense. And when James Madison proposed the Bill of Rights, the Second Amendment was the least "debated" amendment.

In fact, the right to bear arms was not debated at all at the Constitutional Convention in 1787. During the 1788 state ratification debates, Federalists and anti-Federalists often campaigned on opposing platforms. However, on this issue, there was a consensus regarding the importance of the right to own and use guns. But politics being politics, a "debate" ensued. On one side, anti-Federalists lobbied for the right out of a fear the government would disarm individuals and impose a standing army or select militia. On the other side, Federalists argued the right was adequately protected because the Constitution embodied the limited powers of the federal government.[2] Consequently, the "debate" turned into a competition as to who would take credit with constituents for the virtues of the Second Amendment.

The Founders formed a consensus as to the meaning of the amendment. The Second Amendment is not a collective right, but rather an *individual* right. There is no record of the Founders viewing a "well regulated Militia" as only state militias, such as the National Guard or police departments, but rather the sum of individuals in a state who choose to create a militia. Furthermore, "the right of the people" in the Constitution is always in reference to individuals, not to some state entity.

The Founders may have agreed on the necessity and meaning of the Second Amendment, but subsequent governments fought to curtail this right. However, because the right to keep and bear arms is a modern-day extension of the right to self-defense, it is natural, or fundamental, and these governments had no legal authority to take away an absolute right without due process. Yet, despite the unconstitutionality of their actions and the clarity of the Founders' vision, progressives in American governments have continuously attempted to create controversy over the true meaning of the Second Amendment and used this controversy to disarm the nation's individuals to seize more power for government.

## Give Me Your Guns, and I'll Protect You

Government's quest to strip us of our ability to defend life, liberty, and property is not unique to this nation. The Nazis used this method to disarm the Jews in Eastern Europe. Once the Nazis overtook a town, Hitler ordered them to seize all guns and other weapons from the Jews and forbade the Jews from acquiring new arms. Not surprisingly, Hitler exempted members of the Sturmabteilung, Hitler's paramilitary organization (the "brown shirts"), and Nazi Party members from the existing gun laws. The tragedy during the night of November 9th through the early hours of the 10th, 1938, or Kristallnacht, demonstrates the success of this method. The Nazis unleashed a series of pogroms against the German Jews in response to a November 7th 1938 assassination of a German diplomat in Paris, Ernst vom Rath, by Herschel Grynszpan, a Jewish teenager. In a matter of hours, the Nazis killed at least 91 Jews, injured countless others,[3] destroyed 7,500 Jewish businesses,[4] and burned 267 synagogues.[5] The Nazis arrested about 30,000 Jews and transported them to concentration camps.[6] The Nazis' previous denial of the Jews' natural right to keep and bear arms left them without a chance to defend themselves, their homes, businesses, or synagogues.

In contrast, those able to hold onto their arms and their basic right to self-defense were much more successful in resisting the Nazi genocide. Take, for example, the Warsaw Ghetto uprising of April 1943. Without notice, Wehrmacht troops arrived in the Jewish ghetto in Warsaw, Poland, with orders to liquidate the remaining Jewish population and transport survivors to concentration camps. Yet, to their surprise, they met resistance from a loosely organized group of Zionists, the Jewish Combat Organization (ZOB). The ZOB never totaled more than 220 individuals,[7] who were ill equipped to fight the Nazis. With only small arms and grenades, they were able to kill about three hundred members of the German military and hold them off for almost a month. More impressively, not one ZOB member was brought to the concentration camps; they either died in combat, escaped, or committed suicide. While there was no way for the Jews to know the Holocaust was occurring or about to occur, if they were able to maintain arms and fight for their lives like those of the ZOB did, then perhaps the six million Jews would never have suffered their tragic horrific fate.

Unfortunately, despite the widespread knowledge of the Holocaust, it is surely not the only case of dictators using the power of disarmament to their advantage. In fact, the Chinese, the inventors of gunpowder, are forbidden from owning any firearms or ammunition. In 1996, the Chinese government imposed a blanket ban and outlawed the private manufacturing, sale, transportation, possession, importation, or exportation of bullets, guns, and replicated guns. The irony is that as the Chinese government continues to disarm its citizens, it makes a fortune off the arms trade.[8] In fact, as of 2009, China was the seventh largest exporter of arms in the world.[9]

Why would a government making large profits exporting arms, prevent its people from owning these arms? The answer is simple: To retain power. As Mao Zedong famously remarked, "Political power grows out of the barrel of a gun." A disarmed citizenry allows China's growing military to maintain the status quo; a status quo involving complete governmental dominance of all non-government persons. In fact, the timing of the blanket prohibition is evidence of this. The Chinese government initiated the prohibition after political unrest and social tensions rose with pro-democracy demonstrations in 1989.

Unfortunately, despite what we are taught, our own nation's history in the realm of gun laws is more similar to Eastern Europe's and China's history than we would like to believe. Currently, the federal government reaps the tax and trade benefits of our nation being the number one producer and exporter of arms; yet, restricts the right to keep and bear arms.[10] The trend in disarming American individuals is not new. During the period after the Civil War, southern governments enacted Black Codes, which prohibited freed slaves and all blacks from owning and bearing firearms. By disarming the former slaves, the Codes made it virtually impossible for them to defend themselves from the violent actions of the KKK. KKK-inspired assaults on self-defense soon spread to the North, and similar statutes were enforced in states, such as New York, which disarmed blacks, Irish, Italians, Jews, and other immigrant groups.

Partly in response to and partly in anticipation of the southern governments depriving blacks of their basic liberties, Congress enacted the Fourteenth Amendment. The Fourteenth Amendment generally applies the protections of the Bill of Rights to the states. Stated differently, the Fourteenth Amendment imposes the same restraints on the states that the first eight amendments impose on the federal government. There are some exceptions to this; though, for the most part, it is the case.

Statutes such as those enacted after the Civil War and in subsequent periods are exactly the atrocities the Second Amendment and Fourteenth Amendment were meant to prevent. And while it does not take a wise man to recognize the advantages of an unarmed citizenry, if we are unable to learn from history's lessons, we are fools destined to repeat them.

## Federal Denial of the Right to Keep and Bear Arms

The Founders envisioned a nation where the government held limited powers and the people were able to live their daily lives with little interference from any government. Within this vision was the power of individuals to defend their property from criminals, other foreign entities, and tyrannical domestic governments. Yet, our current and past governments continually seek legislative tools to circumvent the Second Amendment. The initial efforts of state governments were shamefully blatant in their attempts to disarm the black citizenry, but over time, the state governments and the federal government sought to impair the right of all non-government persons to keep and bear arms.

The first of the federal acts interfering with the right to self-defense was the National Firearms Act of 1934. In the guise of raising revenues, the government began to require registrations and taxation on the transfer of weapons. Today, the registration of a gun is the status quo, and we are taxed on everything from food to the shampoo we buy at the store. However, the National Firearms Act placed a two-hundred-dollar tax on the registration of shotguns. This tax is even more exorbitant when you consider that a brand-new shotgun only cost $6.95 in a 1938 Sears catalogue. The government claimed it was trying to raise revenues and not prohibit guns; yet, what other conclusion can one come to when a tax is thirty times more than the price of the product?

Continuing the assault on natural rights by the feds, the Supreme Court got in on the action. On June 22nd 1938, Treasury agents looking to make a bootlegging bust stopped Frank Layton and Jack Miller as they drove through Arkansas. To their despair, Layton and Miller's car contained no illicit bootlegging equipment; however, the men were in possession of an unregistered sawed-off shotgun. The reason for the arrest was the length of the gun's barrel. Had it been two inches *longer*, and thus comparable in size to those used by the military at the time, Miller and Layton would not have been arrested. The comparability to military weapons was the premise—a historically inaccurate, profoundly unconstitutional, and Natural Law–violating premise—of the 1934

Act. Progressives in Congress took the phrase "a well regulated Militia" in the text of the Second Amendment and falsely claimed that the Framers intended to protect the ownership of military-style weapons only, those fit for use by a well-regulated militia. The newly enacted National Firearms Act prohibited the unregistered gun, and the men were subsequently arrested.

Under the Act, the men faced fines and up to five years in jail. Layton and Miller appealed their conviction all the way to the Supreme Court. Unfortunately, by the time their case reached the Court, the men were unavailable, and their counsel could no longer afford to represent them without compensation. Yet, their case moved forward, and the Court heard oral arguments on behalf of the government only. The government argued that the statute was for revenue purposes and held no relation to the Second Amendment or the right to keep and bear arms. This one-sided oral argument resulted in the Court incorrectly ruling in favor of the government and the constitutionality of the National Firearms Act. The justices accepted the government's false claims that firearms with a barrel shorter than sixteen inches were not used by the military. Consequently, the government successfully argued these arms were not protected by the Second Amendment because it only protects arms used by the militia, and the militia can only be armed by guns used by the military. The failure of the Court to investigate the truth and reject this narrow and obviously incorrect interpretation of the Second Amendment created a wide-open door for the enactment of gun regulations over the next seventy years.

By 1968, the government took the opportunity to intrude even more on the natural right to keep and bear arms by enacting the Gun Control Act of 1968 and Omnibus Crime Control and Safe Streets Act. These Acts required all gun owners to be over the age of eighteen and prohibited the sales of arms between residents of different states. Moreover, a gun-licensing program was implemented, and a manipulative "sporting test" was developed. Yet, after allegations of abuse and a complete about-face by the government, the Firearms Owners Protection Act of 1986 was enacted. The Act resulted from a 1982 bipartisan Senate subcommittee. The subcommittee was tasked with investigating the Second Amendment and found,

The conclusion is thus inescapable that the history, concept, and wording of the second amendment to the Constitution of the United States, as well as its interpretation by every major commentator and court in the first half century after its ratification, indicates that what is protected is an *individual* right of a private citizen to own and carry firearms in a peaceful manner.[11]

While the subcommittee concluded the above, the Act did not reinstate the natural right to self-defense. Instead, the Act banned the manufacture, transfer, and civilian use of machine guns not manufactured as of the date of the Act. But, of course, there was one exception: Those for the police.

By 1993, the government was up to its old tricks, and President Clinton signed into law the Brady Handgun Prevention Act (Brady Act) on November 30th 1993. The Brady Act was named in honor of James Brady. During the attempted assassination of President Ronald Reagan, a stray bullet hit Brady, Reagan's press secretary, and left him permanently disabled. Consequently, he and his wife have devoted their lives to assaulting the right to self-defense. The main purpose of the Act was to provide "for a waiting period before the purchase of a handgun, and for the establishment of a national instant criminal background check system to be contacted by firearms dealers before the transfer of any firearm."[12] In doing so, the Act imposed a five-day interim measure before a licensed importer, manufacturer, or dealer may sell, deliver, or transfer a handgun to an unlicensed individual. While the interim measure applied only in states without an acceptable alternate system of conducting background checks on handgun purchasers, it expired on November 30th 1998, and the waiting period ceased to apply when the computerized instant check system came online.

Finally, the government enacted the Violent Crime Control and Law Enforcement Act of 1994, or more appropriately the "Federal Assault Weapons Ban." The main thrust of the Act was to prohibit the sale of specified semiautomatic firearms, which were defined as "assault weapons," to civilians. Additionally, the Act designated nineteen weapons as assault weapons and then provided a definition of assault weapons based on certain senseless combinations of a variety of non-lethal features.

Now, at first you may be sympathetic to a ban on "assault weapons," but in reality, these weapons are no more potent than your or your neighbor's legal hunting rifle. In fact, the bullets are fired one at a time, at the same speed, and produce the same damage as a hunting rifle. So then, what is the difference? The rifle's plastic casing. That's right, the government is not protecting you from machine guns producing a spray fire; no, it is restricting your right to own a dangerous-*looking* hunting rifle.

Fortunately, the Violent Crime Control Act expired in 2004, and not surprisingly, the United States did not dissolve into chaos. Rather, there was no uptick in crime rates, and the FBI reported a 3.6 percent drop in violent crimes the following year. This was the first drop in five years, and the states that maintained the assault weapon ban experienced the smallest drop in murder rates. Of course, the government claims we were safer with the ban, and the drop in crime rates did not make the national news; but the numbers do not lie.

By creating gun bans and stripping you of your natural right to protect your personal property, the government is not keeping you any safer; rather, the government is giving criminals more firepower for their crimes. This can only be exemplified through a close analysis of the numbers, numbers which the government continually chooses to ignore.

## Numbers Don't Lie; People Do

The argument is simple: *More guns mean less crime.* Year after year, the statistics prove the number of gun crimes committed lessens as prohibitions on guns are weakened. Yet, if you were to listen to the mainstream media and government bureaucrats, they would like you to believe the opposite. Whether it is for political gain or their own personal beliefs, our government officials continuously preach the myth that guns create, instead of prevent, harm.

Currently, there are approximately 300 million privately owned firearms in the United States. This includes nearly 100 million handguns. On average, the number of firearms rises by more than 4 million annually. There are about 70 to 80 million gun owners in the United States, which is about 40 to 45 percent of all American households. In 2009, about 125 million Americans lived in households with guns. As of 2007, there were 5 million Americans carrying concealed handguns, and thirty-nine states maintained right-to-carry laws, with another nine states maintaining "may-issue" laws. Only two states, Illinois and Wisconsin, completely ban all people who do not work for the government from carrying handguns.[13]

The reality is that almost every year, guns kill about 30,000 Americans, and about 1,000 of these deaths are accidental. While these numbers appear staggering, fewer than 2 percent of handguns and 1 percent of all guns in this country will ever be used to commit a violent crime.[14] Thus, the use of blanket prohibitions against owning guns is like burning a haystack to get to a needle. The individuals using guns to kill crime victims are most likely already prone to crime and are not going to refrain from these actions simply because their gun's registration has not come in the mail or they failed to pass a background check. Have you ever seen a TV show in which a convicted felon claims he did not commit more crimes because he was afraid he'd be arrested for an unregistered gun? Have you ever even heard such nonsense? Probably not. No one watching would believe it.

However, the statistics do show criminals refrain from crimes when they know the victim may be armed. Take, for example, the disparity of "hot burglaries" in Canada and Great Britain compared to the United States. A "hot burglary" is one where a resident is at home when the criminal strikes. In Canada and Great Britain, both with stringent anti-gun laws, nearly half of burglaries are "hot"; the burglars are not concerned with the victims being armed. Comparatively, the rate is only 13 percent in the United States, where we have relatively less restrictive gun laws. Moreover, convicted American felons reveal that they are much more worried about armed victims when committing a crime than they are about running into the police. In fact, interviews with convicted felons, in ten state correctional systems, reveal that 56 percent would not attack a known armed citizen.[15] When one burglar entered a Colorado home, the owner promptly aimed a gun at him and waited for police to arrive. Police Sergeant Roderick O'Connor recalled that the intruder pleaded, "Those guys pointed guns at me. They should be arrested." Apparently, the government would agree with him.

STICKS AND STONES WILL BREAK MY BONES

Another example of this is Switzerland, where gun ownership rates are high and burglary rates are low. James A. Donald describes Switzerland as a nation where in peacetime, there are no generals or a central command; rather, every individual is his own policeman. As Donald explains,

> Almost every house in Switzerland contains one or more automatic weapons, the kind of guns that the American federal government calls "assault rifles with cop killer bullets." Switzerland has strict gun controls to keep guns out of the hands of children, lunatics and criminals, but every law abiding adult can buy any kind of weapon. Almost every adult male owns at least one gun, and most have more than one, because of social pressures and the expectation that a respectable middle class male citizen should be well armed and skillful in the use of arms. It is also no coincidence that respect for property rights in Switzerland is amongst the highest in the world, possibly the highest in the world.[16]

This description clearly demonstrates the importance of the right to keep and bear arms in relation to our property rights.

In America, you are instilled from a young age with the belief, "guns kill," but you are never informed of your natural right to own and use a gun to save your own life or defend your property. You never learn how vital guns or weapons were in securing the independence of this nation and many other nations. You are never taught that guns can help prevent crimes by deterring criminal activity, nor are you taught how gun laws can actually increase crime.

For example, take the 2010 case of Michael Lish, an Oklahoma homeowner. Upon returning home with his wife around 10:00 p.m., Lish noticed the back door ajar and a window open. Lish then entered the house and searched it to make sure everything was okay. Unsuspectingly, a nineteen-year-old intruder, Billy Jean Tiffey III, jumped out at Lish while brandishing a sword. Lish, who had a concealed-weapon permit, pulled out his gun and shot Tiffey in the abdomen. Tiffey dropped to his knees and reached behind his back, upon which Lish fired a second and third shot, killing him. Investigators found Tiffey was carrying not only a sword, but also a .38-caliber pistol, the homeowner's 9 mm pistol, a knife, and a stun gun. Fortunately for Lish, he did not face prosecution because

Oklahoma maintains the "Make My Day" law, where a person can use force—including deadly force—to defend his home.[17] In my home state of New Jersey, had Michael Lish endured this ordeal, he'd have faced twenty years in prison.

## What Could Have Been: Two Fewer Days of Remembrance?

As the previous statistics prove, these bans do not help protect you. In fact, you are worse off with gun prohibitions because you are unable to protect yourself, and criminals know this. This can only be exemplified by two tragic incidents at the beginning of the twenty-first century. The events leading up to the collapse and destruction of the World Trade Center do not need to be repeated. However, it is important to consider what would have happened if the passengers or pilots of those planes were armed. I believe it is unlikely the terrorists would have been as "successful" in causing destruction and taking American lives.

You may argue the idea of armed pilots or airline passengers is frightening, but to do so, you are ignoring history. Until 1963, American commercial passenger pilots were required to carry guns on any flight carrying U.S. mail in order to protect the mail—not the passengers, but the mail—in case the flight landed away from an airport. Moreover, until 1987, pilots could legally carry guns on their flights. In fact, the pilots' union for American Airlines and the Airline Pilots Security Alliance claim that until 1987, up to 10 percent of all pilots regularly carried guns. Okay, so pilots carried guns on the planes, but how many injuries or diverted flights resulted from this practice? None. That's right; there are no recorded instances of any significant gun-related problem arising from a legally armed pilot.[18]

Additionally, since 2003, pilots have been legally able to carry guns on their flights. Yet, in order to do so, the pilots must receive extensive training and psychological evaluations. In the time between 2003 and the writing of this book, there has been only one reported incident where a pilot accidentally discharged his gun. However, it is ironic, because the gun was discharged when the pilot was attempting to follow federal regulations calling for pilots to put a trigger lock on a loaded gun as the plane is landing. The incident caused no flight problems, and the plane landed safely. This is just another example of federal regulations causing more harm than good.[19] What is the value of a handgun when it is incapacitated by a trigger lock? Absolutely no value. It's kind of silly not to trust a pilot with a gun but to trust him or her with a passenger plane, essentially a guided missile.

On April 16th 2007, a monumental, yet avoidable, shooting took place on the campus of Virginia Polytechnic Institute and State University (Virginia Tech) in Blacksburg, Virginia. The attacker, Seung-Hui Cho, killed thirty-two persons and wounded many others before taking his own life. The events took place over a period of two hours, and once called, the police took nearly six minutes to enter a barricaded building. Keep in mind, this was six minutes *after* the shooting stopped. The first shooting had occurred two hours earlier. While the events are tragic, one must wonder what would have happened if individuals were permitted to carry concealed guns on Virginia Tech's campus and not compelled to keep their weapons in their cars.

Perhaps even more heartbreaking, is that in January 2006, prior to the shootings, legislator Todd Gilbert introduced a bill, HD 1572, to the Virginia House of Delegates. HD 1572 was intended to forbid public universities in Virginia from preventing students from lawfully carrying a concealed handgun on campus. The bill was defeated, and the defeat was praised, but we can only wonder whether we would be marking April 16th as a day of remembrance if just one student or professor on the Virginia Tech campus had been armed. While it cannot be guaranteed any individual involved in the incident would have been armed, the effect of armed faculty and students is demonstrated by other school shootings.

Take, for example, the school shooting at Appalachian School of Law in Grundy, Virginia. On January 16th 2002, Peter Odighizuwa, placed on suspension and failing out of school, sought to take revenge. He entered the campus and waved a gun while yelling, "Come get me." In a matter of seconds, he killed the school's dean, a professor, and a classmate. As panic ensued, and the gunshots were heard around campus, students Mikael Gross and Tracy Bridges ran to their cars in order to retrieve their guns. Both Gross and Bridges, unaware of the other, approached Odighizuwa from different directions. Ultimately, they cornered Odighizuwa, and he dropped his weapon and surrendered to police. Fortunately for the students of Appalachian School of Law, their peers were armed and able to prevent more killings.[20]

A similar case occurred at the University of Texas at Austin on August 1st 1966. Charles Whitman, a student at UT, ascended the tower on campus to use as a sniper's perch. Once there, he engaged in a shooting spree, killing fourteen people. Shortly after he initiated the attack, both police and armed civilians—including an English professor armed with a deer rifle—started to return fire. Officer Ramiro Martinez later reflected that it was owing to these armed civilians that the body count wasn't even higher; without them, Whitman would have been able to take aim freely at whomever he wished. We should be honoring—not incapacitating—these heroic civilians for exercising their natural rights in order to prevent further bloodshed.

The lack of media coverage on the advantages of guns on campus feeds into the ignorance of Americans with regard to firearms in government-owned schools. Just fifteen years ago, many states allowed concealed-handgun permit holders to carry guns on school property, and there were no major incidents. Yet, with the passage of the Federal Safe School Zone Act, these states no longer allow schools to permit concealed handguns. Fortunately, some states (New Hampshire, Oregon, and Utah), in defiance of the federal law, have taken the lead in restoring our natural right to bear arms and now allow permit holders to carry guns at school.

## The Supreme Court Restores Gun Rights

While you must remain eternally vigilant to protect your natural right to keep and bear arms, the Supreme Court recently began to do the work for you. Almost seventy years after the Supreme Court permitted the feds to restrict Second Amendment rights in the *Miller* case, it decided what is now lauded as a "landmark" decision. The Supreme Court in *District of Columbia v. Heller* (2008) held the Second Amendment protects an *individual's* right to bear arms in the home. In so doing, Justice Scalia in his majority opinion referred to the right to bear arms as a "fundamental right." By enshrining the right as fundamental, the Court acknowledged the right is natural, and thus cannot be stripped by any government, federal, state, or local, without due process. However, the Court failed to go far enough in this case. The majority did not address the language "shall not be infringed." In fact, the Court listed a number of infringements it deemed acceptable. By doing so, the Court ignored the plain language of the Second Amendment and the Founders' original intent. The Founders did not write "should not be infringed," which would give government leeway in creating restrictions; no, they wrote "shall not," which means the government *must not* infringe on your right to bear arms.

Unfortunately, mayors such as Mayor Richard M. Daley of Chicago ignored *Heller* and kept their gun control laws in place. This resulted in the Supreme Court agreeing to hear the case of *McDonald v. The City of Chicago* (2010). The named plaintiff, Otis McDonald, was a seventy-six-year-old African American residing in Chicago. McDonald had lived in his neighborhood since the 1970s, and over time, the neighborhood became overrun with gangs and drug dealers. In fact, McDonald received threats on the street, and his home was broken into numerous times.[21] While McDonald felt it was his natural right to protect his family and his home from the neighborhood's increasing violence, Chicago's 1982 gun control law prevented him from doing so. It effectively banned possession of handguns by all persons living in Chicago, except certain employees of the government. Some argued McDonald could still legally own a shotgun in his home, but what use is a shotgun to a seventy-six-year-old man? As McDonald pointed out, "Yes, I own long guns . . . but how long do you think it will take me to get up, get out of bed, and get my hands on a shotgun if someone is breaking in through the bedroom window?"[22]

Fortunately, for McDonald and the rest of this nation, the Supreme Court woke up and applied the Second Amendment to the states. Justice Alito, writing for the majority of the Court, wrote a reasoned and careful analysis of the Second Amendment issue at hand. In doing so, he noted how Chicago's murder rates actually increased after the ban was enacted, and Chicago residents "now face one of the highest murder rates in the country and rates of other violent crimes that exceed the average in comparable cities."[23] Again, the numbers don't lie. Alito concluded the *Heller* decision answers the question as to whether the right to keep and bear arms is *fundamental* to our nation's scheme of liberty. The Court held it is *"unmistakable"* that this right is fundamental (natural) and explains, "Self-defense is a basic right, recognized by many legal systems from ancient times to the present day,"[24] and no government may interfere with it.

While the ultimate application of the Second Amendment to states was correct, the Court again failed to restore our natural right to bear arms. The Court refused to hold the Chicago ban explicitly unconstitutional, but instead remanded the case to the lower federal appeals court to reconsider its ruling. Additionally, the majority again acknowledged a number of infringements the Court deemed constitutional. Yet, how can *any* infringement be constitutional when the Constitution plainly states "shall not be infringed"? Just as you do not need to register your books with the government in order to exercise your First Amendment rights, you do not need to register your firearms in order to exercise your Second Amendment rights.

The likely result of the recent Supreme Court decisions is a number of test cases. Cities, such as Chicago and New York, already declared they will enforce new regulations prohibiting gun ownership and seem prepared to face the Supreme Court again in future legal battles. When will the government bureaucrats get the point? You have the natural right to protect your life, liberty, and property. No matter how narrowly tailored or what governmental purpose the government argues it is protecting, nothing trumps your natural rights. How long shall we tolerate plutocrats who elevate their judgment and power over the Constitution? What has become of their oath to uphold it?

## Conclusion

Until the government recognizes our natural right to keep and bear arms, the fight against gun control cannot wane. While the recent Supreme Court decisions are in the right direction, they are not enough to restore your right to defend your life, liberty, and property. If only one Justice in the majority voted the other way, any progress made may be quickly revoked. Moreover, the government's claim that it is only trying to protect you is clearly false. The government's regulations do not change criminals' attitudes on guns or where they carry their guns, but only where and how they get their guns. By enabling criminals to arm themselves and preventing potential victims from defending themselves, we are bound to repeat history's tragedies. I do not know what it will take for the people to wake up and realize the power the government is currently seizing, but I urge you to do so, before it is too late.

# Chapter 9

# You'll Hear from Me:

*The Right to Petition the Government for Redress of Grievances*

In 2002, the non-profit organization We the People Foundation for Constitutional Education petitioned the government to answer for violating the following provisions of the Constitution: The War Powers Clause with the undeclared Iraq War, the money clauses with the Federal Reserve System, the right to privacy with the Patriot Act, and the tax clauses by levying a direct, un-apportioned tax on labor. After having those petitions ignored, We the People, including 1,450 individuals, commenced a lawsuit against the United States government seeking to enforce their constitutional right to petition, and to compel the government's corresponding duty to respond. They argued that if the government failed to respond to petitions, then the people of the United States had a right to sanction the government, namely, in the form of withholding taxes. They thus adopted the mantra "No Answers, No Taxes," citing in part the following excerpt from the *Journals of the Continental Congress*: "If money is wanted by Rulers who have in any manner oppressed the People, they may retain it until their grievances are redressed, and thus peaceably procure relief."

A federal district court judge dismissed *We the People v. United States*. The court pointed to two inapposite Supreme Court cases as support. Specifically, the district court reasoned that if employment-related petitions made by government employees did not trigger a duty to respond, neither did petitions made by United States citizens for the enforcement of constitutional rights.

The U.S. Court of Appeals for the Second Circuit in New York affirmed, and the Supreme Court declined to hear the case. To further silence the petitioning activities of organizations such as We the People, the Congress amended the Tax Relief and Health Care Act of 2006 to provide for five-thousand-dollar fines for anyone who submitted a so-called "specified frivolous submission" to the IRS. Among a host of others, frivolous submissions included arguments that "a taxpayer may withhold payment of taxes or the filing of a tax return until the [IRS] or other government entity responds to a First Amendment petition for redress of grievances." Thus, the government not only took the stance that it was not bound by the Constitution, but that individuals could be punished harshly for attempting to exercise their constitutional right to hold the government accountable for its illegal conduct.

Why is it that a government can transgress our natural rights, and then so easily avoid responsibility when organizations such as We the People attempt to hold the government responsible? Isn't there a fundamental human yearning to right those wrongs which have been committed against us, regardless of whether the transgressor was an individual or a government, American or foreign? As we shall see, the right to petition the government for redress of grievances guarantees individuals a liberty to demand that legislatures take a particular action, and to sue the government when it breaks the law. For centuries, this has been one of the most jealously guarded rights in the Anglo-American legal systems. Moreover, implicit in this right is the self-evident truth that government is the servant of the people, and not the other way around. Understanding the crucial role that the right to petition plays in free governments, our Founders enshrined it in the Constitution so that future generations might enjoy the blessings of liberty.

Nonetheless, growing weary of receiving complaints regarding slavery during the antebellum era, the federal government took the position that it had no duty to respond to or even read petitions. Moreover, the government has enacted rules which allow for sanctions against parties bringing so-called frivolous lawsuits. All of these rules and doctrines have swept away those components of the right which history has taught us is necessary for liberty, and in so doing eviscerated one of our constitutionally mandated protections from government interference. As in all of these chapters, we shall see that the culprit has been a push for larger government and unconstitutional legislation. Only when our rights, especially the right to petition, have been cut down, can government gain complete control of our lives and fully sate its thirst for power.

## The Right of the People over Their Government

The right to petition the government for redress of grievances is one of the oldest and most well-established rights in our legal history, leading the prominent lawyer Norman B. Smith to call it in 1986 "the cornerstone of the Anglo-American constitutional system[s]." The development of the right to petition paralleled an increasingly stable government in medieval England. Rather than use warfare and coercion to effectuate political change, barons were able to petition the King peacefully to redress their grievances. In fact, petitions became an early form of legislation, as laws would typically be submitted by Parliament to the King in the form of petitions to adopt a particular policy. Moreover, the political stability offered in part by the right to petition was an essential component in the development of the modern state as we now know it. As historian Joseph R. Strayer, who taught me history when I was an undergraduate, once noted,

In any political unit where there was some stability and continuity, one could expect that there would be efforts to create judicial institutions which would improve internal security and financial institutions which would provide the revenues necessary for defense against an external enemy.[1]

Such institutions are indeed the proper role of government and were particularly necessary amidst the violence of the Middle Ages.

The alternative to the right to petition was a violent regime change. When grievances go unanswered, history demonstrates that the aggrieved will inevitably seek to overthrow those in power. The English were acutely aware of the role that the right played in maintaining a healthy political system: "To traduce such petitioning [is] a violation of [royal] duty, and to represent it to his majesty as tumultuous and seditious is to betray the liberty of the subject, and contribute to the design of subverting the ancient legal constitution of this kingdom, and introducing arbitrary power."[2] Many historians posit that Britain was able to avoid the bloody revolutions on the European continent in the eighteenth and nineteenth centuries because the right to petition secured for the people a participatory role in government. Thus, the stability of the political system was largely based upon the ability of the King's subjects to request that certain actions be taken, and the corresponding expectation that the King would respond to those petitions and evenhandedly redress their grievances, and enhanced by the transparency that petitions necessarily brought about.

The right to petition was also essential to the development of popular sovereignty. This theory holds that, in the words of Benjamin Franklin, "the rulers are the servants and the people their superiors and sovereigns." The right to petition furthers popular sovereignty by making the government accountable to the people for all of its wrongs and misguided policies; petitions are not mere prayers or requests, but demands made by the masters (the people) to their servants (the government). If, however, the people were the servants of the government, then the government's interests would always be superior to those of the people, and it would be oxymoronic to demand that the government redress its violations of the people's natural rights. President John Quincy Adams succinctly stated the role that the right to petition plays in our political system: "The right of petition . . . is essential to the very existence of government; it is the right of the people over the Government; it is their right, and they may not be deprived of it." Thus if we lose the ability to petition the government, we also lose our right to demand that the government protect our freedoms instead of merely enhancing its own power.

One of the most essential features of the right was that the people remain immune from punishment for petitions made to the government. The most important event in securing this component of the right was the famous Seven Bishops Case. During the seventeenth century, the English Parliament seriously curtailed the rights of Catholics to participate in government. As a response, in 1687 the Catholic monarch King James II issued his Declaration of Indulgence which negated those restrictions, and later demanded that the Declaration be read aloud during Protestant church services. The predominantly Protestant English citizenry nonetheless perceived this action as an encroachment upon the sovereignty of Parliament and an initial attempt to re-establish Catholicism as the state religion. Believing the command to be an illegal exercise of authority, a number of senior Anglican bishops, including the Archbishop of Canterbury, petitioned the King, requesting that they be exempt from the duty to read the Declaration. This nationally published request outraged King James, who responded by charging them with the crime of seditious libel, "written or spoken words . . . that tend to . . . embarrass, challenge, or question the government."[3] Doesn't this sound eerily like the Alien and Sedition Acts of 1798 and the Espionage Act of 1917? History repeating, again.

The public was enraged by the arrests, appearing in droves to support the bishops as they were brought to the Tower of London. When ordered to enforce the Declaration, almost all soldiers in the army refused to do so. William III of Orange, who sought to replace James II, captured the significance of the case: "[King James's] evil counselors have endeavored to make all men to apprehend the loss of their lives, liberties, honors and estates, if they should go about to preserve themselves from . . . oppression by petitions, representations, or other means authorized by law."[4] If petitioners could be punished for making a humble request that the government do something differently, then the people would no longer be free to seek justice, and the right would be eviscerated. What could be a more fundamental human yearning than freely and uninhibitedly to right wrongs which have been committed against oneself? Consequently, the primary defense raised was not that the bishops were innocent, but that statements made as petitions could not be a valid basis for prosecution, even if they were genuinely seditious. As we have seen, it is dangerous to be right when the government is wrong.

Although the bishops were later acquitted, the real significance of the case was in prompting the adoption of the English Declaration of Rights. Seeking to prevent further transgressions of the right, the drafters of the Declaration enshrined the "right of the subjects to petition the King, and all commitments and prosecutions for such petitioning are illegal." Thus, it is clear from both the broad text of the Declaration and its history that its drafters were acutely aware of the effects that penalties could have on the right of the people to petition, and consequently sought to outlaw them forever.

The right to petition the government not only traveled to, but flourished in colonial America. In fact, it was deemed so essential a right that it was one of the few which were guaranteed to those traditionally disenfranchised members of society: Women, Indians, and even slaves. As one scholar notes, the right to petition therefore "vested these groups with a minimum form of citizenship: petitioning meant that no group in colonial society was entirely without political power."[5] Moreover, it was the right to petition the government from which other First Amendment rights, such as speech and assembly, are made more effective: If the right to petition was to be truly absolute, then the people compiling those petitions needed to be able to assemble, and speak freely. In sum, the right to petition the government can be considered a foundational right in our legal system; it is the right by which most other rights are enforced. After all, the Constitution cannot defend itself; its provisions will only ever take effect through the constant vigilance of those who wish to remain free.

One of the essential features of the right in the American colonies was that it imposed a correlative duty on the part of the government to hear those petitions and give them due regard. It is telling to note how legislatures dealt with an increasingly large number of petitions: "Whereas conditions of admissibility, such as amounts in controversy [i.e., a fee for submitting a petition], were manipulated to ease the pressure of petitions, the judicial guarantee of full consideration for those petitions still heard remained inviolate."[6] For example, a Connecticut Assembly provision passed in 1769, which abolished the right to appear before it, was shortly thereafter repealed as being contrary to fundamental individual rights (i.e., the Natural Law). Moreover, one of the principal reasons that America declared its independence was the British government's refusal to hear petitions from the colonies. It is only when we examine this history that we can begin to appreciate our Founders' belief that the right is "essential to the very existence of government." It should therefore come as no surprise then that they, and their predecessors, associated subversion of the right with tyranny and oppression.

More fundamentally, it should be clear that the right is useless if the government has no obligation to consider petitions; without it, the petitions might as well go straight into the waste basket, along with any hope of the people to seek a redress of their grievances. In essence, the duty of government to give petitions due consideration gives the right its meaning. A right to petition without any consideration of that petition is nothing more than a mere pretense of government accountability to the people.

When the Founders incorporated the right to petition into the Constitution, they also enshrined all of its essential protections, namely, the proscription of penalties for petitioning and the duty of the government to respond. They were thoroughly educated in its history and political theory, and the inevitable consequence of an out-of-touch government which results when the right is transgressed. By incorporating this right into the Constitution, the Founders could ensure that the new federal government would not commit the same wrongs as the government from which they had declared independence fifteen years earlier. Moreover, they wished that no future generation would have to fight another war just to have their natural rights enforced. Why would they ignore these lessons and grant to we the people far fewer freedoms than were guaranteed to their English counterparts and colonial ancestors? To suggest otherwise is to suggest that the Constitution was a radical shift away from a rich tradition of liberty and individual rights. Nothing could be further from the truth.

## Judicial versus Legislative Petitions

It is important to note that there are two kinds of petitions, both of which serve different interests. The first is the traditional *legislative* petition, which typically comes in the form of a letter sent to one's representatives. The second is the *judicial* petition, which is essentially a lawsuit against the government. We will explore both, and the important role they have played in securing individual liberty.

In early English legal history, common law courts lacked the power to compel the government to take an action. Thus if the people wished to take up a grievance with the King or Parliament, they would have to "petition" them directly with a request for a redress of grievances. The petitions themselves were actually received by the chancellor—a sort of chief operating officer of the government and chief justice of its courts—who was appointed by the King, with the consent of Parliament. My hero, St. Thomas More, once held this position.

If these petitions demanded the adoption of a different policy, they took the form of what we now know as *legislative* petitions. The legislative petition served the crucial function of ensuring government accountability to the people: "The people used this newfound right to question the legality of the government's actions, to present their views on controversial matters, and to demand that the government, as the servant of the people, be responsive to the popular will."[7] The formal petitions which activists draft and gather signatures for today are the descendants of these early petitions made to the King.

However, some of these claims were based not on a mere request that government do something differently, but that the government had violated an established legal right. Imagine the difference between petitioning the government to build a road around Boston instead of New York, and petitioning the government to release you from unlawful imprisonment; in the latter case, you actually have a legal right to be free from that kind of action, whether perpetrated by an individual or a government (in the Boston Road Case, you do not have a legal right); if that right is transgressed, then you are able to sue the offending party in court for a remedy.

If the King found that the claim against him was legitimate, then he authorized courts to hear the claim, with the attorney general representing him as a party. These are the antecedents of what we now know as *judicial* petitions; lawsuits against the government, heard and decided in a court of law. Gradually, the requirement of formal consent withered away, and the King lost the right to say when and if the government could be sued by virtue of judicial doctrine (the King himself would never have voluntarily agreed to such a large-scale waiver of immunity). Thus, historically the government and its officials were not above the law, but held accountable to it. In addition to accountability to the people, judicial petitions have the essential benefit of ensuring that disputes between individuals and the government are resolved by a neutral arbiter. As James Madison proclaimed in *Federalist* No. 10, "No man is allowed to be a judge in his own cause." Every child knows what happens when you get to cut the pie *and* choose the first piece. Eventually, the King lost that right.

Judicial petitions became especially important in early America because, as James Madison suggested in the statement above, individuals distrusted legislatures and favored the neutrality offered by an independent judiciary. In fact, the need for courts unbiased in the government's favor was one of the primary reasons for the creation of the judiciary as a separate branch of government: The Founders recognized the danger of the government being a judge in its own cause. The Chief Justice of the Virginia Court of Appeals once summarized the proper role for courts:

> The Legislature are to form rules for the conduct of the citizens. . . . The province of the Judiciary [is] to decide all questions which may arise upon the construction of laws or contracts, *as well between the government and individuals, as between citizen and citizen.* . . . If a contract is entered into on behalf of the government pursuant to an existing law and a contest shall arise about the meaning of the contract, it belongs to the Judiciary to decide what the contract was, and, if the Legislature shall decide the question, they invade the province of the Judiciary, *contrary to the Constitution.*[8]

The ability of the government to be sued in courts of law was therefore not only necessary for government accountability, but also to the doctrine of separation of powers implied in the Constitution's structure. To violate the right to petition the government in courts of law jeopardizes the integrity of the entire system. Thus at the time of the founding, the Petition Clause included both a right to sue the government and a right to request the government to take or abandon a particular action. Both were based upon the interests in government accountability to the people and the resolution of disputes by a neutral arbiter, and both are essential features of liberty.

## "You Got Served!!! But Only if You're Okay with It."

Following the September 11th terrorist attacks, family members of the victims filed suit against the Saudi government and four princes of the Saudi royal family. They alleged that the princes had knowingly funded Al Qaeda vis-à-vis the Saudi High Commission for Relief to Bosnia and Herzegovina, a Saudi charity, and thus should be held accountable for the attacks. The relevant statute for establishing whether the Saudi princes could be sued in America was the Foreign Sovereign Immunities Act (FSIA), which creates a presumption of immunity from suit.

In the case *In re Terrorist Attacks on September 11th 2001* (2008), the trial court dismissed the case for lack of jurisdiction. The Second Circuit affirmed the dismissal, ruling that the Saudi government was immune, the FSIA's protections applied to the princes as well as the government (despite the absence of text in the statute granting government officials immunity), and the charity was acting as an "organ" of the government, thus immunizing it as well. Interestingly, the Act was amended to allow for terrorism-related claims against foreign states. However, the federal government maintains a list of which states remain immune, and which may be sued. Unfortunately for family members of the victims, Saudi Arabia was not on that list of states that may be sued. In other words, those entities could not be held to answer for their actions in American courts because President Bush personally immunized them, and federal law permitted him to do so.

Now consider that foreign businesses which manufacture some kind of component part can be held liable in American courts if they purposefully targeted the American market, even though those component parts were incorporated into a final product elsewhere. This makes perfect sense: If you expect that your actions may harm someone, you should also expect to be held accountable in the place where the harm is caused. And yet, foreign governments, their officials, and even charities acting on their behalf, are free to fund terrorist organizations that they know are intent on killing innocent American civilians, and still escape responsibility in our courts when their officials are friends of the president.

Despite the crucial role which the right to petition plays in our constitutional system, the government has managed to shield itself from judicial petitions via the doctrine of sovereign immunity. Why can the government say when it will be sued and when it will not? What is the basis for treating a government which harms innocent persons differently from businesses and individuals who harm innocent persons? As you may have guessed, sovereign immunity cannot be reconciled with the right to petition the government judicially for redress of grievances: It is the negative of a judicial petition. As we shall see, the doctrine of sovereign immunity has vastly changed from its understanding at the time of the adoption of the Constitution, and in so doing has become one more legal device which government has crafted to eviscerate the right to petition, and therefore escape accountability to the people for its violations of the law.

The Supreme Court has said that any lawsuit is against the government if a finding for the plaintiff "would expend itself on the public treasure or domain, or interfere with public administration, or if the effect would be to restrain the Government from acting, or to compel it to act." So long as one of these conditions is met and the government has not specifically consented to be sued, then the government is immune from lawsuits, no matter how severe the violation of natural rights is. How could this be anything but the divine right of kings over the people, which popular sovereignty explicitly rejected, recast in a modern-day form? Moreover, this current state of the law distorts traditional common law, which allowed for suits against government officials and the government itself in some cases. The most well-known common law action against the government—the writ of *habeas corpus*, which allows for petitioners to challenge the lawfulness of their detention—is even enshrined in the Constitution.

Interestingly, the original justification for the notion of government accountability to the law was that government is the "fountain and head of justice and equity," and thus we can assume without further inquiry that the government would consent to having those wrongs redressed. Surely, the government would not mind being sued if doing so would accomplish its true purpose—justly protecting our freedoms. Thus, there can be no legitimate reason why government should remain immune from continuous accountability. Think of the sneaky child with his hand behind his back, whose parents assure him that "if you don't have anything to hide, then you don't have to worry about showing me what's in your hand."

More fundamentally, sovereign immunity dictates that the government is superior to the people, since it is not accountable to the law. As we have seen elsewhere in this book, this violates the Natural Law by suggesting that the temporal (in this case, a man-made government) is superior to the immutable principles of nature. And although the government claims that sovereign immunity is a *public necessity*, this is a hopelessly subjective term, and the government's own actions demonstrate this claim to be false; when government does consent to being sued, it is always because of the public outcry at the heinousness of individuals being left without a remedy, not because immunity is somehow less necessary. Why else would the Congress amend FSIA to include terrorism-related claims against foreign governments? And even if it were important not to draw down upon the public coffers and distract officials from their duties, how could it be rationally argued that this is an evil worse than the transgressions of the Natural Law which are facilitated by sovereign immunity?

Why then does the government insist upon sovereign immunity? The answer lies in what St. Augustine referred to as *libido dominandi*, the lust to dominate, or in other words, a desire to exert control over others. As St. Augustine described, there are two cities; the realm of God (the divine), and the realm of man (the earthly). He noted that "the two cities have been formed by two loves: the earthly by the love of self, even to the contempt of God; the heavenly by the love of God even to the contempt of self." We experience this on a daily basis when we initiate an argument with our loved ones; we do so not because there is a dispute that genuinely needs to be resolved, but because we lust for the feeling of "winning."

So, too, our politicians, though they may claim to have our best interests at heart, are corrupted by this human desire for power. Moreover, a position of power only facilitates *libido dominandi*, because one can so easily forget that he is supposed to be the servant of the people and not their master. An excellent example of this corruptive nature of power is the Alien and Sedition Acts; although our Founders enshrined a right of free speech, those same men later enacted an outrageous law punishing those who criticized the government, a direct contravention of that right. Thus, even the men who promised future generations liberty in perpetuity were not immune from *libido dominandi*.

Not being held accountable to the law—in the form of immunity from a lawsuit—is extraordinary power. After all, the law not only endeavors to restrict individuals from taking actions which are harmful to others, but seeks justice; the promise that those who do in fact break the law and harm others will have to suffer the consequences, or in other words, that wrongs will be made right. When one escapes justice, he becomes free to trample on the natural rights of whomever he pleases. Thus, there can be no better example of *libido dominandi* than the government's evisceration of the judicial petition, in direct contempt of God—the Natural Law. When the government escapes justice, not only are innocents harmed, but the escape establishes a precedent for future governments to do the same. Wilson relied on Lincoln's assaults on innocents, and FDR relied on Wilson's, and George W. Bush relied on FDR's.

## "Your Constitutional Rights Are Getting in the Way of Our Unconstitutional Power"

As we have seen, the right to petition imposes a duty on the government to respond to petitions. This is essential to the meaning of the right, and was historically one of the most jealously protected components. Nonetheless, it was abolished during the antebellum era, and has not been restored since. In particular, it stood in the way of a large government, which simply did not have the patience, respect for constitutional guarantees, or inclination to respond to petitions. When asked what ever happened to this fundamental right, courts today will simply respond, in the words of Justice Oliver Wendell Holmes Jr., that "where a rule of conduct applies to more than a few people it is impracticable that every one [*sic*] should have a direct voice in its adoption."[9] In other words, since the Founders enshrined the great right to petition in the Constitution, the government has taken the stance that the right is simply not "practical" in today's world of large, complex governmental institutions.

The annihilation of the duty to respond has a particularly unsavory history. When the abolitionist movement gained momentum during the antebellum era, activists began petitioning Congress in droves. In essence, abolitionists rightfully saw slavery as oppression and tyranny in their most extreme form, and thus felt a need to petition the government to redress this grievance. One abolitionist stated that "the District of Columbia fastens on the whole nation the guilt of slaveholding. . . . And I hold it the duty of every man in the free States . . . by solemn remonstrance to Congress, to purge his conscience of the nation's crime."[10] What could be a more righteous application of the right to petition than a demand that human bondage, the ultimate crime, be forever abolished? The right to petition was intended to provide a means for making right those wrongs committed by government, and thus, the abolitionists' petitions to the federal government were as proper an exercise of that right as any in the annals of history.

Congress, however, ultimately passed a "gag rule" in 1840 which barred the reception of petitions "praying the abolition of slavery." Slave states argued that the government could refuse to hear such petitions, because official government behavior was higher than and of a different order from the wishes of the people themselves. Stephen Higginson, professor of law at Loyola University New Orleans, notes,

[John Calhoun contended that] assemblies would be little more than "passive receptacles" were petitioners' rights held superior to legislative necessities. Thus, Calhoun supported a sharp demarcation between citizenry and legislators. The right of the former to assemble and communicate opinions to the government ceased upon presentation of a petition; thereafter, the legislative domain was absolute and the assembly had full discretion to interpret and devise its own rules.[11]

Thus, the argument against a duty to respond was an explicit rejection of popular sovereignty and the notion that the government should ultimately be answerable to the people as their servant.

For reasons discussed earlier, we may start with the assumption that the right to petition *mandates* a governmental duty to respond to those petitions. Without that guarantee, the right would be meaningless, and we could only hope that government was desirous of listening to our protestations.

Robert Schulz is a tireless defender of constitutional freedom. As the founder of We the People, he articulated, "The very philosophical premise of the Sovereignty of humans over the governments they create to serve them requires a corollary obligation in the Law to respond, and respond responsively." Constitutional rights have never been so tenuous as to rest on a mere hope that the government will choose to hold itself accountable to the people. Therefore, to read out the duty to respond from the Constitution is to read out the right to petition.

Although some may argue that the right is not suitable to current times, this violates a fundamental principle of constitutional interpretation: Chief Justice John Marshall once pronounced, "It cannot be presumed that any clause in the constitution is intended to be without effect." Thus, every word of every clause must be treated as law. The only process for altering the Constitution is by amendment. If slave states, and the generations of large government proponents after them, wished to do away with the duty to respond to petitions, then they were free to propose an amendment to that end. It should, however, not be surprising that such a proposal has not occurred: As history shows, time and time again such proposals have always failed due to public backlash. Moreover, as history also shows, the government abdicates a duty to respond because it wishes to prevent the people from exercising their sovereignty over it. Thus, for courts to uphold Congress's refusal to respond to petitions is to violate both the Constitution and popular opinion. Could there be a better example of judicial activism? After the Civil War, the Constitution was quite properly amended to prohibit slavery; but the right to petition was never restored.

Moreover, the arguments for annihilation of the duty to respond are simply illogical, and misconstrue the very purpose of a constitution. Critics of the obligation, like Justice Holmes, argue that the right is not practical; it hampers governmental exercises of authority. But let us examine exactly what is impractical about the duty to respond. It is impractical because it conflicts with a constitutional assurance of government accountability to the people. Our rights were enshrined in the Constitution so as to restrict which actions government can take. Government cannot then argue that the right to petition should be done away with because it is too, in a word, restrictive. Thus, the entire purpose of our rights is to make unconstitutional government actions "impractical." Could a basketball player sensibly argue that he should be able to carry the ball because dribbling it is too restrictive? Why can the government?

Nor are these mere abstract ruminations. As noted before, the right to petition ensures government accountability to the people. By eviscerating this right, government has been able to grow large and out of touch with the freedom of the electorate, not an unsurprising result given the political philosophy of John Calhoun discussed above. Anyone who feels disillusioned by the Iraq and Afghanistan Wars, health care reform, or government bailouts, can appreciate the purpose that the right to petition serves, and the hypocrisy of government's claiming that it is impractical.

More fundamentally, to read out the right to petition because it is impractical does harm not only to that right, but also to our entire constitutional system of government. When we allow shifting attitudes about what is the proper size and scope of government to trump the Constitution, then the Constitution itself loses its entire meaning: It is no longer law. Justice John Marshall Harlan once said that "the Constitution is not a panacea for every blot on the public welfare, nor should this Court, ordained as a judicial body, be thought of as a general haven for reform movements." Thus, even if a large welfare state, which of necessity did not have the time or resources to hear all legislative petitions, was genuinely in the public's best interest, it could not change the fact that it is unconstitutional, and thus illegitimate. To abolish the duty to respond does violence not just to the right to petition, but to our entire Constitution, and the notion that we are a nation of laws.

The very idea that the government can pick and choose which parts of the Constitution it will defend and leave other parts unenforced belies the self-evident truth that the Constitution—the entire Constitution—is the supreme law of the land.

YOU'LL HEAR FROM ME

## Rule 11 Motions

The final component of the right to petition, the proscription of penalties, has also come under attack since our founding. One such device used by the government to punish petitioners is what is known in federal civil procedure as a Rule 11 motion. The rule provides that

> by presenting to the court a pleading . . . an attorney or unrepresented party certifies that to the best of the person's knowledge, information, and belief, formed after an inquiry reasonable under the circumstances . . . the claims, defenses, and other legal contentions are warranted by existing law or by a non-frivolous argument for extending, modifying, or reversing existing law or for establishing new law.

If judicial petitions, even if made to the government, fail to satisfy this requirement, then a federal judge may punish the petitioner accordingly. When asked how this rule can be reconciled with the right to petition, one of the drafters would simply respond, "There is no constitutional right to make frivolous petitions."

Although as a simple matter this rule clearly violates the historical proscription of punishments appended to the right to petition, it is worthwhile to discuss precisely how it infringes upon the right. First, *frivolous* and *well researched* are not the same thing. The problem is that Rule 11 only punishes those petitions which are inadequately researched, rather than those which are genuinely frivolous. Consequently, it will punish those petitions which are meritorious, but have not been adequately researched. Imagine, for example, that a government official is caught accepting payments in exchange for awarding subsidies to one particular company. When one business owner in the industry does further research and discovers that he has a claim against the government, he files suit. Having discussed the complaint with a few of his friends who are also business owners harmed by the grant of subsidies to the competitor, they copy the original complaint (a kind of petition, for our purposes) and also file suit. Although they no doubt have meritorious claims against the government, they will face punishment for simply not doing the research themselves. How can this be squared with the Seven Bishops Case, and the understanding at the time of the founding?

Moreover, the threat of fines can deter otherwise meritorious claims, particularly where those claims are "novel or controversial." This is often the case for suits against the government, since petitioners are frequently challenging a traditional and entrenched governmental practice, such as segregation. And as has been noted before, "today's frivolity may be tomorrow's law." Thus, in addition to discouraging the redress of legitimate grievances, punishing petitioners who take up these difficult cases stifles the beneficial growth of the law.

One of the best examples of so-called frivolous lawsuits which eventually became today's law is the *Brown v. Board of Education* line of cases. These petitioners in 1954 stood for the position that "separate but equal is inherently unequal," a difficult argument to make in light of *Plessy v. Ferguson*'s explicit rejection of that position in 1896. Are these the sorts of developments that we should be discouraging? Or weren't these exactly the kinds of popular movements which the right to petition the government was intended to protect?

The *Brown v. Board of Education* (1954) case is particularly instructive. Governments throughout the United States, mainly in the South, were stubbornly unwilling to cease making public school–related decisions—building schools, hiring and firing teachers, allocating school budgets—based on race. The Congress was unwilling to use its Fourteenth Amendment powers to intercede. Only a petition to the courts to redress grievances liberated generations of African Americans from ignorance spawned by the states.

As one might then imagine, Rule 11 motions have a well-documented, disproportionate impact on civil rights petitioners; although civil rights claims made up 7.6 percent of total filings in the first two years of the rule's existence, they made up 22.3 percent of Rule 11 cases. It is time that we abolish Rule 11 and encourage, rather than punish, petitioners to take up their grievances with the government and modify the existing law.

So why is it that Rule 11 motions have remained the law? A federal judge once said, "Insubstantial lawsuits against high public officials . . . warrant firm application of [Rule 11 because they] undermine the effectiveness of Government."

However, we have already rejected the claim that effectiveness of government can *ever* trump the need for robust protection of constitutional rights. Fortunately, this judge was not presiding over the legally "insubstantial" *Brown v. Board of Education* line of cases, which no doubt undermined the effective administration of a segregated school system. If he had, then the dream of Martin Luther King Jr. that one day "the sons of former slaves and the sons of former slave owners will be able to sit down together at a table of brotherhood"[12] would have remained just that: A dream.

## Conclusion

Let us now rekindle King's dream with renewed vigor and petition the government to right all of its wrongs. In his famous speech, Dr. King posed the following question to his audience, and I now pose it to you: "When will you be satisfied?" Will it be while our government tortures suspects? Will it be while the government can take away our economic liberties, and hence our ability to earn a livelihood, for nearly any reason it chooses? Will it be while the government can say what kind of healthy, non-abusive personal unions are entitled to legal benefits, and which are not? Will it be while a government, which has dropped an atomic bomb on innocent civilians before, is prepared to do it again? When we are asked that question, we, like Jefferson and King, must answer: "No, no, we are not satisfied, and we will not be satisfied until justice rolls down like waters and righteousness like a mighty stream." And this time, we shall not be silenced when told that our clamoring for liberty is "impractical."

Does the government work for us, or do we work for the government?

# Chapter 10

# War . . . War . . . What Is It Good For?:

*The Right to Enjoy Peace*

The year was 1941. Nazi Germany had conquered most of Europe and invaded the USSR. America, having suffered through the Great War and the Great Depression in the prior twenty-five years, remained staunchly opposed to intervention. Franklin Delano Roosevelt, although eager to enter the war against Germany, recognized this popular opinion and promised to remain neutral, so as to secure his reelection: "I have said this before, but I shall say it again and again. Your boys are not going to be sent into any foreign wars."[1] This presented an obvious problem for FDR. In order to "justify" breaking this promise and intervene in the war, he would need a strategy.

His plan? Provoke the Japanese navy into killing American sailors. On September 27th 1940, Japan, Germany, and Italy entered into a mutual assistance treaty called the Tripartite Pact. The Pact required the three nations to come to each other's aid and protection if one of the others in the Pact was attacked. In other words, if Japan attacked the United States, the United States would surely retaliate against its aggressor; in doing so, Germany would then come to Japan's assistance. Essentially, the signing of this mutual assistance treaty gave President Roosevelt exactly what he desired: The window of opportunity to go after Germany. FDR responded to Churchill's pleas to enter the war, "[Although] I may not [constitutionally] declare war, I may make war."

Roosevelt had a number of ways to go about prosecuting this strategy.

Shortly after the treaty between Germany, Japan, and Italy was signed, Lieutenant Commander Arthur McCollum of the Office of Naval Intelligence submitted a memorandum proposal to the director of Naval Intelligence, now known as the "McCollum memo." The memorandum explored the United States' options when it came to potential actions taken by the Japanese in the South Pacific. The memo included an eight-part plan stating, "It is not believed that in the present state of political opinion the United States government is capable of declaring war against Japan without more ado. . . . If by [the eight-point plan] Japan could be led to commit an overt act of war, so much the better."[2] Demonstrating adherence to and belief in this very provocation strategy, Roosevelt fired Admiral James O. Richardson, commander in chief of the U.S. fleet, who voiced objection to the provocation plan at the White House during a discussion with the president.

Part of this strategy involved sending U.S. ships into Japanese waters on so-called pop-up missions. FDR himself confessed, "I just want them to keep popping up here and there and keep the Japs guessing. I don't mind losing one or two cruisers, but do not take a chance on losing five or six."[3] Keep in mind, two lost cruisers equal the deaths of 1,800 men—roughly the number of men killed at Pearl Harbor. Moreover, Secretary of War Henry L. Stimson's diary reveals the intent to provoke an attack when the United States issued an ultimatum to Japan twelve days prior to Pearl Harbor, demanding that she remove all troops from China and Indochina, and break the tripartite treaty with Germany and Italy. As Stimson himself said, "We face the delicate question of the diplomatic fencing to be done so as to be sure Japan is put into the wrong and makes the first bad move—overt move."

Further, the U.S. government began marshalling its resources in preparation for a full-scale war, including the purchase of "$3.5 billion worth of military supplies from automobile plants alone."[4] When questioned about the institution of the draft, FDR responded that "[your boys] are going into training to form a force so strong that, by its very existence, it will keep the threat of war from our shores." As history would later prove, this was a complete and utter lie.

Eventually, FDR's strategy paid off. The United States continued to monitor

Japanese communications, but consciously chose not to prevent the attack. One such message indicated that the Japanese consul in Hawaii was sending information to Tokyo about U.S. naval ships at Pearl Harbor. Another, received just three days before the attack, contained the message "war with the U.S." and suspiciously disappeared in Washington shortly thereafter.

And when the attack did eventually come, all remained quiet and orderly in the White House. As Eleanor Roosevelt would later recount,

> In spite of his anxiety Franklin was in a way more serene [after the attack] than he had appeared in a long time. I think it was steadying to know finally that the die was cast. . . . [It] was far from the shock it proved to the country in general. We had been expecting something of the sort for a long time.[5]

What was the ghastly result of Roosevelt's provocation and failure to prevent the attack? At Pearl Harbor, 2,403 Americans died, and 405,399 Americans were eventually killed throughout the course of World War II.[6] As Bettina Bien Greaves, a senior scholar at the Mises Institute, has said, "The Japanese attack on Pearl Harbor made war inevitable. But the attack was not Roosevelt's reason for going to war. It was his excuse."

## War Is the Health of the State

> Never let a serious crisis go to waste. What I mean by that is it's an opportunity to do things you couldn't do before.
>
> —RAHM EMANUEL, THEN CHIEF OF STAFF TO
> PRESIDENT BARACK OBAMA

As outrageous as FDR's warmongering was, it raises larger questions about the state's inescapable motives in declaring war against another. Why is it that FDR was so eager to enter World War II? Was it because he recognized the evil of Fascism, and sought to liberate millions of oppressed individuals around the world, as our history books teach us? When governments enter into wars, is this *ever* their true intent? Or is there something in the very nature of war that has irresistibly tempted every government since the beginning of organized society?

The truth is that the ultimate crisis—war—is a dear friend of the state. In fact, the government uses war as the ultimate means to expand its own power, size, and scope. It does so in a multitude of ways, to which we will return below: Tax and budget increases, security laws and regulations, nationalization of industry, censorship of speech and expression, suspension of due process, warrantless searches and seizures, and blanket arrests of war resisters.[7] This list goes on and on. Every one of these measures grossly swells the size and scope of government, thereby stripping us of the freedom to live as we please. The "opportunity," as Rahm Emanuel states above, to grow, to expand, and to garner power is too alluring and too easy a feat for the state and its politicians to pass up. Mr. Emanuel's remark fundamentally exemplifies the government's cavalier and exploitive attitude when it comes to war. The government rejoices in war and utilizes it to leverage its own power. The president's poll numbers rise in war, the Defense Department's budget is of no importance, defense contractors close to the government make money, and elected officials get reelected merely for "staying the course."

The dire result: The state *intentionally* exploits war to circumvent the Rule of Law—the United States Constitution. Unfortunately for the government, the Constitution is not suspended during wartime. Professor Robert Higgs of the Independent Institute explains it this way:

> The Constitution makes no provision for its own evisceration during wartime or other crisis, yet time and again during national emergencies the [Supreme Court] justices have allowed the legislative branch and especially the executive branch of government to transcend their constitutionally enumerated powers and to nullify individual rights proclaimed in the Constitution.[8]

In other words, war is the time during which the Constitution should be most adhered to and embraced. In reality, the government purposely looks in the other direction.

162

Unfortunately, we as a nation have not yet learned from our mistakes. This ugly pattern of warmongering, provocation, and government growth has repeated itself through history, time and time again. When a major crisis erupts—whether it is a world war or economic depression—there is a public outcry for the government to act in some way. The state, in turn, pounces on the political opportunity to make a grab for power and to do things it does not have the constitutional power to do. The government then acquires authority and political clout, ultimately obliterating the Founders' deliberate and carefully considered relationship between individual freedom and government.

More fundamentally, however, war is the most effective assertion of the primacy of the collective over the individual. As Randolph Bourne notes in his essay "War Is the Health of the State," in times of peace "the sense of the State almost fades out of the consciousness of men"; we go about our daily lives, subject to no one's will but our own. Moreover, we are naturally concerned with only our affairs as individuals—our jobs, our spiritual development, our families, and our friends. Bourne continues:

> With the shock of war, however, the State comes into its own again. . . . The moment war is declared . . . the mass of the people, through some spiritual alchemy, become convinced that they have willed and executed the deed themselves. They then, with the exception of a few malcontents, proceed to allow themselves to be regimented, coerced, deranged in all the environments of their lives, and turned into a solid manufactory of destruction toward whatever other people may have, in the appointed scheme of things, come within the range of the Government's disapprobation.

In other words, the state *needs* warfare in order to continue its existence as a coercive force intruding upon our lives. War is the state's way of saying, "I am still important, and am owed your continuing support and allegiance." Without war, the government would fade away, with no more power over us than Ozymandias's crumbled, long-forgotten statue lying impotently in the desert. War is the state's justification for its own existence.

## The State's Toolbox: Provocation, Fear, and Hysteria

> The Constitution supposes, what the history of all governments demonstrates, that the executive is the branch of power most interested in war, and most prone to it.
>
> —JAMES MADISON

FDR's lie to enter World War II was not the first time a president lied to rally support for war, nor will it be the last. A brief examination of our country's short history demonstrates that many presidents have used self-created fear and hysteria to justify war.

To garner American support for the "impending" Spanish-American War, President William McKinley touted the sinking of the USS *Maine*. McKinley claimed a Spanish mine caused the ship's destruction, when in reality, the ship's American captain determined that a coal bin explosion was the cause of the *Maine's* sinking.

Similarly, President Woodrow Wilson created the illusion that his soon-to-be World War I enemy—Germany—fired the first shot at the United States, when in reality, Germany was trying to play fair. The German Embassy in Washington notified Wilson's secretary of state, William Jennings Bryan, that the British passenger ship the *Lusitania* carried illegal weapons and would become a German target in open waters. Bryan tried to convince Wilson that he should warn Americans of the ship's danger, but Wilson refused to do so. He saw an "opportunity" in the form of lost American lives, which would present him with a clear and decent motive to enter the war. When the *Lusitania* went down near the coast of Ireland, 114 Americans went down with it. Thereafter, Secretary of State William Jennings Bryan resigned.

Scheming like FDR, McKinley, and Wilson, President Lyndon B. Johnson provoked an attack to spark the Vietnam War, claiming that America was shot at first. To carry out his charade, President Johnson pushed the Gulf of Tonkin Resolution, which was itself based on false reports of attacks on American naval forces, through a pliant Congress. In turn, Johnson built up American forces in Southeast Asia and eventually collected more than five hundred thousand American troops to fight in that catastrophic war. Millions of Vietnamese, Cambodians, and Laotians were killed and wounded in the conflict, along with fifty thousand dead young Americans. To what end?

Turning to the War on Terror, we see that the more things change, the more they stay the same; presidents in the twenty-first century lie just like their nineteenth- and twentieth-century counterparts. Throughout most of his presidency (and particularly after September 11th), George W. Bush purposefully inspired fear and anxiety in Americans through every channel of communication available to him: "We are in imminent danger of attack." "The terrorists are out there." "The terrorists want to destroy our way of life." Bush and his team, not having presented any form of convincing evidence of so-called weapons of mass destruction, lied us into war with Iraq. Professor Robert Higgs elaborates:

> The 9-11 attack, then, is to the Bush administration as the Pearl Harbor attack was to the Roosevelt administration: an enduringly evocative pretext for whatever "retaliatory" measures the government chooses to take, even if, as in the present case, the retaliation is aimed in large part at parties who had nothing to do with the initial attack.[9]

Moreover, if the government truly believed that we were all in grave danger, then surely it would shift all of its resources toward eliminating that threat; protecting Americans' personal freedoms would take precedence above all other government initiatives. However, this has been far from the case. For example, the government enacted an enormous farm bill in 2002 immediately after September 11th which purported to spend $180 billion over the next decade, a 70 percent increase.[10] This vast farm bill can be coupled with the $40 billion (and growing . . . ) the federal government spends on education along with the $11 billion dished out annually for "community and regional development."[11] If terrorists are lingering in our airports, what is Congress doing spending money on fertilizer, math books, job training programs, and peonies? Professor Robert Higgs argues convincingly:

It is all too clear that either we are not really in grave danger, and hence the government's actions, though sufficiently objectionable in many ways, are not lethally reprehensible, or we really are in grave danger and, given that condition, the government is acting in a completely irresponsible and utterly immoral manner. If semi-organized gangs of suicidal maniacs numbering in the thousands are out to kill us all, the government ought not to be fiddling with kindergarten subsidies and the preservation of the slightly spotted southeastern screech owl.[12]

In none of these cases were McKinley's, Wilson's, Roosevelt's, Johnson's, or Bush's actions morally, legally, or constitutionally justified. Article II, Section 2 of the Constitution states that the "President shall be Commander in Chief of the Army and Navy of the United States, and of the Militia of the several States, when called into the actual Service of the United States." Nowhere does the Constitution state the "President may willfully and intentionally fool the people into war."

## Land of the Free? Barely

If tyranny and oppression come to this land, it will be in the guise of fighting a foreign enemy.

—JAMES MADISON

Now that we have seen that throughout our history the state has used warfare merely as a means of expanding its power and control, we must next ask, In what way do wars encroach upon our own freedoms and thus violate the Natural Law? While war is being fought in the name of "freedom" abroad, war is bringing the opposite effect to Americans back home; we are *less* free because of war. While this statement may seem contradictory, the irony becomes clearer as we helplessly witness losses of liberty brought on by our power-hungry government in the form of higher taxes, greater government debt, increased government intrusion in markets, more pervasive government surveillance, manipulation, and control of the public.[13] Every single one of these reactions to war restricts our freedoms and fundamental liberties as human beings. Our Founding Fathers would be appalled.

The most tried and true way of limiting Americans' freedom during times of war is the draft. Whatever happened to the *inalienable* right "to life, liberty, and the pursuit of happiness"? President Wilson drafted almost 2.8 million men during World War I.[14] This involuntary servitude (violating all natural rights) was found to be constitutional by the Supreme Court at the time, a prime example of how crisis allows people to pull off unconstitutional measures. Draft supporters will argue that conscription fundamentally "unifies the country," "levels the classes," and offers the opportunity to "share in our national fate."[15] This rationale, however, is empty and completely counters the individual freedom our Founding Fathers had in mind for their new, burgeoning, and free nation. The Founders' thoughts are relevant in every age and at every encounter between the government and any individual: *Does the government work for us, or do we work for the government?*

Repressive and freedom-limiting actions by the government continued during World War I in the form of jailed draft objectors. Resisting conscription led to the arrest and imprisonment of hundreds of Americans throughout the Great War. Of the 450 conscientious objectors found guilty of evading the draft at military hearings, 17 were sentenced to death, 142 received life sentences, and 73 received twenty-year prison terms![16] Similarly in World War II, more than 10 million men were drafted to fight. Those who chose to stand up to the government and refuse to fight due to their religious affiliations were jailed just as they were in World War I (the government just does not seem to learn). The state locked up 6,000 of these conscientious objectors, most of whom were Jehovah's Witnesses.[17]

But the most shocking and dehumanizing restrictions during World War II took the form of concentration camps for Japanese Americans. In the wake of the Pearl Harbor attacks, President Franklin Delano Roosevelt signed Executive Order 9066, which authorized the removal of people of Japanese descent from the West Coast of the United States.[18] This executive order took away civil liberties on a whole new level. It singled out a group of people based upon their race, accused the group of sabotage and espionage without consideration of the presumption of innocence or due process of law, and then locked them all up as a "security measure."

Born in California, Fred Korematsu was an American citizen of Japanese heritage. As we have seen in an earlier chapter, he was convicted of being in one of the areas restricted under the Civilian Exclusion Acts. In the appeal of his conviction, *Korematsu v. United States* (1944), the Supreme Court held that the government could ship Japanese Americans off to internment camps in the name of national security, and that protections guaranteed under the Constitution could be curtailed based on race—or perceived collective guilt—when national security was at stake. Along with Korematsu, more than 112,000 men and women were kidnapped from their homes and forced to inhabit concentration camps without due process of law, in reaction to the attacks on Pearl Harbor. The Court believed that "pressing public necessity may sometimes justify the existence of such restrictions." In other words, during war—a "special circumstance"—the government can use an end to justify the means.

Justice Frank Murphy believed that no such vague showing of public necessity could ever justify government racism. In his dissent, he responded that "racial discrimination [by the government] in any form and in any degree has no justifiable part whatever in our democratic way of life. It is unattractive in any setting, but it is utterly revolting among a free people who have embraced the principles set forth in the Constitution of the United States." Those principles are the Natural Law, and Justice Murphy was absolutely correct.

## More "Covert" Freedom-limiting Rules and Regulations

Civil and economic liberties always suffer when it comes to the lengthening list of laws, regulations, and agencies implemented during times of war. From Woodrow Wilson's Espionage Act of 1917 to George Bush's Patriot Act of 2001 to the creation of the Department of Homeland Security to governmental business controls, the government continuously finds ways to violate our freedom under the guise of "it's for your own security."

The government implemented the Espionage Act of June 1917 to silence critics of the draft. Penalizing willful obstruction of enlistment services with fines of ten thousand dollars and imprisonment as long as twenty years, the federal government stripped away civil liberties at the most fundamental level: Both freedom of speech and religion. The feds censored all printed materials, deported aliens, and encouraged warrantless searches and seizures. People were even arrested for reading the Bill of Rights and the Constitution in public.[19]

How far have we come since World War I? Not very far. Almost a century later, the Patriot Act creates some of the same consequences as the Espionage Act. It lets the government snoop around your private communications and personal records. It expands the size and power of federal agencies and allows searches and seizures of your property without a warrant or probable cause. It permits the president to detain you without counsel for indefinite periods. And all of this conduct can be accomplished without the scrutiny of a judge. Whatever happened to the freedoms the Constitution was written to guarantee?

Controls on business during both World War I and World War II also severely restricted Americans' economic freedoms. The feds "nationalized the railroad, telephone, domestic telegraph, and international telegraphic cable industries," asserting control over prices, people, and corporations.[20] Regulations in the forms of manipulation of "labor-management regulations, securities sales, agricultural production and marketing, the distribution of coal and oil, international commerce, and markets for raw materials and manufactured products" highly constricted private enterprise and free market practices.[21] These economic controls must not be disregarded as simply unimportant economic liberties (as opposed to civil liberties).[22] The penalties for violation of economic controls were severe, ranging from fines to prison.

Moreover, unnecessary agencies are created during wars. Typically, they grow in size and lengthen the list of regulations under which we live. After war, some disappear, while others magically morph into the "solution" of other government problems. The War Finance Corporation, for example, was founded during World War I "to provide funds for various munitions enterprises."[23] After the war, the War Finance Corporation turned into an agricultural cooperative financing tool, which exported agricultural products to Europe. It died in 1925. In 1932 it was brought back to life again to bail out railroads and other bankrupt companies during the Great Depression. It was laid to rest in the 1950s due to scandals, but was yet again revived and combined with the Small Business Administration. Do you see how the government uses war to grow in size and scope surreptitiously?

And lastly, we come to the ultimate theft and restriction of property: The government's withholding of income taxes. The withholding practice was not implemented until World War II: A seemingly new custom wholly unsupported by our Founding Fathers whatsoever. In an effort to raise funds for the war effort, Congress passed the Revenue Act of 1942 which imposed a "Victory Tax" on income, which was to be withheld by the employer and paid directly to the government. Gradually, this practice increased in scope to constitute the present system of income taxation in America.

There are several evils inherent in this practice. First, by allowing the government to seize property directly and send the taxpayer back any surplus, it portrays the government as a beneficent caretaker. Second, it deprives the taxpayer of the use of his money for a period of time; that is money that could have flowed into investments and generated a return while the government was holding on to it. Finally, it enables the government to increase in size, as it would be infinitely more difficult to wrest tax dollars from the taxpayers themselves than secreting them away from their employer. And it was all made possible because of war.

Constitutionally and philosophically, withholding taxes presumes that we exist to serve the government. In an historic irony, the idea of withholding income taxes was proposed as a short-term war-financing measure by a young Treasury Department clerk named Milton Friedman. That would be the future Nobel Laureate who championed the free market and who would one day condemn the extension to peacetime of his wartime-only proposal with his sharp and witty tongue: "There is nothing more permanent than a temporary government program." Too late, professor.

## "The Purse Is Now Open"

When the government does not comply with its own laws, it is rewarded with more power. When it overspends its budget, it is rewarded with a bigger budget. Furthermore, "most of the defense budget increase has little to do with winning the war on terrorism," observed an Independent Institute defense analyst, Ivan Eland. In war, the government's bank account (filled with your tax dollars) flies open to the joy of an interconnected web of governmental and quasi-governmental actors: The president, the Defense Department, defense contractors, and elected officials.

Consider the size of the Defense Department's budget, and more importantly, the government's justification for the size of that budget. When President Bush signed the defense authorization bill for fiscal year 2004, everybody knew the price tag was big, but nobody understood how big. At $401.3 billion, President Bush attempted to legitimize the 42 percent rise in budget by claiming it was for the security of the American people. He vowed the government "will do whatever it takes to keep our nation strong, to keep the peace, and to keep the American people secure." Perhaps, but in any event, unborn taxpayers are picking up the bill. How about keeping us free—free to make our own choices, free from debt, free from Big Government?

And the $401.3 billion price tag was not even the whole of it. Hidden elsewhere in the nation's budget were allocations to other departments that constituted defense spending. The Department of Energy, the Department of Homeland Security, the Department of Justice, the Department of Transportation, the Department of Veterans Affairs, and the State Department were just some of the places where further defense items were concealed. Professor Robert Higgs of the Independent Institute perused the federal budget to estimate the actual total. Higgs's suggestion: Take the Pentagon's budget total and nearly double it. His estimate came to a whopping $596.1 billion.[24] In the same vein, if the Defense Department was not defending the security of the "homeland" prior to the Homeland Security Department's creation after September 11th, what precisely *was* it defending?

To make the government's theft and deceit even more glaring, the Defense

Department's accounting practices are a disaster. The Department of Defense has never been able to fulfill the government's auditing requirements because its records are in such disarray. To date, no major part of the Department of Defense has been able to pass the test of an independent audit.[25] In other words, the government consistently breaks its own laws! (As Mark Twain once remarked, Congress truly is "America's only native criminal class.")[26] Instead of focusing on the flaws of its own system, the federal government chooses to go on a witch hunt against corporate America, demonizing the likes of Enron, WorldCom, Xerox, and Arthur Andersen for their accounting practices in the full view of the public. While these companies grossly misbehaved with billions of dollars, the federal government has grossly misbehaved with trillions of dollars.[27] Only the government can prosecute, with a straight face, entities for engaging in the same behavior as it does.

Equally important as the amount of waste is the identity of its intended recipients. With war, the government forms a criminal organization with large business to transfer money away from taxpayers fraudulently and place the lives of innocent soldiers at stake. General Smedley Darlington Butler, one of the most lauded marines in U.S. history, wrote and spoke extensively on the nature of this criminal organization in *War Is a Racket*:

> In the World War a mere handful garnered the profits of the conflict. At least 21,000 new millionaires and billionaires were made in the United States during the World War. . . . And what is this bill? This bill renders a horrible accounting. Newly placed gravestones. Mangled bodies. Shattered minds. Broken hearts and homes. Economic instability. Depression and all its attendant miseries. Backbreaking taxation for generations and generations.

The military-industrial complex (a term coined by President Eisenhower, another decorated war hero, no less) is the biggest, bloodiest, and most culpable criminal organization in American history. It grows fat off of the blood and gold of everyday Americans, and continually evading justice, has no incentive to cease its piracy during our lifetimes or our children's.

Despite the fiscal irresponsibility and waste which necessarily accompany war, progressive historians and Keynesian economists have argued that war actually creates prosperity (as opposed to simply transferring it to the fortunate few). This argument, however, is flawed. As economist Ludwig von Mises noted, "War prosperity is like the prosperity that an earthquake or plague brings."

This argument's strongest case for war prosperity is based on the drop of unemployment rates and rise of gross domestic product during World War II. To be fair, unemployment numbers did in fact plunge, falling from 14.6 percent to 1.2 percent between 1940 and 1944.[28] However, there is a simple answer to this analysis. The unemployed were drafted by the feds to serve in the armed forces; unemployment rates only fell because the government was conscripting its very own unemployed population. Of the sixteen million who served in the armed forces at some time during the war, ten million were drafted. Many of these men volunteered so as to avoid the draft and the likelihood of assignment to the Army infantry.[29] With this line of reasoning, shall we reinstate the draft to alleviate our high unemployment rate today?

The war prosperity argument will also contend the gross domestic product (GDP) soared during World War II. However, upon closer inspection, this calculation consisted entirely of military goods and services; there were planes to build, guns to manufacture, and food items to ship.[30] Real civilian consumption and private investment actually *dropped* after 1941 and did not recover until 1946.[31] Professor Robert Higgs asserts "it is high time that we come to appreciate the distinction between the government spending, especially the war spending, that bulks up official GDP figures and the kinds of production that create genuine economic prosperity."

More fundamental is the fact that, although resources may be redistributed toward those Americans who are manufacturing military supplies, there is no actual wealth being created. When the farmer grows his corn crop, he exerts labor toward creating something that will literally nourish society, thus making us all better off. It is for this wealth creation that he receives money in exchange, and it is for this value that we are willing to give money. Transactions for defense supplies do not, however, share this attribute. War creates no more prosperity than hiring one hundred individuals to dig a hole and fill it back up again. After the defense contractor has received his pay for building nuclear submarines, precisely who is it that is "nourished" by their standing idly at the bottom of the ocean? Unlike a Web site that connects consumers with sellers, neither a submarine in the sea nor bullet in a soldier's gun produces wealth. What benefit is it that we as taxpayers are receiving from this exchange? There is none; it is wealth redistribution by another name.

Wartime prosperity: We are anything but prosperous during times of war. War is a time of death, grief, and tragedy. The only entity that prospers in war is the state and its close friends. And as General Butler asks, "How many of these war millionaires shouldered a rifle?" No, my readers, war creates no prosperity; it only bankrupts our savings accounts, our cradles, and our sense of human decency.

## Perpetual War: The "New Normalcy"

Of all the enemies to public liberty, war is, perhaps, the most to be dreaded, because it comprises and develops the germ of every other. . . . No nation could preserve its freedom in the midst of continual warfare.

—JAMES MADISON

Sadly, the need to limit the government's use of war is greater than ever. The War on Terror could go on forever. In fact, shortly after the attacks of September 11th, Vice President Dick Cheney stated that the war on terrorism "may never end. It's the new normalcy." While this statement may prove to be true, the government is not there to ensure that war goes on; the government is there to ensure that war stops. This, however, is not the reality. War is the health of the state, and the state will do whatever it can to ensure that war continues in some form or another because, in the words of President Bush, "the war on terrorism is a new kind of war." Once the government knows the power and the control it can hold over its people, it is unlikely ever to give them up.

## Conclusion

President John Quincy Adams stated that this country "goes not abroad in search of monsters to destroy" while President George W. Bush claimed, "We must take the battle to the enemy, disrupt his plans, and confront the worst threats before they emerge." As long as presidents continue to spout comments that induce fear and anxiety, the government will continue to be "in business." Our most recent culprit, President Bush, taunted that "intelligence gathered by this and other governments leaves no doubt that the Iraq regime continues to possess and conceal some of the most lethal weapons ever devised" and that "the danger is clear." There is no doubt danger exists, but as discussed throughout this chapter, the state is merely using alarm and despair as a platform for government expansion in size, scope, and power. As for President Bush's disingenuous, alarmist nonsense about Iraq and weapons of mass destruction, he conveniently omitted the historical fact that Iraq purchased them with the approval of the Reagan administration and their acquisition was negotiated by then Secretary of Defense Donald Rumsfeld. The very same Donald Rumsfeld. Of course, whatever Iraq bought via Rumsfeld under Reagan in the 1980s was consumed—destroyed—by the time Bush via Rumsfeld went looking for them twenty years later.

Fortunately for the state, the world is rampant with brutal regimes and dictators. While the United States cannot be expected to extinguish them all, the government will surely seek to capitalize on trying. Unfortunately for individuals, spreading the gospel of democracy is anything but in the interest of liberty. If the government cannot deliver the mail, how can it be expected to bring democracy to Iraq and Afghanistan?[32] Professor Robert Higgs recommends that we "decline the fool's errand of perpetually enforcing our political standards on the entire world."[33] When will the government listen?

The war in Iraq has demonstrated the intense tragedy of war. Through every graphic photograph and newspaper caption, the public has been exposed to its horror and heartbreak. President George W. Bush, nonetheless, told a *Time* magazine reporter that the war in Iraq was a "catastrophic success."[34] That it was a catastrophic success cannot be doubted, nor can for whom it was a catastrophic success be doubted: The federal government.

# Chapter 11

# When the Devil Turns Round on You:

*The Right to Fairness from the Government*

Consider the following hypothetical, taking place in Danistan, a country with no courts to hear disputes. Recently elected Governor N'ameyore Price decides that there is a pressing public need to convert your land into a reserve for the rare Saharan penguin. After doing some research, you discover that your state constitution grants each individual a right to be secure in his property, which can only be abridged if there is (1) an exceptional public necessity, and (2) the government provides fair and just compensation. Despite your pleadings that the high school nearby would make this an unsuitable location (Saharan penguins are terrified of Danistanian teenagers, and refuse to eat or reproduce on the same continent as them), Governor Price decides to go ahead with his plan. To make matters worse, the governor refuses to pay anything more than the market value of the property as of 1908, insisting, "If I have to suffer as a Cubs fan, then it is only fair and just that we all do." Two days after taking the property, Governor Price announces that, on second thought, the land would better serve the public interest if it was auctioned off to the pharmaceutical industry (not surprisingly, a key contributor to his political campaign).

Outraged, you do some more research and discover that your state constitution also grants a right to free speech, "except for speech tending to promote hatred against an identifiable group." Consequently, you try to oust Price from political office by holding up signs outside voting booths which say "no land for penguins." Governor Price orders you off the premises, insisting that your protest is not protected since it constitutes hate speech, as it incites public resentment toward "a discrete and insular minority of Saharan penguins, seriously curtailing the operation of those political processes ordinarily to be relied upon to protect minorities." (The governor is a disbarred lawyer.)

Think for a moment: What exactly is *legally* wrong in the hypothetical above? In other words, if you were a legislator, what laws would you want to pass to prevent such future transgressions of natural rights? Although it is undeniable that you have robust rights to property and speech, the law extends only as far as the government desires if the government does not need to follow certain procedures in applying those laws to you. In short, substantive rights become no more than an instrument of propaganda intended to convince the public that we live in a free society.

This chapter discusses those procedural requirements which are most essential for the protection of individual liberties and their origins in the Natural Law. We can think of due process as those procedures which government must follow before life, liberty, or property can be taken away by law. Although we typically think of these as juries, neutral judges, and warrant requirements, there are other procedures which government must follow as well. For example, no one can be deprived of liberty by an *ex post facto* law, that is, a law that was passed after the commission of the act which it condemns. In such a case, the law itself, rather than just its application to a particular case, violates due process.

There are two components to due process: Requirements which ensure that the essence of a law is just, and can therefore be called legitimate (called *substantive due process*), and procedures which ensure that the application of a law is just (called *procedural due process*). As we shall see, it is the Natural Law which is the source of these substantive and procedural constraints on government. Moreover, in no other area of law has the Natural Law played a more important role; the Due Process Clauses of the Fifth and Fourteenth Amendments have been, as noted by the late UCLA professor, Charles Grove Haines, "the main provision[s] through which natural law theories were made a part of current constitutional law." Although due process may at times seem abstract and removed from the realities of our modern world, such as terrorism and immigration, as we shall see, its subversion is the single biggest threat to our natural rights today.

## "Laws Must Be Fair to Be Just and Enforceable"

It should be clear from the hypothetical above that certain fundamental principles are necessary in order to protect all of those substantive rights discussed elsewhere in this book. However, before we discuss what those protections are, it is necessary to examine how they are derived from the Natural Law. The need for due process arises out of the fact that there are circumstances where the government can, and should, lawfully deprive the people of their liberty. After all, if one does harm to another, that is, "an intentional physical invasion or aggression of another person's body or rights or property," then, under those limited circumstances, the government is right in prosecuting that individual.

This is known as the concept of "waiver" of rights: The thief or invader, by his theft or aggression, waives the permanency and inalienability of his natural rights by violating the natural rights of another. As stated elsewhere, my right to swing my arms ends several inches from your nose. Beyond these "contours" (i.e., on your side of your nose), I voluntarily surrender possession of those rights. In this sense, the government can never deprive one of his rights to life, liberty, and property; when the government prosecutes a genuinely guilty individual, these rights were already waived by him, and him alone. Although this may sound abstract, it is simply an application of the principle of personal responsibility. Only *you* can waive *your* rights.

The specific problem highlighted by the hypothetical at the beginning of this chapter is that the government can use this power to prosecute improperly, punishing the wrong individuals and thereby eviscerating any meaningful protection of substantive rights. In short, there must also be some scheme of procedural constraints which ensures that our natural rights are actually enforced, and liberty is only deprived when its possessor has given it up.

There are several ways in which due process is based in the Natural Law. First, due process is comprised of those principles of justice prescribed by the

Natural Law itself. Could anyone doubt that there is a fundamental human yearning to be treated fairly and justly under the law? Why else is it that we are outraged at the punishment of the obviously innocent, or government theft of property, or any government classifications based on an immutable characteristic inherited at birth? Take public school segregation. Just because separate treatment might be technically equal, we nonetheless recognize the manifest injustice in a scheme of forced segregation. After all, it is a central precept of the Natural Law that all humans are to be treated the same, since no temporal being could be treated as "higher" than another; the Natural Law commands that the government and its laws be applied fairly and justly to all, and devoid of any racial classifications whatsoever. Thus, we can say that there is a procedural requirement, dictated by the Natural Law, that politicians and judges draft and apply the law to individuals in a fair manner. In this sense, a procedural right to be treated fairly under the law is not only a protection of other natural rights, but also is its own fundamental right implicit in the natural order of things.

To cite an example of the natural right to be treated fairly, why is it that the government is prohibited from passing an *ex post facto* law? This is clearly not an outgrowth of another substantive right, such as a right to property. By contrast, it should be clear that as a matter of principle and without more, it is manifestly unfair to punish someone for behavior that wasn't a crime when he engaged in that behavior. In other words, an *ex post facto* law does not need actually to deprive you of property or liberty before it can be considered unfair, and thus in violation of fundamental human yearnings; it is a *per se* transgression of the Natural Law. Stated differently, its wrongness is self-evident.

This notion that the Due Process Clause of the Constitution imposes unenumerated principles of fairness and justice on all branches of government has been adopted by the Supreme Court; specifically, the federal government via the Fifth Amendment and the state governments via the Fourteenth Amendment. For example, when deciding if a state court can hear a dispute involving a particular defendant, it must be shown that he has personal dealings with that State, such that requiring him to defend himself there "does not offend traditional notions of fair play and substantial justice." Otherwise, a plaintiff could sue you in a faraway State, and force you to settle simply because the cost of defending yourself there could be greater than what the plaintiff is seeking. Thus, the Supreme Court itself has recognized that the Due Process Clause imposes a requirement of fairness and justice in how laws are applied.

Second, due process comprises those implied procedures which are necessary to protect our immutable natural rights (and other political rights guaranteed by the Constitution) from unwarranted encroachments. In this sense, when we enter into the social contract with government for the protection of our natural rights, there are certain procedures implied in the contract which ensure that the government will execute that duty with good faith. As an example, juries and burdens of proof ensure that if someone is found guilty, then it is an accurate finding and therefore genuinely just to deprive him of his freedoms by imprisoning him. By contrast, without these procedures we could have no assurance that deprivations of liberty are in fact just, and there would be no such thing as a government which respects natural rights; judges could determine guilt by flipping a coin, or worse, on the basis of the defendant's race or political ideology.

In thinking about how rules of procedure can be implied by the need to protect our natural rights, it is helpful to think of a rule deemed so fundamental that we often forget its existence: The accused is innocent until proven guilty. As a purely practical matter, our natural rights would be meaningless if we could only avoid their deprivation by "proving otherwise." First, in many, if not most, cases there will be a lack of clear and convincing evidence that we did not in fact commit a crime. Thus if we could not prove via security camera footage that we were at home on Friday at 11:00 p.m. instead of at the scene of the crime, then we will summarily lose our liberty. Second, it is simply unfair to make an individual prove why he should be free; the government should always be forced to prove why he should not be free. If anything should be clear from this book, it is that inherent in a scheme of Natural Rights is the notion that liberty is the rule and not the exception. Thus "guilty until proven innocent" cannot be reconciled with the Natural Law. Liberty is the presumption.

Thus, we can think of procedural requirements not as the Natural Law itself, but as being implied by the Natural Law. To be fair, if human beings could be trusted to apply the Natural Law, then many rules of procedure would be

IT IS DANGEROUS TO BE RIGHT WHEN THE GOVERNMENT IS WRONG

superfluous; as James Madison once said, "If men were angels, no government would be necessary. If angels were to govern men, neither external nor internal controls on government would be necessary." Our politicians would only ever pass just laws, and prosecutors would only charge criminals who had so much evidence against them that a jury would certainly find them guilty. However because governments are run by individuals just like Governor N'ameyore Price, there must be this additional set of procedural laws to safeguard our liberties.

Having discussed the basis for due process in the Natural Law, we turn to ask: How do we then determine what that process is? The best answer is to look at history, and determine which procedures have, over time, proven themselves to be necessary for the protection of our natural rights. They are those restrictions on government which the people, having lived under the yoke of oppression and tyranny, have crafted for their own protection. For the duration of this chapter, we shall turn our attention to just such an examination.

## The Requirement of Expediency and Public Necessity

Regardless of whether a law infringed upon your natural rights or not, can the government pass a law for absolutely any reason it chooses? Before you answer that question, consider the following laws. In Maine, it is illegal to keep up Christmas decorations after January 14th. In Connecticut, the only thing worse than jaywalking is doing so upside down on one's hands. In North Dakota, you had better not order beer and pretzels at a bar, because doing so just might make you guilty of soliciting a crime. In New Jersey, the state government posted signs saying "Bear Free Zone" as if to warn the bears to stay out. And, being a dog lover, my personal favorite: In Denver, dogcatchers are required to post notices of impoundment for stray dogs to see.

As noble as giving dogs an opportunity to avoid the kennel might be, according to Positivism, such laws are perfectly valid merely by virtue of being the pronouncement of the government. But, you might ask, "Isn't the government supposed to pass laws only for certain purposes?" William Blackstone, the eminent English jurist, proclaimed that laws are only permissible where *"necessary and expedient* for the general advantage of the public." By *necessary*, it is meant that the law is a sort of "last resort" in solving whatever problem the government is seeking to remedy; surely, there are more effective ways of keeping our streets free of stray dogs than to post signs threatening them with time on the inside. By *expedient*, it is meant that those laws are in direct furtherance of the good of innocent individuals. Thus, according to Blackstone, a law which criminalized consuming beer and pretzels together would not be expedient, whereas a law which criminalized consuming beer while driving a car that caused human injury could be.

Why does this requirement of necessity and expediency exist? Because the only reason government exists is to secure our liberty, and thus when it criminalizes drinking beer and eating pretzels, not only is it infringing upon the natural right to drink and to eat, it is acting outside the scope of its entire purpose. Thus, the first requirement that government must abide by in the process of drafting and enacting a law is that it is necessary to protect the freedom of persons within the jurisdiction of that government.

## The Presumption of Liberty

How then is this procedural requirement of public necessity and expediency enforced? The answer is by means of judicial review, which allows courts to invalidate unconstitutional laws. When learned judges have adequately scrutinized our officials' commands and determined that they stem from the Constitution and do not infringe upon our natural rights, only then are those laws legitimate, giving rise to a moral obligation to obey them. The same moral imperative that lets me do as I please in my own house prevents me from doing as I please in my neighbor's house. That imperative is freedom: The unfettered ability to make personal choices.

By contrast, without judicial review, we would have to trust the legislature and the executive to abide by the Constitution's protections, which for reasons already discussed, is entirely inadequate. For all of their consistent and plentiful historical abuses of the Constitution, we should have no reason to believe that Congress and the President will remain within their constitutionally permitted bounds. It is for this reason that our Founders intended that "the Judges, as expositors of the Laws would have an opportunity of defending [our] constitutional rights."[1]

Sadly, judicial scrutiny of legislative and executive commands has been woefully inadequate, allowing our natural rights to be circumvented time and again. Consider the case of *United States v. Carolene Products* (1938). In 1923, Congress enacted the Filled Milk Act, which banned the interstate sale of skim milk reconstituted with coconut oil. Filled milk became popular during the era as an inexpensive alternative to comparable dairy products; the dairy industry lobbied Congress to eliminate this new source of competition. Although the purpose of the statute was purely to shield the government's friends in the dairy industry, it was not so cleverly passed under the guise of a public health and consumer fraud law: Congress claimed that filled milk was unhealthy, and that it was manufactured to look like real milk, thus confusing consumers. The difficulty was that there was no evidence whatsoever that it was injurious to public health, and the claim that consumers would be "tricked" into buying it was as ridiculous as it sounds; and Congress had no authority to regulate for health or safety. Those bases for law were retained by the Tenth Amendment for the states.

In the *Carolene Products* case, the Supreme Court, ever the "impenetrable bulwark against every assumption of power in the legislative or executive,"[2] addressed the constitutionality of the Filled Milk Act. Although it clearly transgressed fundamental economic liberties, interfered with the natural workings of the market, and deprived consumers of the natural right to choose a cheap and perfectly healthy food product, the Court upheld the statute, notwithstanding its constitutionally illegitimate purpose. The Court's reasoning was that the statute should be *presumed* constitutional, and thus the burden was on the defendant company to prove that Congress could have no constitutional authority and no lawful basis for regulating the sale of the product; a nearly impossible showing. By requiring a presumption of constitutionality instead of a presumption of liberty, the Court permitted Congress to transgress economic liberties for almost any reason it wished.

The presumption that legislation was constitutional unless proven otherwise first arose during the New Deal era, and its significance in facilitating the growth of the welfare state cannot be overstated. Prior to the presumption of constitutionality, legislatures were required to prove that legislation was necessary (and hence an acceptable regulation of one's liberties) with empirical information; the very information that the legislature would presumably have used in formulating its policy. Thus, if upon surveying the relevant facts, the legislature found there was a dire need for the regulation, the state would of necessity present to a judge its moral and constitutional bases for enacting the legislation, and if the neutral judge agreed, the legislation could be upheld. Only then could laws be legitimate; we could assume that after judges closely scrutinize legislative commands for their constitutional basis and fidelity, those commands really were necessary to safeguard our liberties, and therefore just.

The Court in *Carolene Products* summed up the shift to a presumption of constitutionality as follows:

> The existence of facts supporting the legislative judgment is to be presumed, for regulatory legislation affecting ordinary commercial transactions is not to be pronounced unconstitutional unless in the light of the facts made known or generally assumed it is of such a character as to preclude the assumption that it rests upon some rational basis within the knowledge and experience of the legislators.

This presumption of constitutionality, however, was not to be limited to economic liberties, but was to be the norm; the burden would only shift in very limited circumstances—circumstances so limited that they did not warrant reference in the main body of the opinion, but merely a footnote. Those limited circumstances would be where the statute violates an express provision of the Constitution, where it infringes upon the workings of the political process, or targets discrete and insular minorities.

Later cases, such as *Griswold v. Connecticut* (1965), established that certain judicially hand-picked "unenumerated" rights would also be entitled to similar treatment. In that case, Justice Goldberg, in his concurrence, noted that there was a "right of marital privacy," which extended far enough to protect the decision to take contraceptives, and sufficient to force the government to prove its case criminalizing the use of contraceptives.

Related to this burden of proof—the legal obligation of producing evidence and making a persuasive argument to a court—was what the individual actually needed to prove to demonstrate that legislation was unconstitutional. In the *Carolene Products* case, the Court stated that the individual challenging the law must demonstrate that there could be *no rational basis* for the statute; a legal element which has proven itself to be nearly impossible to satisfy. As for those limited, judicially determined circumstances where the burden shifts to the government, cases established that the state must have a compelling interest, and the means used to actuate that interest must be narrowly tailored so as to do the least amount of damage to fundamental liberties. This legal doctrine has resulted in a jumbled mess where racial affirmative action is scrutinized more closely than gender discrimination, and there is a fundamental right to take contraceptives, but not to establish paternity over a biological child. In essence, it is a system where recognized rights rest on tenuous legal grounds, and liberties on which our Constitution bases its legitimacy are only marginally protected.

The presumption of constitutionality is the central flaw of this entire system. It will be the individual who will have the burden of presenting that evidence. However, one must ask, Why should the individual have to present empirical data, rather than the governmental officials who gathered and relied upon that data in crafting policy? It is simply inefficient to place this burden on the individual; doing so is more burdensome. Might the government have advanced and secured the presumption of constitutionality—and the concomitant burden of disproving it upon the persons whose liberties the government has violated—in order to assure its maintenance and possession of its coercive powers? In a word: *Yes.* Thus, because the individual has inadequate access to information, it increases the chance that he will lose even where that evidence clearly and convincingly shows that the statute was unconstitutional.

As a simple matter of fundamental fairness, shouldn't it be the one who encroaches upon liberty who has to show why he is justified in doing so? Certainly, this principle would apply to individuals; why not government as well? If someone on the street walks up to you and randomly punches you in the face, is it fair to assume that he was acting in self-defense, and you should carry the burden of proving otherwise? Would your answer change if the puncher was a police officer instead of a private citizen? Recall that all individuals are subject to Natural Law, as are all governments, which are merely human inventions. To suggest that governments should somehow be treated differently from individuals in how Natural Law applies to them is to violate the truths that Natural Law transcends the temporal, and that the order of things governs those things themselves.

Moreover, shouldn't the burden of proving the justification of an action which is adverse to another always fall on whoever is trying to take that action? Why is it that you said in our hypothetical above that the puncher should have the burden of showing he was acting in self-defense? Because the person taking an action which is adverse to freedom always has the moral duty to justify his actions. It is the same moral imperative not to restrict your neighbor's unfettered ability to make personal choices, like the choice to buy filled milk. To say otherwise is to assume that actions which are adverse to freedom are acceptable, and thus you are superior to your neighbor. Similarly, every government command restricts liberty. *Government is, in essence, the negation of liberty.* The burden of showing why government is justified cannot morally shift to the individual, the object of that restriction of liberty. To say otherwise is to say that the individual is inferior to the government, a myth which we have thoroughly rejected by now.

Another problem with the presumption of constitutionality arises where the evidence of unconstitutionality is of a "controversial and indeterminate" nature. In these cases the presumption will invariably win the day for the government. Thus, as a practical matter, the government is no longer bound by the Constitution unless evidence is clear and convincing. This has allowed government to circumvent constitutional constraints and encroach upon our liberties. Its justification? "You couldn't prove otherwise." Or, in other words, the government can violate your liberty if you cannot provide a legally sufficient answer to the question "Why not!?"

Such has been the case with nearly any restriction of economic liberties. In *Williamson v. Lee Optical* (1955), the Court upheld an Oklahoma statute which made it criminal for an optician to repair lenses without the patient first obtaining a new prescription every time. Did it matter that the statute had no ostensibly legitimate purpose, and was not even rationally related to any purpose at all (except to reward the lobbying efforts of Oklahoman optometrists)? Writing for the Court, Justice Douglas stated that "the law need not be in every respect logically consistent with its aims to be constitutional." In another, less subtle word: NO.

What is even more infuriating is the belittling view of our rights adopted by the Court, which necessarily accompanied this deference to the legislature (recall that government is the negation of liberty). What of our economic liberties? Those were viewed by the Court as vestiges of an outdated economic "school of thought" (laissez-faire). And in *Plessy v. Ferguson* (1896), good law until *Brown v. Board of Education* (1954), the Court chided that if African Americans felt humiliated by racial segregation, "it is not by reason of anything found in the act, but solely because the colored race chooses to put that construction upon it." In sum, if we felt morally outraged by these statutes, it was purely the product of our own heterodox views, not the transgression of our constitutionally protected natural rights.

But, one may ask, doesn't it cut the other way? That is, won't there be a number of cases where the government was genuinely authorized by the Constitution to take some action, but it just couldn't prove why or how it was constitutional with evidence? The answer is NO, because the only time government is supposed to act is when it is morally and constitutionally justified in doing so, that is, when it has evidence demonstrating not only a rational basis, but a necessity. Anything less would permit arbitrary—or even worse, invidious—government restrictions of liberty. Thus, the presumption of constitutionality can serve no legitimate purpose other than to increase the scope of the government's authority beyond the Constitution.

It should be clear at this point that the presumption of constitutionality disparages our Constitution in principle, and our unenumerated natural rights in practice. But as a practical matter, how then are we to protect all of our unenumerated liberties, as the Constitution requires, without actually listing them? The answer is, of course, *a presumption of liberty.*

## What Is a "Law," After All?

In *Papachristou v. City of Jacksonville* (1972), the Supreme Court considered the constitutionality of the following ordinance, which provided for the arrest and conviction of

> rogues and vagabonds, or dissolute persons who go about begging, common gamblers, persons who use juggling or unlawful games or plays, common drunkards, common night walkers, thieves, pilferers or pickpockets, traders in stolen property, lewd, wanton and lascivious persons, keepers of gambling places, common railers and brawlers, persons *wandering or strolling around from place to place without any lawful purpose or object*, habitual loafers, disorderly persons, persons neglecting all lawful business and habitually spending their time by frequenting houses of ill fame, gaming houses, or places where alcoholic beverages are sold or served, [and] persons able to work but habitually living upon the earnings of their wives or minor children. (emphasis added)

Essentially, the purpose of the statute was to enable police to arrest those people who just have that certain "up to no good" look about them; stated differently, to permit Jacksonville, Florida, police to arrest anyone they wanted to arrest. Although eventually you will find a genuine criminal if you arrest enough people who fit those descriptions, clearly such a law is unjust to the clumsy amongst us who were confused for common drunkards. For quite obvious reasons, the Supreme Court struck the statute down for being too vague.

Lest one believe this statute was an isolated incident, consider the text of the following Act:

> For any lawful stop . . . made by a law enforcement official . . . where *reasonable suspicion exists that the person is an alien and is unlawfully present in the United States*, a reasonable attempt shall be made, when practicable, to determine the immigration status of the person. (Emphases added)

As many readers were probably able to guess, this is the pertinent text from Arizona's recent infamous immigration law, the constitutionality of which is being challenged and the enforcement of which has been enjoined, as this book is being written. How is the phrase "reasonable suspicion . . . [of being] unlawfully present in the United States" any less vague and ambiguous than "strolling around . . . without any lawful purpose"? If one wants to avoid getting stopped by the police while driving, he can simply avoid speeding or swerving. But how does one avoid looking like an illegal immigrant, or how does one walk without looking like a "habitual loafer" for that matter? And similarly, how are the police to recognize such persons?

The law, as I have said before, must have standards. If it did not, then Congress could simply speak words proclaiming that gambling is illegal, and without more, it would be. Or it could sneak the law itself into a drawer and never speak of it again (similar to what it does with earmarks). Even Positivists concede that, at a minimum, the law must be "written." Thus, there are certain minimum requirements which a law must satisfy. By contrast, if it was not enacted according to these "procedures," then it cannot be called a law.

So what exactly are these standards? The late, great Lon L. Fuller, former professor at Harvard Law School, outlines eight requirements. Laws must be

1. expressed in general terms, and
2. publicly promulgated, and
3. not retroactive, and
4. easily understandable, and
5. consistent with one another, and
6. not impossible to obey, and
7. not changed so frequently that the subject cannot rely on them, and
8. administered in a manner consistent with their wording.

What is Professor Fuller's basis for identifying these eight requirements? He notes that without them, laws would be, as a practical matter, without any effect, since the purpose of the law is to "subject human conduct to the governance of rules." Consider the Jacksonville vagrancy and Arizona immigration laws once more. How can one subject one's conduct to such rules? In other words, I ask these questions: How does one avoid looking like an illegal immigrant, or a habitual loafer for that matter; and can the government proscribe the way people appear; and whose freedom do these laws protect? Without these standards in place, a legal system would fail to guide individuals' conduct, and thus, it would not be successful as a legal system. Although many contend that society would degrade into a lawless, kill-or-be-killed disarray under a libertarian regime, we can see from Professor Fuller's requirements that it is in fact when Natural Law principles are not abided by that true anarchy occurs.

Although Professor Fuller's analysis is more focused on the efficacy of a legal system, these requirements are equally necessary in ensuring that we are deprived of liberty only when genuinely warranted, the true purpose of due process. Consider how just a system would be if it did not comply with each of these requirements. For example, what if the law was so hopelessly complex that one couldn't understand what it in fact prohibited? We could then be punished for doing something we didn't even know was illegal. Moreover, criminals would be able to get away because police didn't know that what they were doing was illegal either. Even worse, if laws were impossible to obey, the government could charge only its political enemies, and win a guilty conviction every time.

To this extent, consider the use of vagrancy statutes in the Jim Crow South. Because overly vague criminal statutes offer no standards, as suggested above, they also give law enforcement officials no guidance in how to apply those laws. This not only facilitates, but encourages discriminatory application of the law. Such was precisely the intended effect of such vagrancy statutes in the Jim Crow South. Recall that the vagrancy statute in *Papachristou* criminalized the act of "loafing" or, in other words, appearing lazy. These statutes would be used to pressure unemployed African Americans or unwanted Caucasians to enter into unfair labor contracts; many would accept unconscionable terms since the alternative was criminal penalties. Thus, these laws were used to perpetuate an economic system which resembled slavery.

But, one may retort, the Arizona immigration law is just "different," that is, it is seeking to address a legitimate problem, and these legal requirements of definiteness are not protecting liberty, but simply inconvenient and impeding law enforcement efforts. It is therefore "unfair," so the argument goes, to compare the law to vagrancy statutes in the Jim Crow South. The answer is that, although the Constitution was intended to set up an effective government, it was not intended to be "convenient" or, in other words, to be relaxed when we deem it proper to do so. Moreover, the Founders specifically warned us that the biggest threats to our rights were not sudden, outrageous transgressions (such as internment of Japanese Americans during World War II), but gradual, piecemeal erosions of liberty. Due process does not prevent Arizona from dealing with immigration problems in an efficient manner, merely from using arbitrary and vague laws which give police officers no guidance and permit them to violate *anyone's* natural rights. Even if this constitutional "problem" may seem small relative to the problem of illegal immigration, that cannot change the fact that we are a nation of laws, and laws are required to have standards.

## Jury to the Rescue

In 1733, the newly installed New York colonial governor, William Cosby, had caused quite a controversy by prosecuting and removing a number of important government officials who had opposed him. Outraged at this manifest injustice, a number of influential citizens established the *New York Weekly Journal*, the first independent political newspaper in the colonies, in order to criticize the governor and his actions. John Peter Zenger was hired as its first editor and printer.

Floored at public criticism, Governor Crosby had the *New York Weekly Journal's* newspapers burned and Zenger arrested and charged with the crime of seditious libel. The prosecution argued that the newspaper sought to "traduce, scandalize, and vilify" the governor, and thus, Zenger should be punished accordingly. Andrew Hamilton, the lawyer for Zenger, responded that it would be manifestly unlawful to punish "the just complaints of a number of men who suffer under a bad administration." The difficulty for Hamilton was that he had no established cases supporting this position; truth could not be a defense to a charge of seditious libel.

Hamilton, one of the most brilliant lawyers in the colonies at the time, thus devised the following strategy: Convince the jury that the law was not just, and they should therefore acquit Zenger, even if he was genuinely guilty according to the established law, a device known today as *jury nullification*. In his address to the jury, Hamilton framed the significance of the case:

> [T]he question before the Court and you, Gentlemen of the jury, is not of small or private concern. It is not the cause of one poor printer, nor of New York alone, which you are now trying. No! It may in its consequence affect every free man that lives under a British government on the main[land] of America. It is the best cause. *It is the cause of liberty.* And I make no doubt but your upright conduct this day will not only entitle you to the love and esteem of your fellow citizens, but every man who prefers freedom to a life of slavery will bless and honor you as men who have baffled the attempt of tyranny, and by an impartial and uncorrupt verdict have laid a noble foundation for securing to ourselves, our posterity, and our neighbors, *that to which nature and the laws of our country have given us; a right to liberty of both exposing and opposing arbitrary power . . . by speaking and writing truth.*[3] (Emphases added)

The jury, roused by the eloquence of Hamilton, disregarded the established law and returned a verdict of not guilty. Stated differently, the jury ignored corrupt man-made laws and ruled according to the Natural Law. Unable to control the jubilations of the courtroom spectators, the governor's Chief Justice sulked out of the courtroom, having failed to suppress the right to speak out against the government's injustices.

Unlike the discussions here which have dealt with the process of drafting and promulgating a law, litigation procedure relates to how those laws are actually applied to individuals. Typically when we think of due process, it is these sorts of laws that come to mind: Juries, rules of evidence, *habeas corpus*, and so on. The importance of these rules of procedure is brilliantly highlighted in the John Peter Zenger trial; without a jury, the governor's judges would have found Zenger guilty and thrown him in jail, thus eviscerating his natural right to criticize the government. As Hamilton urged the jury, they were capable of countering tyranny in their capacity as jurors, thus ensuring the just application of the law. There are much too many rules of procedure to cover even briefly in this remainder of this chapter. Thus, we shall focus on the role that litigation plays in properly constraining the government and on one of the most important components of any lawsuit: The right to a jury. Despite being one of the most fundamental procedural rights rooted in our legal tradition, we shall see that it has still come under attack in recent years.

Even if a legislative command is passed according to all of the procedural protections discussed above, how must the government go about depriving people of their liberty? Can the government extort twenty billion dollars from BP merely by demanding and threatening (as was done) or by passing a law which satisfies Professor Fuller's eight requirements (as was not done)? Sadly, the Supreme Court has oftentimes taken the stance that the act of passing a law itself satisfies the requirement of due process. This view, however, entirely disregards the other "half" of due process: Fair hearings in neutral courts, preceded by ample notice of litigation and an opportunity to appeal. This is procedural due process. The government can under no circumstances deprive one of life, liberty, or property without litigating it in courts; in essence, the government, like any other entity or individual, must persuade a jury that BP has violated the law, and that for whatever reason, the federal government itself is entitled to compensatory damages in the amount of twenty billion dollars. Without access to courts and fair hearings, then the propriety of a government action is entirely in the opinion of the very government that took it. It therefore violates James Madison's famous truism that "no man is allowed to be a judge in his own cause" and subjects us all to the tyranny of the majority.

In order to ensure that one is deprived of liberty only when genuinely warranted, that deprivation must take place in a neutral court and possess the following elements: Notice, hearing, fairness, and a right of appeal. These elements are as old as our legal culture. As has been proven over time, each is essential before a deprivation of liberty can be considered proper. For example, could the government commence a lawsuit against you without first notifying you, and then collect a default judgment after you fail to defend yourself in court? Clearly not; there is a requirement that interested parties receive adequate notice. Moreover, the right of appeal plays a crucial role by ensuring that judgments are in fact correct, and that a litigant was not the victim of a judge's improvident behavior.

Like the above requirements, juries have ancient roots in our legal system. When the Magna Carta proclaimed in 1215 that "no freeman shall be hurt in either his person or property, unless by the lawful judgment of his peers, or by law of the land," it thus guaranteed a right to have convictions determined by juries. Blackstone adamantly praised the role of the jury in securing justice: He contended that they served as a crucial restraint on improvident judges. This is so for two reasons. First, without a jury, litigants could be at the mercy of a corrupt or prejudiced judge. Similar to the problem with vague statutes described above, a judge could determine guilt for nearly any reason he wished, regardless of actual guilt or innocence. Second, judges possess a bias by virtue of being appointed by some machinery in the government or elected by voters for partisan reasons, which is mitigated by the presence of a jury comprised of the people themselves. In essence, without a jury there could be no such thing as separation of powers, and the government would be, in the words of James Madison, "a judge in its own cause."

To illustrate the crucial role that juries play in our legal system by ensuring that deprivations of liberty only occur when warranted, imagine how the John Peter Zenger trial would have come out differently, if he did not have a jury trial. As noted above, the judges were appointed by the very same governor who had charged Zenger with the crime of seditious libel. Interestingly, Zenger's initial attorneys were disbarred after they challenged the judges for their loyalty to the governor. Consider the Chief Justice's instructions to the jury, issued before they took leave for deliberation. As we can see, arrogance was just as common then as now. Imagine the Chief Justice's face when the jury didn't follow these orders:

> The great pains Mr. Hamilton has taken to show how little regard juries are to pay to the opinion of judges, and his insisting so much upon the conduct of some judges in trials of this kind, is done no doubt with a design that you should take but very little notice of what I might say upon this occasion. I shall therefore only observe to you that as the facts or words in the information are

confessed, the only thing that can come in question before you is whether the words as set forth in the information make a libel. And that is a matter of law, no doubt, and which you may leave to the Court.[4]

In other words, in light of the content of the newspaper's articles, the Chief Justice all but commanded the jury to return a guilty verdict. More fundamentally, however, these instructions highlight not just the potential biases of judges, but how juries will oftentimes be more faithful to the Natural Law and its principles of justice, rather than simply whatever is customary and dictated by precedent.

This crucial protection provided by juries has parallels in other political institutions as well, what I will collectively refer to as *tripartite nullification*. In addition to jury nullification of state prosecutors, the states retained the power to nullify the unconstitutional behavior of the federal government. Under this concept, states are obligated to refrain from enforcing unconstitutional federal laws. Third, individuals should have the right to withdraw their consent to state and local governments, in effect nullifying governmental actions taken in violation of their natural rights. This tripartite nullification should sound familiar: It is, in essence, checks and balances as between federal, state, and local governments, and the people themselves. What would happen if checks and balances were wholly eliminated at the federal level of government, that is, the Supreme Court could no longer strike down laws as unconstitutional, the president himself could declare war, and Congress could pass any legislation without fear of an executive veto or a judicial invalidation? Government would expand even further than it has already. Tripartite nullification is just as essential to keeping government within its proper scope. Sadly, however, it has been wholly ignored.

As an example, consider how the crucial right to jury trials in criminal proceedings has come under attack. Currently, defendants in the juvenile justice system are not given a constitutional right to a jury trial. Nonetheless, findings of guilt as a juvenile can be used to elevate sentences for later convictions as an adult. This is a particularly troubling concern given the recent proliferation of three-strikes laws, which provide for drastically elevated sentences if the defendant has a past criminal record. Thus, those who received prior convictions in juvenile courts without a jury are to be punished the same as those who received those prior convictions in adult criminal courts. Lest one dismiss this difference as trivial, it is worth noting that racial and socioeconomic biases have been well documented amongst juvenile court judges, thus creating a risk that a child discriminated against in juvenile court could receive fifteen more years in prison later in life than if he had access to a jury and all of its crucial protections.[5]

> The history of American freedom is, in no small measure, the history
> of procedure.
>
> —Justice Felix Frankfurter

Sadly, we live in a society today that has forgotten the lessons of the Zenger trial, and decries the granting of due process to certain persons more than their deprivation to others. Many question the principles espoused in this chapter by challenging: Why is it that we have to give "terrorists" the same rights that upstanding American citizens enjoy? Why should "murderers" receive the dignity of a trial and a jury? Moreover, this stance so often dovetails with both American exceptionalism and legal Positivism. Here is how this perverse argument goes: Because the government grants us our rights, and we as a people are created superior to others, then it follows that we as a people are to enjoy greater rights than others. Similarly, we are not wrong to transgress against individuals born in other countries.

This line of argumentation should however sound shockingly familiar: It is the ideological justification for the Third Reich. It also conflicts with moral universalism, the philosophy that all humans are subject to the same moral standards. Thus, if it is wrong for a group of people to be aggressors against us, it is wrong for us to be aggressors against them, and similarly, if it is right for us to receive certain procedural protections, then it is also right for all people to receive those protections. The source of moral universalism is the Natural Law: Because we are endowed with inalienable rights by virtue of being human, then all humans are endowed with those rights, and must be treated equally, irrespective of the place of their birth or what the government says they have done. The modern-day empire which we have fashioned, meddling as it does in the affairs of foreign countries, violates moral universalism in every way possible and predictably leaves us and our children at home with a bloated, broken system.[6]

Millennia of history have taught us that tyranny is the inevitable consequence of assigning justice to the discretion of government officials. To say that alleged terrorists shouldn't enjoy the same procedural rights as Americans is to place our full and abiding trust in the government's ability to determine who is guilty and who is not. Anyone who espouses the prudence of such a policy should know the story of Mohammed Akhtiar, an Afghan citizen who was mistaken for a terrorist and detained in Guantanamo Bay for three years. Ironically, he was maliciously abused because he supported America and rejected the teachings of hatred; his tormentors were not the U.S. military, but his fellow inmates.

But more fundamentally, how can we allow the clear intent of the Founders and the struggles of Zenger to be cast aside by the simple assertion that "we are fighting an unconventional war"? Aren't such claims of public necessity always the excuse? Why is now any different? A quick examination of history will show that these same words have been spoken in nearly identical language, by nearly every government for hundreds of years. Although the war might be unconventional, the claim that it justifies suppression of procedural rights is anything but.

Some may contend, however, that they are not complicit in suppressing due process because they trust the government, but because they have a "gut feeling" that the suspect is in fact guilty. But if we are capable of intuiting guilt without the rigors of the judicial system, then why would we ever need procedural rules? It is precisely because human intuition and judgment have proven over time to be insufficient that these rules of procedure were devised.

Moreover, if we genuinely prefer that innocents remain in prison (and believe me, they do) than actual terrorists go free, then the issue becomes one of sacrificing liberty to security. To do so in the context of procedural due process is even more outrageous than in other contexts: You are giving up someone else's liberty for your own security. How else shall we define tyranny of the majority? It is because of the manifest injustice of sacrificing another's liberty for greater security that William Blackstone believed it "better that ten guilty persons escape than that one innocent suffer." And even if we as a people are still prepared to deprive others of their rights and impugn the role of justice in our society, we must ask: How long will it be until it is you or I who is sacrificed in an effort to keep our neighbors more secure?

## Conclusion

Robert Bolt's question to us in *A Man for All Seasons*, as the individuals who will ultimately shape government policy:

> What would you do? Cut a great road through the law to get after the Devil? . . . And when the last law was down, and the Devil turned round on you—where would you hide, Roper, the laws all being flat? This country is planted thick with laws from coast to coast, Man's laws, not God's, and if you cut them down—and you're just the man to do it—do you really think you could stand upright in the winds that would blow then? Yes, I give the Devil benefit of law, for my own safety's sake!

No, my readers, there is no security in such policies; only tyranny, oppression, and the death of liberty. As Justice Felix Frankfurter once said, "It is a fair summary of history to say that the safeguards of liberty have been forged in controversies involving not very nice people." It is at precisely times like these that we must each decide for ourselves: Are we to secure our liberties, or cast them aside?

# Chapter 12

# A Dime Isn't Worth a Penny Anymore:

*The Right to Sound Money*

The evils of the Federal Reserve System (the Fed) run so deep that its proponents understand its operations must take place in full secrecy. Murray N. Rothbard once said this about the Fed:

> [T]here is a federal agency that tops the others in secrecy by a country mile. The Federal Reserve System is accountable to no one; it has no budget; it is subject to no audit; and no Congressional committee knows of, or can truly supervise, its operations. The Federal Reserve, virtually in total control of the nation's vital monetary system, is accountable to nobody—and this strange situation, if acknowledged at all, is invariably trumpeted as a virtue.[1]

This fact, in tandem with the current financial crisis, has recently prompted calls for transparency of this system as a means to bring about a realization of all it does. Congressman Ron Paul (R-Texas), for example, has authored a bill to audit the Fed; a bill that enjoyed majorities in both houses of Congress, yet never became law. What is the purpose behind this push for transparency? The belief is that once the American people become aware of what these central bankers are clandestinely doing with our hard-earned money, the people will demand an end to the Fed.

Supporters of the Fed maintain that secrecy is the only way the system can achieve its twin goals of "maximizing full employment" and "stabilizing the currency." If the system became politicized and open to public criticism, so the argument goes, it would not be able to achieve those two goals. Yet, since the institution of the secret Federal Reserve in 1913, the U.S. dollar has lost about 93 percent of its value, and the U.S. economy has seen countless boom-and-bust cycles that have destroyed private wealth and caused massive unemployment. Moreover, as we are currently witnessing, the temptation to spend through crises, as is facilitated by the Federal Reserve System, is too great for most politicians to resist.

The Founders and drafters of the Constitution understood this danger, having witnessed it when the unsound Continental (the predecessor to the dollar, and basis of the phrase "not worth a Continental") fell victim to hyperinflation in the early days of the nation. Accordingly, the Constitution made clear that only gold and silver could be used as legal tender. Nonetheless, what should have ended with a simple question of constitutional interpretation has grown into a massive system which has handicapped the ability of individuals to exercise their natural right to seek prosperity. As we shall see, the Fed, cloaked in its secrecy and esotericism, has offended the Natural Law as surely as any government agency we have yet witnessed.

## Money Does Not Grow on Trees

This system of secrecy, conspiracy, and fraud naturally had its origins in secrecy, conspiracy, and fraud. To understand truly and appreciate fully why this system is so dangerous and unstable, we must understand where money comes from, how it led to the earliest banking systems, and how government management of it has caused economic chaos.

When human beings first started trading goods and forming societies, the method of trade was direct exchange, or *barter*. Persons who wished to engage in trade had to come across a double coincidence of wants; if you produced apples and wanted oranges, you had to find someone who produced oranges and wanted apples. This system was obviously cumbersome and inefficient. What happens if the orange farmer did not want apples? Then the apple farmer was out of luck. Also, it is very difficult for producers to calculate their profits, how well they were engaging in trade, and how much each good was actually worth. Moreover, apples only stay fresh for a few weeks and are only produced at certain times of the year, so the apple farmer is forced to flood the market with all of his excess apples. Apples are, in other words, a poor store of economic value.

## Gold Is the Gold Standard of Currencies

Humans responded to these inefficiencies by using goods that were in very high demand, durable, easily divisible, available in large quantities, and hard to produce (or counterfeit) as a universal medium of exchange, or a currency. In this system, the producer trades not for goods with the immediate intention of consuming them, but with the intention of trading them for other goods which he may consume at a later time. To use a simple example, consider the use of cigarettes as a medium of exchange amongst inmates in prisons. Not every prisoner who collects cigarettes smokes them, but the prison population's demand for cigarettes is so high that they can always be traded for practically anything available within the prison's walls.

Over time, the best mediums of exchange became gold and silver. Both of these metals were attractive because they have always had a high value-to-weight ratio, are very durable, are difficult to counterfeit, and are easily divisible. Also, neither metal could be easily produced, since mining them was and is a slow process. Throughout history individuals remained calmly assured that the two metals' value would remain stable if they wished to save their profits for future consumption, rather than consume them all at once.

## Fool's Gold

A goldsmith's original job was to transform the gold that was extracted from the earth into coins of equal weight and value. They had very secure buildings in which to store the gold, safe from the reach of thieves. Since people also began to stockpile these highly valuable metals for future security, they, too, had to protect their gold from thieves, and to keep their gold in the gold-smiths' vaults (for a fee, of course). This was a very lucrative business for the goldsmith. When people deposited their gold in the goldsmiths' vaults, in return they received a certificate which was a claim for the amount of gold they had stored in the vaults; not the very same gold which they brought to the goldsmith, but its precise equivalent. Since it was very inconvenient to go back and forth continually to the goldsmiths' vaults to claim your gold in order to trade at the market, people started leaving their gold in the vaults and trading the claim certificates.

Goldsmiths started realizing this, and saw an opportunity. If most people were leaving their gold in the vaults for safekeeping, goldsmiths typically did not have to worry about exchanging all of the gold in their vaults for the claim checks at once. Thus, they could start loaning out claim checks for a fee (i.e., interest payment), for more gold than they actually had in their vaults. If someone wanted to claim his own gold, or see if there was gold in the vault, there was still a significant amount there to make good on the small day-to-day transactions. When people became aware of this fraud, they panicked and frequently rushed to the goldsmith to claim their gold (this panic is now commonly known as a *bank run*), only to find out they were conned, and there was not enough gold to be claimed for all the outstanding claim checks. People were furious to have been robbed of their hard-earned gold; furious because their natural rights to property had been violated.

## I Now Pronounce You Bank and State

Kings and governments saw great opportunity with this system, however, since it created an institution that could provide massive funding for projects and wars which would in turn expand their empires and power. Thus, government-sponsored fractional reserve banking was born. Since government-chartered (authorized) banks were able to loan out more currency than they had in their vaults as reserves (just as the goldsmiths had done), there still remained a possibility of a bank run. In an attempt to mitigate this possibility, the government created a *lender of last resort*: A government-sponsored, and privately owned, central bank, that would control the issuance of all currency within the nation. If banks suffered a run, they could always turn to the central bank for immediate loans to keep them in business. In other words, this system of central banking "propped up" the fraud highlighted above.

Like any action which possesses the capacity to violate the Natural Law, this power should never have been given to a person, institution, or government. The famous rags-to-riches banker Mayer Amschel Rothschild reflected on this power: "Let me issue and control a nation's money and I care not who writes the laws." Thomas Jefferson expressed his own concerns for a central banking system (and a prescient anticipation of our present woes) which printed and loaned money to the government: "And I sincerely believe, with you, that banking establishments are more dangerous than standing armies; and that the principle of spending money [today] to be paid by posterity, under the name of funding, is but swindling futurity on a large scale." Jefferson understood that the Natural Law can be violated not just with guns, steel, and fire, but also with the printing of money.

The first central bank in America, the First Bank of the United States, was chartered to pay off the debts that accrued from the Revolutionary War. This bank spread the debt evenly among the colonies, and was relatively small, controlling only about 20 percent of the nation's money supply. Jefferson, however, was not fooled into believing the bank's influence would remain this small, and while president wisely allowed the bank's charter to expire.

The Second Bank of the United States was chartered five years later in 1816 by Congress and signed into law by President James Madison. This second bank's life only lasted until 1833, when President Andrew Jackson allowed the charter to expire after a bank panic. Jackson faced the hard decision of letting banking institutions fail, causing unemployment in the short term, or bailing them out with the central bank system, causing erosion in the value of the nation's currency in the long term. He explained to the managers of the bank:

Gentlemen, I have had men watching you for a long time and I am convinced that you have used the funds of the bank to speculate in the breadstuffs of the country. When you won, you divided the profits amongst you, and when you lost, you charged it to the bank. You tell me that if I take the deposits from the bank and annul its charter, I shall ruin ten thousand families. That may be true, gentlemen, but that is your sin! Should I let you go on, you will ruin fifty thousand families, and that would be my sin! *You are a den of vipers and thieves.*[2] (Emphases in original)

President Jackson expressed concerns about banks funded by a central bank because bankers would have an incentive to take as much risk as possible, sharing the profits amongst themselves, and the losses amongst the taxpayers as the ultimate lender of last resort. The future of this country would be brighter had all presidents since Andrew Jackson possessed both his understanding of the dangers of "too big to fail" and his personal courage necessary to resist its temptations.

## State-sponsored Moral Hazard

To illustrate President Jackson's fears, as relevant today as ever, take, for example, the real estate boom and bust during which banks were making massive profits from extremely risky lending practices. They were lending money to people they knew could not pay them back, investing in extremely risky collateralized debt obligations (CDOs), and utilizing exorbitant leveraging ratios (lending out forty dollars for every one dollar of actual bank equity, for example) in order to maximize gains on their investment. That also maximized their risk of loss, and the size of that loss should it occur, as it eventually did. When the banks profited, the bankers gave themselves million-dollar bonuses; and as spoken by Andrew Jackson, when this system failed, the "den of vipers and thieves" were bailed out by taxpayers' money.

About thirty years after Jackson ended the Second Bank of the United States, the debt accumulated by the federal government during the Civil War made a return to a system of central banking extremely attractive to the Lincoln administration. This debt prompted Congress to pass and President Lincoln to sign the National Currency Act of 1863 and the National Bank Act of 1864. Although the American economy continued to grow despite being dominated by this third system of central banking, it nonetheless saw great turbulence with many boom-and-bust cycles, and bank panics. In 1873, 1893, 1901, and 1907, massive panics caused a series of bank failures, and proved how unstable this central system of fractional reserve banking was. The response to the 1907 bank panic, caused by the Morgan-Rockefeller–dominated fractional reserve banking industry, was the Federal Reserve Act of 1913, discussed in greater detail below.

## Hayek Busts the Bubble of Conventional Economic Wisdom

Austrian economist Friedrich A. Hayek did not accept the conventional view and foundational assumption of the Federal Reserve System, that the boom-and-bust cycle was inexplicable and unavoidable. Hayek provided an explanation of why there was a period with such a large cluster of entrepreneurial errors that led to the shrinking of businesses and increased bankruptcy, which in turn led to bank failures. His explanation of the boom-and-bust cycle laid the foundation for the Austrian Business Cycle Theory (ABCT) (later expanded upon by Ludwig von Mises, Murray Rothbard, Henry Hazlitt, and other very influential Austrian economists), and would eventually win Hayek the Nobel Prize in economics in 1974. (*Austrian* is the name of the economic school of thought, not the personal ancestry of those who espouse it.) But what exactly were Hayek's findings?

In brief, this theory is centered on the time-coordinating feature that interest rates play in the economy. There are two ways in which interest rates can fall. The first way is when individuals save more of their money in banks. When the supply of money which banks have to lend rises, banks then compete for borrowers' business in order to clear this increase in the money supply. At the same time, when people save more of their money in banks, they defer some of their consumption (i.e., demand) from the present to the future. This causes a shrinking of the retail sector of the economy. The three productive resources of land, labor, and capital that were being used in the retail sector are now freed up and can be purchased cheaper for use in other sectors of the economy such as mining, manufacturing, and technology. These projects are farther away from the consumer and take a longer time before they can start churning out profits, so these businesses will be taking out long-term loans to complete these projects. When the interest rate is low, it makes long-term borrowing and production cheaper, incentivizing investment.

In sum, when consumers save more, interest rates decline. This will cause a net flow of capital from consumption to long-term investment projects necessary to sustain a healthy economy. You can see how interest rates play a very important role in coordinating the economy over time, by matching up the markets for goods and markets for capital.

The second way interest rates can fall is if a central bank with governmental authority commands lower interest rates, or through fractional reserve banking or money printing, injects more money into banks' vaults, inducing them to lower interest rates. The current consumer is incentivized to borrow and spend since interest rates are low (think of the teenager who just received his first credit card), causing a growth in the retail sector which bids up the cost of the three productive resources—land, labor, and capital. The low interest rate once again incentivizes long-term production projects, but this time there are no resources being freed up from the retail sector, so they cost more money. Moreover, since consumers have not deferred any of their consumption to the future, the pool of resources these long-term projects seek to draw from is either much smaller than they calculated, or does not exist. Since these long-term projects do not churn out profits while being completed, and thus are not able to make profits once they are completed because of the unchanged or smaller pool of resources, they are forced into bankruptcy. This means all of these projects constituted a waste of the three productive resources since there was never a profit being made, or an increase in wealth; these resources will be lost forever. All this because interest rates were artificially low; that is, they were brought low by government command or money printing, not by free market forces.

Hayek concluded that the causes for bank panics and the boom-and-bust cycle were the increase in credit brought about by a government- or central bank–induced lowering of interest rates and a massive increase in the money supply through the fractional reserve central banking system. When a bank can loan out more money than it has on reserve, automatically the money supply can be greatly expanded. Stated differently, it was the system of fraud and counterfeiting, which violated every individual's property rights with respect to their money, that was distorting the free market of exchange so grossly that it caused massive depressions and severe economic harm.

This boom-and-bust cycle could never happen if there was a 100 percent reserve banking system.[3] Let's look at this. You deposit $1,000 in your checking account at your bank. If there was a 100 percent reserve banking system, you would just pay a fee to the bank for the safekeeping of your money. There would be a decrease in your currency holdings by $1,000, and an increase in your checking account by $1,000; the total money supply in the economy would remain unchanged.

The only way the bank could loan out the funds you deposited without risking a violation of your property rights is if you agreed not to withdraw your money for a certain period of time. During this time, you would be free to monitor the loans the bank has given with your money, thus ensuring that the loans are sound and profitable. In this system, banks could never get too big to fail, banks could never collapse an entire economy, and banks could never increase credit to create the mal-investment that leads to a boom-and-bust cycle. Moreover, people would never be at risk of losing the money they deposited in their checking accounts; they would only be at risk for the money they voluntarily agreed to allow the bank to loan out. Thus, a 100 percent reserve system is not only congruent with, but necessary for the enforcement of the Natural Law.

### Forget a Money Tree; We Create It Out of Thin Air

Let us return to our history lesson. In stark contrast to Hayek's insights, the solution to the boom-and-bust cycle proposed by the deceptive bankers was to cartelize it and have it backed by the government. A cartel is an agreement amongst competing firms to fix prices and to refrain from serious competition. The prices are normally set above the market rate so these firms can make larger profits. However, there is an extremely strong incentive for firms to bust the cartel, because there is a great amount of untapped demand at the normal market price. Because of this temptation, someone always ends up breaking the cartel, and thus there needs to be some form of coercion to ensure all firms do not lower prices to their natural, market level. Coercion? This is where the government steps in.

The way bankers make profits in this system of counterfeiting and fraud is simple. Take the same example above. You deposited $1,000 in a checking account at your bank. In a fractional reserve system, your bankers would only have to keep 10 percent of your deposit on reserve, giving them the opportunity to loan out up to 90 percent of your money. In other words, once you deposit $1,000 in the bank, its reserves would be increased by $1,000, and the bank now has $900 in excess reserves that it can loan out.

So let's presume that your bankers found Bob, a business owner who needed a loan. The bank would loan out the $900 and charge Bob 5 percent interest for a one-year loan. Right away, the money stock in the economy would have increased by $900, now totaling $1,900: The $900 issued to Bob, plus the $1,000 note given to you, which effectively functions like cash ($100 is kept on reserve at the bank). Bob, a widget manufacturer, then pays Carl the $900 for raw materials. Carl then deposits this $900 in a different bank, which can now loan out $810 to Dan (holding 10 percent, or $90, on reserve). Now, we have a total increase in the money supply of $2,710, compared with a mere $1,000 initial deposit. This process continues, the money supply growing larger and larger until it has vastly outstripped the amount of your original deposit.

In normal economic times, this wouldn't present much of a problem; Dan would repay his loan, and Bob would repay his. Thus, there would never be a shortage of cash as the depositors make withdrawals. The problem, however, arises when depositors get scared that numerous investments will go sour, and thus they will lose their money. They then rush to the bank to make withdrawals—legal claims which the bank is clearly not capable of honoring under this system of fractional reserve banking. The end result, of course, is that you have lost your hard-earned savings. As we discussed earlier, this process is known as a bank run.

It is because of this process that banks in this system pushed for centralization of control with government backing, or a government-backed banking cartel. With this cartel the commercial banks could utilize cheap (sometimes free) loans from the central bank, so the commercial banks would have access to all the money they needed to conduct daily transactions, and honor legal claims in the event of a bank run. Moreover, the government would set up an insurance system, the Federal Deposit Insurance Corporation (FDIC), to protect deposit accounts from the risk of losses. The FDIC is funded, of course, by taxpayers' dollars.

If the banks received government backing, they would then be able to profit from their gains and pass their losses along to the taxpayers in the form of bailouts, just as President Andrew Jackson warned about and predicted 180 years ago. Big Government, constantly needing money to fund its military adventurism, welfare state, and campaigns for more power, would clearly benefit from this system, as would the cartel members. Everyone else, by contrast, would be outright robbed of their savings through inflation.

Inflation, a rise in prices, is caused by an increase in the money supply. The reason this happens is, as explained before, money or currency is just a medium of exchange you use to acquire other goods or save for the future acquisition of goods. When money printing and fractional reserve banking increase the money supply, there is more money bidding up the prices on the same supply of goods. Moreover, an increase in the supply of money does not increase real wealth, since money is used only in exchange.

To illustrate the actual effects of inflation as caused by the Fed, consider that what cost $25,000 in 1913 would cost about $536,000 in 2010. If a person had $25,000 in 1913 and did not keep it in a bank or a (risky) investment account, by 2010 he would have lost 93 percent of his money's purchasing power, or the amount of goods or services that can be purchased per unit of currency. Even if someone had saved $25,000 in a savings account at the average interest rate yield of 1.3 percent over the same ninety-seven-year period, he would have $87,500 in the bank. He would still need an additional $339,000 to buy in 2010 what his $25,000 would have purchased in 1913. Thus, even by saving his $25,000 for ninety-seven years, he would have lost 83 percent of the money's purchasing power at the end of the ninety-seven years.

## The Creature from Jekyll Island

Now that we can see the fractional reserve system's propensity to cause bank runs, and the role of central banks in creating inflation, let us return to the foundation of the Fed. On November 22nd 1910, Senator Nelson W. Aldrich (R-Rhode Island), with five companions, set forth under assumed names in a privately chartered railroad car from Hoboken, New Jersey, to Jekyll Island, Georgia, allegedly on a duck-hunting expedition. The need to maintain secrecy was extremely important to the men who were aboard the train traveling to J. P. Morgan's private retreat at the Jekyll Island Club. The full guest list would be later revealed as including Senator Aldrich (Rockefeller kinsman), Henry P. Davison (a J. P. Morgan partner), Paul Warburg (a Kuhn Loeb & Co. partner), Frank A. Vanderlip (a vice president of Rockefeller's National City Bank of New York), Charles D. Norton (the president of Morgan's First National Bank of New York), and Professor A. Piatt Andrew (head of the National Monetary Commission research staff), who had recently been made an assistant secretary of the treasury under President Taft, and who was a technician with a foot in both the Rockefeller and the Morgan camps.[4]

These powerful banking elites would devise the new central banking system and draft what is now known as the Aldrich Plan. However, the plan was defeated in 1912 after the Democrats took the White House and Congress. A later change in power revived it. After losing the Republican nomination to Taft, Teddy Roosevelt founded the United States' Progressive Party, or the Bull Moose Party, in 1912. The Bull Moose Party and the Republican Party would split votes, which subsequently led to the election of Democratic candidate Woodrow Wilson, the perfect candidate for U.S. banking interests. The Aldrich Plan formed the substance of the Federal Reserve Act which, once

Wilson took office, was passed in 1913. The Federal Reserve would cause the first Great Depression only sixteen years later.

Professor Murray N. Rothbard described this system here:

The Fed was given a monopoly of the issue of all bank notes; national banks, as well as state banks, could now only issue deposits, and the deposits had to be redeemable in Federal Reserve Notes as well as, at least nominally, in gold. All national banks were "forced" to become members of the Federal Reserve System, a "coercion" they had long eagerly sought. This meant that national bank reserves had to be kept in the form of demand deposits, or checking accounts, at the Fed. The Fed was now in place as lender of last resort. With the prestige, power, and resources of the U.S. Treasury solidly behind it, it could inflate more consistently than the Wall Street banks under the national banking system. Above all, it could and did, inflate even during recessions, in order to bail out the banks. The Fed could now try to keep the economy from recessions that liquidated the unsound investments of the inflationary boom, and it could try to keep the inflation going indefinitely.[5]

Shortly after the Fed was established, the United States entered World War I, and abandoned the gold standard, thus enabling the Federal Reserve to print money to fund the war effort. One way the government generates money to fund its conquests is by issuing bonds. When the Federal Reserve starts to purchase the bonds, it sends a signal to all other investors. This signal that is sent is one that says come what may, this bond will always be paid off, either at the bond's maturity date by the government, or by a private investor who might purchase it, or by the Federal Reserve. When these bonds are auctioned off, people are willing to pay more money for them, since payment is guaranteed. The higher the amount of the bond means the lower the yield; a lower yield means a lower interest rate. A lower interest rate means it is less painful for the government to borrow money. This system led to the national debt ballooning from $2.6 billion in 1910 to $25.9 billion in 1920, which also led to the sharp spike of inflation that followed.

This caused massive expansion, and eventual contraction, and the Fed was forced to raise interest rates to stabilize the volatile economy. Once the economy stabilized in the early 1920s, the economy saw massive growth, but beneath the surface most of this growth was distorted by a Fed-generated inflationary credit expansion which lowered interest rates, causing a boom in the stock market. This was Hayek's worst nightmare come true. The bust that Hayek's theory explained was caused by the massive credit expansion and lower interest rates and came in the form of the Wall Street stock market crash of October 1929.

Congressman Ron Paul, in his book *End the Fed*, has described this same process as it occurred in the context of the current financial crisis:

> Prosperity can never be achieved by cheap credit. If that were so, no one would have to work for a living. . . . Artificially low rates of interest orchestrated by the Fed induced investors, savers, borrowers, and consumers to misjudge what was going on. Multiple mistakes were made. The apparent prosperity based on the illusion of such wealth and savings led to misdirected and excessive use of capital.[6]

History, it seems, has an odd habit of repeating itself.

Armed with Federal Reserve funding, President Franklin D. Roosevelt attempted an interesting solution to the 1929 stock market crash. This plan was to spend our way out of the depression and into prosperity, which is the exact opposite of rational logic and what the economy needed. This recklessness turned the stock market crash into the Great Depression, which lasted for fifteen years.

Unable to fund the massive debt he contemplated, FDR, during his first month in office and acting as a ruthless dictator, abandoned the gold standard for individuals, and confiscated every American's gold.[7] As well, FDR made ownership of gold illegal. The abandonment of the gold standard only made the Great Depression that much greater. Many of the policies of the New Deal exacerbated the Great Depression, and many economists believe these policies kept the country in the depression until after World War II.

The easy credit that led to the Great Depression, as explained by the Austrian Business Cycle Theory, was only made easier by the abandonment of the gold standard. Commercial banks now only needed to keep Federal Reserve notes as bank reserves, and the Federal Reserve was the only bank that needed to store gold. With a reduction of the fractional reserve ratio to 10 percent, the Federal Reserve could loan out ten dollars for every one dollar it had on reserve in gold. These loans went to commercial banks, and could be used as these banks' reserves. The commercial banks could then loan out ten dollars for every one dollar they had on reserve in their bank's vault. So a dollar's worth of gold in the Federal Reserve Bank can be turned into one hundred dollars of loans to the public.

## Getting Out of the Woods

The great nations of the world would abandon the gold standard in order to print money to fund World War II. With the massive debt accrued by European nations to fight the war, as well as the need for the United States to pay its bills for the war, a new monetary system had to be formed. Shortly after World War II, Lord Keynes and Harry Dexter White, a U.S. Treasury official, prepared the plans for a new global financial system. Representatives of the financial rulers of the United Nations assembled in Bretton Woods, New Hampshire, and they enacted the new global monetary system. This system fixed the price of gold at thirty-five dollars an ounce, and created a fixed exchange rate between all currencies of the world and the dollar. The Federal Reserve would store the world's gold, and the rest of the world's banks would store Federal Reserve notes as their reserves. Only foreign central banks were able to redeem their Federal Reserve notes in gold; individuals were denied this right. Since the right to trade is a natural right, the prohibition on gold ownership assaults that right.

The federal government would succumb to the temptation of printing more money than it had reserves in gold; and once the different international bankers became aware of this, they started to claim their share of the gold reserves. On August 15th 1971 came the nail in Bretton Woods's coffin. President Nixon on that day instructed his treasury secretary to cancel the dollar's convertibility into gold—only temporarily, he claimed. Recall Milton Friedman's warning about the permanence of temporary government programs. This meant the dollar was backed by nothing, except the laws that made it the nation's legal tender, and the government's promise not to print too much of it. Naturally, massive inflation followed.

## Inflation and Its friends

Massive increase in the money supply, or inflation, by way of fractional reserve banking and a fiat-based monetary system (or a monetary system that has currency which is not backed by any intrinsic value and is considered money just because the government says it is; oddly reminiscent of legal Positivism) causes prices to rise as well as the boom-and-bust cycle. The people who benefit from this inflationary system are the ones who get their hands on the money first, the banks. The banks get to make their investments before the prices of assets rise in response to the increase in the money supply. By the time the money trickles down to the rest of the people in the economy, the symptoms of inflation will have begun to settle in and devalued money will mean the money has less purchasing power, which will cause the phenomenon of rising prices.

This inflationary system robs people of their savings. Every time the Federal Reserve expands the money supply through this system, all money that was already in circulation loses purchasing power, and the people who get their hands on the money first gain that lost purchasing power. Normally, the banks loan money to the government by purchasing treasury bills. Treasury bills have been one of the safest investments in the past since the federal government's debt is guaranteed to be repaid with interest, by you and me, the taxpayers. The government can now decide what to do with this money, say, funding any one of its special interest projects, or even our collective welfare, if it feels so ambitious.

As you can see, it is the banks, the government, and the corporations the government favors that benefit from this system, while everyone else is robbed of their purchasing power in order to fund it. This is exactly what Jefferson predicted in a quote attributed to him: "If the American people ever allow private banks to control the issue of their currency, first by inflation, then by deflation, the banks and the corporations which grow up around them will deprive the people of all property until their children wake up homeless on the continent [of] their fathers."

There is no difference between the Federal Reserve's system of fractional reserve banking that inflates the currency to transfer your purchasing power to the special banking interests, government, and corporate interests and a thief who hacks into your bank account and removes funds from it. This inflationary system of theft that causes the boom-and-bust cycle makes it impossible for the average American to save for his own retirement (unless he converts his savings into gold and hopes the ghost of FDR in the White House at this writing doesn't confiscate it). Prior to the abandonment of the gold standard, Americans could work and earn gold as their income, store it in a bank vault, and it would appreciate in value all on its own, serving as their retirement safety net. Fed inflationism depreciates people's savings over time, and the busts the Fed creates wipe out the retirement investments people make in the stock market. The Fed, stated simply, is an abomination to the Natural Law and the Constitution.

## When I Was Your Age!

Surely, any young person today can think of stories told by their parents that sound something like "when I was your age, I could buy a movie ticket for twenty-five cents, a round-trip subway ticket for ten cents, a bag of chips for five cents, and a soda for ten cents!" Now it costs over sixteen dollars to go to the movies—ten dollars for a ticket, two dollars for the chips, and four dollars for the soda, and that's before transportation costs and the tax! This exorbitant increase in price occurred only within a time span of about fifty years; that is a 3,100 percent increase in price! For some reason, people just take price increases for granted as a normal occurrence that happens with the passage of time or blame it on the businesses that charge the higher price and call them evil and greedy.

Let us take a look at the money supply—literally the cash in circulation and in bank accounts in the United States—over this same fifty-year period.[8]

The increase in the monetary base is the reason for such absurd occurrences as the 3,100 percent increase in the cost of attending a movie. The money supply really started to increase drastically in the mid-1960s, and once Nixon took America off the gold standard in 1971; money creation grew out of control. Nixon broke away from the quasi-gold standard of the Bretton Woods agreement because there was no other way to pay for the debt racked up by Lyndon B. Johnson's Vietnam War and Great Society, which provided "guns and butter" for all of America, according to Johnson.

"Guns and butter" is just another way of describing LBJ's warfare agenda abroad in Vietnam—ultimately financed by the Fed—as well as his massive increase in domestic spending. He spent money the government did not have; and he spent wildly on programs such as these: The Economic Opportunity Act of 1964, which created an Office of Economic Opportunity (OEO) to oversee a variety of community-based anti-poverty programs; his War on Poverty, which began with a $1 billion appropriation in 1964 and spent another $2 billion in the following two years; the Elementary and Secondary Education Act of 1965, which was initially allotted more than $1 billion for inner-city schools; the Higher Education Act of 1965, which gave federal money to universities, as well as created scholarships and low-interest loans for students; and LBJ's Great Society, which created the bottomless pits of Medicare and Medicaid. The two medical programs have been complete disasters that are not only broke, but are unfunded to the tune of $76 trillion and counting.

Moreover, the debt is not just a financial issue. Admiral Michael Mullen, at this writing chairman of the Joint Chiefs of Staff and thus America's highest-ranking military official, proclaimed that "our national debt is our biggest national security threat." Can you imagine that, from a military man! *His greatest fear is not terrorists, but government debt!* Secretary of State Hillary Clinton further explained the nature of this threat: "It undermines our capacity to act in our own interest, and it does constrain us where constraint may be undesirable. And it also sends a message of weakness internationally." There is no chance this debt monster could have grown so out of control if the United States operated on a full gold standard.

Every day the federal budget grows, every person loses more and more freedom. The bigger the government, the smaller the amount of individual liberty; the bigger the government, the more it can regulate every aspect of our lives which strips us of our rights and liberties. Each day the Federal Reserve System exists is one more day that the government can fund its growing budget, increase its size, and deplete our savings and pass them along to its friends. Each day of Big Government is one more day of assaults on our liberties.

## Conclusion

It should be pretty self-evident that neither Alan Greenspan nor Ben Bernanke, or any Fed chairman, can be trusted to achieve full employment and currency stabilization. Throughout the life of the Federal Reserve, we have seen American production diminished, debt rise, inflation wreck people's savings, the boom-and-bust cycle wreck the economy, a widening gap between the rich and the poor, and the value of the dollar drop by 93 percent.

Fed supporters have all sorts of explanations and reasons for these occurrences; but it is no coincidence that from 1870 to 1913, while on a strict gold standard and without a central bank, the American economy grew larger and more rapidly than any other economy in the history of the world, and from 1913 to the present, we have seen our economy fight through years of booms and busts, our living standards decline, and our cost of living increase. This should make it pretty clear that Alan Greenspan's NYU education, as well as Ben Bernanke's Harvard and MIT education, is not worth its weight in gold. When economic growth, prosperity, wealth, safety, and happiness are the goals, nothing can replace the gold standard.

If the U.S. federal government were on a strict gold standard, with a 100 percent reserve ratio, there would be absolutely no way to fund these assaults on the Natural Law, such as wars, welfare programs, and regulatory schemes. We would be forced into having a sensible foreign policy of peace, free trade, and a strong national defense that focused only on legitimate threats. The size of the government would be forced to shrink, allowing us all to keep more of our natural freedoms. People would be left to make the decisions that affect only their life, liberty, and property. We would have sound reasons why we shouldn't go to war, instead of making excuses to go to war, and our men and women in the military would not be needlessly risking their lives. Government would also have to stop making excuses to bail out "too big to fail" corporations, and stop the excuses for why we need this social program or that social program. The government would be forced to stop its assaults on our savings, our economy, our safety, and most importantly, our natural rights and liberties.

This is why the government must stop abusing everyone's natural right to sound money.

# Chapter 13

# Theft by Any Other Name:

*The Right to Spend Your Own Money*

Suppose someone with a gun approaches you as you are getting out of your car. "Your car or your life," he demands. Of course, you give him the keys and walk away. Is this theft? Or is there something that makes it different from theft, that is, a justified violation of your inherent property rights? All of us would say that it is theft, and the person who did this should be punished by the full force of the criminal law.

Would you, however, change your answer if, instead of one, a gang of five men forcefully take your car? Now assume that ten approach you, all armed, but this time they put it to a vote, including you in the vote as well. You, however, are quickly outvoted ten to one, and only then do they take your car. Is this still theft?

What if, after taking your car, they give you a bicycle instead, and they give the car to a person who is particularly poor and needs it to get to work? What if they erected a street lamp in the parking lot, and claimed that they were justified in taking your car because you had enjoyed the benefit of the street lamp by parking there? What if there are one hundred men? Ten thousand? One or two million? What has to change before this *forceful* taking of your property is no longer theft?

Because taxation is compulsory, and therefore a forceful taking of your property, we may assume that it is a *malum in se*—an evil in itself. The question then becomes whether there is some valid justification for it. As we shall see, no such justification exists, and therefore taxation violates natural property rights. That taxes are all justified by some subjective public necessity is an outright lie, which we quite literally can no longer afford to believe. As we have just seen, the two other means government uses to finance itself—the issuance of public debt and printing of money—are simply theft by another name and are even more dangerous than taxation. Does the government exist to protect our freedoms, or do we exist to serve the government?

The real tragedy of public finance is that it acts as the great enabler for all of government's most tyrannical actions. How could wars be fought without money? How could we give aid to corrupt regimes without a source of revenue? As Frank Chodorov, a well-respected critic of taxes, warns, "We cannot restore traditional American freedom unless we limit the government's power to tax. No tinkering with this, that, or the other law will stop the trend toward socialism." If we are really, truly committed to the cause of liberty, then we must cut off tyranny at its source: Public finance.

## The Evil of Taxation

The basic evil of taxation is that it degrades the individual by flouting his natural rights. Taxation in essence establishes a legal right on the part of the government to your property and the product of your labor, a right which precedes and trumps your own. The government's claim of right, however, extends to *all* of your property, not just what it actually takes; otherwise, it would not be able to raise taxes whenever it chooses. Consider in this regard the text of the Sixteenth Amendment, passed in 1913: "The Congress shall have power to lay and collect taxes on incomes, from whatever source derived, without apportionment among the several States, and without regard to any census or enumeration." It is clear from the text itself that there are no constitutional restrictions on what Congress may take (unlike the original Constitution). Thus, whatever portion of your own property it declines to take is simply whatever it, in all of its infinite professed wisdom and charity, decides you may keep. Our retained income has become not a right, but a privilege granted by government. This scheme is one of the fundamental legal precepts of socialism: The government decides what it will take from you and what you may keep from it.

This is also the strictest application of Positivism: If the government can say when our natural rights protect us from aggression and when they do not, then there can be no such thing as natural rights. This tenuous, subjective nature of our rights is itself reflected in the distinction between taxation and theft. *Theft* does not mean a taking of your property, but whatever the government determines to be an unlawful taking of your property. Thus, the contemporary understanding of *theft* extends from lawmakers, and not the Natural Law or any ethical principle. Although natural rights and taxation could theoretically be reconciled if free choice was somehow involved, as we shall see, it is in the nature of Big Government that this will always be an unattainable ideal.

Because natural, inalienable rights are transgressed, the people become sub-human by losing free will. One of the most important property rights is the right to choose how your property is used. If the state is able to take property and allocate it to a different use than the individual would have chosen, then the will of the individual is servile to the will of the state. Even if the entire value of the labor you produced is returned to you in the form of governmental services, you have still lost the *freedom to choose* what should be done with that value. Although the economic consequences of enabling centrally planned investment and spending decisions are disastrous (not to mention the disincentive to labor caused by the reallocation of income), the real tragedy is the cost to human liberty.

Given this inextricable link between property and freedom, it should not be surprising that one of the major civil rights statutes during the Reconstruction era gave African Americans a right "to the full and equal benefit of all laws and proceedings for the security of persons and property as is enjoyed by white citizens." In other words, emancipated African Americans could never truly be free unless they had the same rights as whites to be free from interference with their property. Anything less would be a variant of slavery. Why should we now forget these lessons and expose all of our property, and our temporal welfare, to the government's voracious appetites?

223

So why do we acquiesce to the government taking our property? The answer to that question is wherein the true evil of taxation lies. It slowly convinces the people over time that its subversion of their natural rights is good for them. When our car is stolen by one person, we feel a sense of moral outrage because we know that what happened to us was wrong. However, when we are taught that it is acceptable if the theft of our car is committed by a democratic majority, it institutionalizes a mode of thought that the individual is a servant of the state, clamoring for some small share of its limited resources. In short, as the government sees us, we exist to support it, not ourselves. How better to define slavery?

## The Democratic Majority and the Oxymoron
of a Progressive Tax

The fact that the public need for taxation was decided upon by a democratic majority, instead of a dictator, should make no difference. After all, recall our "how many men" hypothetical. How many men are needed until it is no longer theft? Similarly, how *much* of a majority should be required, until the will of the individual can be trumped and the trump considered moral? Fifty-one percent? Seventy-five percent? Everyone but you? The fact of the matter is that, as far as a transgression of natural rights is concerned, the difference between a dictator and a democratic majority is not only meaningless, but hopelessly subjective. The only cogent distinction is that in a democracy, more of your neighbors desire to take your property than in a dictatorship.

Consider also that when taxation is called for by a majority, it becomes precisely the instrument of tyranny over a minority. That is the identical tyranny that the Founders had witnessed firsthand and sought to prevent by creating a federal system of government. Consider the following. All of us would certainly favor a system whereby we could "purchase" services—say education, for example—for less than they are actually worth; this is simply the human as a rational actor. The problem is that one group will necessarily be paying for this "windfall" that the other group enjoys; all costs must be eventually borne by someone. In a normal market, this unfair result is prevented by a number of laws which prohibit the taking of value by any means other than voluntary transfer. Stated in other words, these laws ensure that the value we get from consuming a good is commensurate to the cost we actually bore in acquiring it.

In a democracy, however, the majority can hijack the coercive power of the state in the form of taxation effectively to sell itself services at a discount, with the discount being footed by the minority. To illustrate this point further, consider a democracy solely made up of a majority of baseball fans and a minority of curling fans. If the baseball fans grew tired of paying for tickets to go see their favorite team, they could demand that the government provide this service, and pay for it by imposing a tax on everyone. Because the total cost of maintaining a baseball team is spread across both groups, baseball fans are now enjoying a windfall; they pay less in taxes than the value they get from going to see a game. This difference is, of course, being made up for by curling fans. In other words, by imposing a tax, baseball fans have effectively sold themselves a service at a discount and stolen from curling fans. As Frédéric Bastiat once said, "Government is the great fiction through which everybody endeavors to live at the expense of everybody else."

It should be clear that the principal problem is not that the government is attempting to provide services, but how it chooses to finance the provision of those services. With coercive taxation necessarily comes this theft. By contrast, if the government possessed no coercive power and services were instead financed by user fees, the government would simply be the same as any other private enterprise in the economy, and no theft would occur.

This reveals taxation for what it really is; simply another form of majority rule cleverly disguised as government initiative, by which one group can live off of another. That this system of taxation simply functions as another instrument of factionalism and wealth transfer, should be clear.

A similar tendency can be seen in long-term changes in American tax rates. Income tax burdens on both median-income families and the highest earning 1 percent (who possess the greatest amount of political power relative to their numbers) have declined since 1960, whereas tax rates on relatively high-earning individuals have risen. How could this be anything less than one tax bracket (i.e., socioeconomic class) waging war on the other vis-à-vis the political system?

Whatever happened to the principle that government is not supposed to recognize castes? Is it any more sensible to have a rule that you can recognize castes, so long as the better-off castes are treated more harshly? The Declaration of Independence (codified as federal law, no less) says that "all Men are created equal," *not* "all Men are created equal in civil, but not economic, matters." This was no mistake. It is no more fair or equitable that a majority could live off of a wealthy minority, than a minority of feudal lords could live off of the labors of a majority of vassals. And today, 47 percent of American households do not pay any income tax.

## Breach of the Social Contract

The justification for taxation is typically that, as part of the social contract, we agree to pay money in exchange for governmental services. If, however, some sort of contract exists between the government and the individual to pay taxes, then it is fitting to analyze it in light of other contract principles, particularly the common law requirement that contracts entail a bargained-for exchange, be made by willing parties, and must have good faith at their essence. Certainly, the government shouldn't be exempt from these rules, which centuries of legal history have taught us are necessary for an agreement to be fair and just. If the government were exempt, then that would itself be an open admission that the social contract is neither fair nor just, certainly a conclusion which critics of libertarianism would be loath to admit. Any contract, as to which a contracting party lacks good faith and voluntary choices, is no contract at all.

In essence, the social contract argument says that we agree to pay taxes in exchange for government services, such as defense, roads, and insurance against times of hardship (in the form of welfare); a sort of *quid pro quo* between the government and the individual. In support of the fairness of this exchange, critics say that if one were to reject it by refusing to consume any government services, life would be unpalatable indeed. One could not use roads, enjoy the protection of the police; not even use money to pay for goods and services. And surely we also benefit indirectly from other forms of spending, such as grants to universities to research and develop socially beneficial technologies. Let us pick apart this argument piece by piece.

One of the central features of contract law is that there needs to be a bargained-for exchange, or in other words, that we are getting something in return for what we give. What is the purpose behind this requirement? It is simply not fair to compel someone to give something up when he is getting nothing in return. It is a hopeless myth that we receive governmental services proportionate to what we pay in taxes. Consider parents who choose to send their child to private school, or the majority of Americans who are not parents of school-age children. They still must pay taxes to support the public school system, even though they receive nothing in return. There is clearly no exchange there.

But, a critic would retort, they are receiving the benefit of living in a more educated society. If this is how we define the benefit, then the parents who do choose to send their children to public school are getting a windfall, paid for in part by the parents who send their child to private schools and by taxpayers who do not have school-age children. Moreover, the law does not recognize such tenuously defined exchanges. If you decided to give your friend a watch as a gift and changed your mind and kept it at the last moment, it is unfair to force you to give up the watch on the grounds that "you are getting the benefit of living in a society that can tell time better." It is clear that that argument is simply trying to circumvent the requirement of a bargained-for exchange and convince someone that the transfer is something it is not.

More fundamentally, the taxation-as-a-social-contract argument fails on the grounds that it is not voluntary. You must pay taxes whether you like it or not, or suffer the consequences of the criminal law. Critics, however, say that it is unethical to receive benefits and then not pay for them, which is certainly true. Thus when you use roads, you voluntarily agree to pay taxes. However, this justification for taxation must fail. First of all, there is no way to avoid all of the benefits which the government provides, such as the safety ensured by the existence of a military. Thus, you cannot be said to accept those benefits willfully. Second, the government has a legal monopoly over the provision of many of its services, and thus it is unfair to require people to go without those services if they disapprove of the "exchange." This would be similar to someone draining all the water on your land, and then trying to sell you water at an inflated price. This exchange could not be said to be voluntary; the alternative is to die of thirst.

Finally, contract law imposes a requirement that parties execute their contractual obligations with good faith. Thus if I enter into a contract with you to purchase cars, and there is a clause which allows me to void the contract if the cars are not fit for use, I cannot get out of my duty to purchase from you if I find one small mark on the inside of one car's bumper. If there is any agreement between the individual and the government to pay taxes in exchange for governmental services, then the Constitution imposes a requirement that the government only make those expenditures which are "necessary and proper" to achieve its enumerated powers. When the government flouts this requirement, as it does when it spends $4.8 million in tax dollars to study bears' DNA, it has breached the social contract. Additionally, many of the "public necessities" at which spending is directed were caused by the government itself, such as war and recessions. This also violates the doctrine of good faith, and amounts to a breach of the social contract.

## A Budget Not Even a Mother Could Love

But social justice legitimizes our system of taxation, right? Before you settle on the image of government as a self-described nurturing caretaker, consider the following statistics. America on average gives Egypt, a country which the Human Rights Watch sought fit to characterize as having a "poor human rights record," $1.3 billion a year in military assistance. Or, what a colleague of mine likes to call "Military Expenditures on Shifty, Suspicious Dictatorships and Unsavory Polities" (MESSD-UP). Interestingly, MESSD-UP's military aid to Egypt works out to around $867 for every homeless child in America, certainly enough to provide each with warm clothes for the winter, that is, if the government were in the business of providing clothes.

"Okay," a critic will concede, "perhaps taxation isn't legitimized by social justice, but what about stimulating the economy and job creation? Are we supposed to just sit in unemployment lines and wait for things to get better?" In the recent American Recovery and Reinvestment Act, for which the federal government borrowed and spent $1 trillion, $389,357 was spent on researching "the concurrent versus separate use of Malt Liquor and marijuana." And rather than pay a cover to get into a comedy club, your college student and his buddies can stay in the dorm and enjoy the fruits of $712,883 spent developing "machine-generated" comedy (i.e., robots that tell jokes). Although no doubt fascinating research topics which will benefit society, precisely how these projects relate to "Recovery and Reinvestment" can only be understood while relishing the concurrent effects of malt liquor and marijuana and joke telling. At least we'll have something to laugh about when the Act starts cutting into our paychecks.

Nonetheless, the government insists that our current system of taxation is justified by social justice, or public necessity more generally. However, this is and always will be a deeply flawed claim. As for social justice, consider the sales tax, which applies both to luxury items and to those goods which are essential to the maintenance of life, such as food and shelter. Everyone pays the same tax on a gallon of milk, irrespective of one's total assets. Thus, the burden of that tax will be much heavier on the poor than the wealthy, because it takes up a higher proportion of their disposable income.

Moreover, taxes on the businesses which produced those goods also raise prices, as do taxes on the materials that went into making them. Thus, the effective tax paid on a good is much higher than the sales tax we see printed on a receipt, especially when considering the numerous hands through which a good will pass before it reaches the end consumer (think of a snowball increasing in size as it rolls down a hill). Ironically, how much of that tax is passed on to consumers is a function of how "essential" the good is. If consumers cannot do without it, such as is the case with food and medicine, then producers can raise prices to reflect the increased cost of doing business without fear of lost sales. This serves to compound the inequitable effect of taxes on the poor.

More fundamentally, the sales tax is a direct affront on the natural right to trade. How can we be free if the government can impair that right? How can we survive in anything more than a hunter-gatherer society without a right to trade? Without this right, the rocket scientist could not trade his services for food, the actor could not trade his services for health care, and the banker could not trade his services for clothes. Infringements upon the right to trade, such as the sales tax, are a substantial impediment to economic development; they reduce the incentive to work hard and trade the product of that labor for other goods and services. In sum, when the middle and lower classes claim that they are being squeezed to death by the skyrocketing cost of living, they should look first to taxation. And lest you think American taxpayers are getting those revenues right back in the form of welfare programs, recall our friend MESSD-UP and its reallocation of wealth abroad.

Furthermore, welfare programs themselves, financed by taxation, so often denigrate the poor more than they help. Consider public housing. Public housing imposes a maximum limit on the earnings of individuals who wish to benefit from use of the program. Thus, once your earnings exceed this level, you are no longer eligible to live there. Not only does this give people a disincentive to earn as much as they can, it also ensures that the poorest members of society will all be living in close proximity to one another with limited opportunities and motivation to escape. In other words, it discourages socio-economic integration. The natural trend of these large apartment complexes is that families lucky enough to be successful will move out, and the majority of residents who remain will likely be single female heads of households. This leads to large concentrations of poor teenagers, who cannot find employment, who lack the discipline and guidance of an older male, and who are left to their own devices. As economist Thomas Sowell has argued, the massive increases in the welfare state have caused the destruction of African American families; "The black family, which had survived centuries of slavery and discrimination, began rapidly disintegrating in the liberal welfare state that subsidized unwed pregnancy and changed welfare from an emergency rescue to a way of life."

Even more infuriating is that this decrease in living standards, caused by the government, ends up serving as the government's justification for increasing public wealth transfers, and thus increasing taxation. In short, it is a self-per-petuating system of inefficiency. Recall when we discussed the government's breach of the social contract: The government cannot create the necessity for providing its own services.

This brings us to public necessity. The problem with public necessity is that, as a term, it is inherently subjective and bears no restrictions; what Chodorov called "unspecified social betterment." Moreover, history teaches us that the size of government has always been a function of the public's distaste for taxation and taste for public spending, not what officials understand to be "necessary." People opt for government programs not because they determine that society cannot function without them, but because they feel uncertain about their ability to provide for themselves. Thus, people favor stimulus spending during a recession not because it is necessary, but simply because it is comforting to think that the government is doing something to fix the recession. In any event, most government spending is not even debatably necessary by any stretch of the imagination. Remember the joke-telling robots?

Furthermore, taxes cannot be necessary, because government programs now financed by taxes could be paid for by user fees instead, or provided by the free market. Not only would this not violate our rights, it would also be better public policy. Take public roads, for example. Why would it be fair for someone who never uses roads to pay taxes to support them? And if we had to pay for roads whether we used them or not, wouldn't more people choose to travel on them, thus congesting highways and diverting consumers away from alternative means of travel, many of which are better for quality of life and the environment?

It is an accepted principle that if you do not pay in proportion to what you consume, then you will opt to overconsume, depleting scarce resources. Assuming we already had a car, we would be much more likely to use a road instead of a train if the road use was free. And the reverse is true. If trains were already paid for by taxes, no one would use roads. Why is it any more sensible to have a user fee for trains (i.e., a ticket), but not roads? The simple solution to both the fairness and the efficiency problems is, of course, to use privately owned tolls instead.

And even then, unless the government relinquishes its monopoly control over toll roads, which effectively taxes us in a different form; if we must drive to work on a government road, and the road has already been more than paid for with tolls, how is the toll at that point anything different from a coercive tax? Only competition can lead to less waste. Consider that the

George Washington Bridge, which was completed in 1931, originally cost $19.6 million, or $273,538,789 today. Nonetheless, the bridge currently collects about $1 million in tolls *each day*. In other words, ignoring maintenance for a moment, its original cost can be made up in a quick nine months. No wonder the government does not want any competition! As we can see, not only is taxation unnecessary; it violates our natural rights and leads to wasteful results.

Moreover, consider the effect that redistribution of wealth has on a market economy. The difficulty with forced taxation is that it discourages the production of goods and services, since the wealth garnered is not commensurate with the amount produced. Why would we choose to work hard if we knew that our money would be taken away from us on our way home from work? As Murray Rothbard notes, "Instead of helping expand the amount and degree of production in society, the robber is parasitically draining off that production. Whereas an expanded market encourages increases in production and supply, theft discourages production and contracts the market."[1]

Additionally, the government's choice of how to spend the money it takes will always be more inefficient than the market. Government spending must, in the long run, come from its citizens, citizens who could be spending it upon the projects which they value the most. By contrast, an out-of-touch government with little access to the information necessary to make prudent spending decisions, cannot allocate those resources in a manner which will maximize our welfare. Consider the recipients of New Deal spending, the most "lauded" spending project in American history: Unused roads, dams, and bridges, and white-collar beneficiaries and the unemployable. How could taxation possibly serve the public necessity if it strangles our economy?

Human history confirms these theoretical arguments. Americans experienced the greatest increase in living standards the world had ever seen during the period from the late nineteenth century up until the early twentieth century. While there was some government intervention in the economy during this time, the interventions absolutely paled in comparison to the interventionist policies which started in the early twentieth century and continue to the present day.

Starting in 1870, prices began to fall sharply in America as a result of a stable monetary supply combined with a massive increase in the American economy's productive capacity. The government, shockingly, lowered the cost of living by withdrawing some of the Civil War greenbacks; and by 1879 the rest of the currency was convertible into gold. Lower prices meant that over time Americans' earnings and savings were gaining purchasing power (the amount of goods that can be purchased per unit of currency) even if they maintained the same nominal value, and thus they were wealthier as a consequence. Since interventionist policies have gained hold, we have experienced lower rates of growth, and numerous financial crises.

In sum, many critics may point to the fact that there is still a shortage of truly necessary charitable donations as evidence that libertarianism doesn't work. However, I think the fact that the government prefers to spend tax dollars on military aid to Egypt rather than provide decent health care for veterans is evidence that a social welfare state, financed by profligate taxation, doesn't work. That taxes are somehow justified by the public necessity is clearly an outright lie which we, quite literally, cannot afford to believe.

## I'll Gladly Pay You Tuesday for a War Today

The government has a few more creative ways of paying for its initiatives, all of which still amount to theft. In this section, we focus our attention on government-issued debt. If the government chooses not to raise taxes in the present to pay for a program, it can issue a bond. In this transaction, someone agrees to give the government money now in exchange for repayment at a later date, plus an interest payment. The problem, however, is that eventually these obligations have to be paid for with taxation. A bond is therefore, as Chodorov notes, a claim on future production. It allows the government simply to defer taxation to a later date.

It is important to reflect briefly on some of the common but erroneous beliefs about public debt, held by both ends of the ideological spectrum. It is theft in the sense that it can only result in more taxation, and thus property will be taken away from you against your will. It is not, however, literally taking money from future generations; clearly, money cannot be "taken" from the future to pay for something today. It is simply reallocated from bondholders to the government, where it is then injected into the economy. It is for this reason that proponents of bond issuance argue that it is not in fact theft: In essence, although future generations will be burdened with a debt obligation on their heads, the money supply increased when the government spent the revenues from debt issuance. Thus, this argument goes, there will be more money flowing in the economy with which the future generations can pay those taxes; money which would not have been there but for the issuance. Moreover, we receive any benefit of money being spent now as opposed to later, for example, in the form of a cleaner environment brought about by government investment in green technologies.

This argument, however, runs into the same problems that we encountered in the section on taxation and the social contract. Because future generations obviously cannot consent to pay for government spending when the debt is issued, taxation cannot be in any sense voluntary. Furthermore, it is also unrealistic that future taxpayers will receive benefits commensurate with their tax burden. One group will always be benefitting at the expense of another. As we shall see in a moment, this is even more likely to occur with borrowing than with taxation.

Debt issuance is more problematic than taxation for several reasons. The first, and most obvious, is that future generations do not get to vote on those government expenditures, thus making it taxation without representation. Moreover, although proponents of debt issuance may paint a sunny picture of our children reaping the benefits of today's prudent investments, they are ignoring the other half of the picture; they will be shackled to the cost of the previous generation's political mistakes. I have yet to hear a cogent argument for why our children should have to pay for our military disasters. Children cannot inherit debt from their parents' debt, so why should they inherit their parents' government's debt?

Second, it is much more likely that profligate spending will result from debt issuance than taxation. Because older folks do not have to pay for as much of

THEFT BY ANY OTHER NAME

the debt as the young (who have a whole taxpaying life ahead of them), it is less costly. This creates an incentive to favor wasteful spending, since the full burden falls on someone else's shoulders. Thus, debt issuance is a surreptitious form of intergenerational factionalism. Nice try, Dad.

Politicians also have an incentive to favor debt issuance, since it allows them to engage in wasteful spending without its typical political consequences; the people get what they think is the benefit of larger social programs, and no corresponding increase in taxes. The key problem with this is that it results in higher spending, and thus higher taxes, than the electorate would have otherwise opted for. A related trick politicians have up their sleeves is simply to cut taxes but not public spending, a tempting "have your cake and eat it, too," policy given that both actions make them look good in the eyes of the public. Assuming, however, that the budget was balanced before those tax cuts, this reduction in government revenues must be met with an equal amount of debt issuance (you can't spend more than you have). Thus the effective tax has not changed, just who pays it and when. Put simply, public debt, like credit cards, facilitates fiscal irresponsibility.

In response to all of these arguments, a proponent of debt issuance may argue that all of these criticisms are outweighed by the fact that government bonds can be a lifesaving tool in times of emergency. There are instances, such as during war or recession, when the government is simply not able to raise taxes to pay for all of its spending. History, however, teaches us that if government must issue debt to pay for its spending, then the odds are it is engaging in something it ought not to be, namely, offensive wars and bailouts of private industry. World War I, and the fifteen million deaths which it caused, would not have been possible if governments could not have issued debt or printed money to pay for it. Thus, the ability to tax is an important fiscal (as opposed to legal) constraint on the size of government.

A final criticism of debt is offered by the economist Henry Hazlitt in his masterpiece *Economics in One Lesson*. Essential to this criticism is the distinction between two possible uses of money—consumption and savings. With both uses, money is being injected into the economy. (If it is saved in a bank, it will be loaned out to businesses and other consumers. Very little money is actually saved as cash "under a mattress" nowadays.) Moreover, both will increase employment. The practical difference relates to the fact that money which is saved is, in the words of Hazlitt, "turned over to someone else to spend on means to increase production"; in other words, it is invested. For any given economy there will be some optimal combination of savings and consumption spending which maximizes total consumption in the long run (we would be poor if we never invested in new technology, or by contrast, never bought the goods which those investments developed).

The government often contends, particularly in times of economic crisis, that it is justified in issuing debt to stimulate consumption and restore the economy to its pre-crisis state. Such was the contention during the Great Depression, and such is the contention during the current financial crisis. The government argues that savings are excessively high, and thus it is proper for the government to convert those savings into consumption spending. There are, however, a number of reasons to reject this claim. The two inescapable effects will be an increase in the price of goods and services by shifting money toward consumption, and a long-term reduction in production levels by shifting money away from investments. Moreover, although banks may be refusing to loan in the midst of a crisis, there is no reason whatsoever to believe that temporary, government-induced consumption spending will be able to restore liquidity. If such were the case, then the economy would be well on the path to recovery at the time of this book's writing. President Obama's explanation of the failure of spending to correct the economy? "We simply haven't spent enough yet!" Perhaps he should have read these words spoken by Henry Morgenthau Jr., FDR's secretary of the treasury, in 1939: "We have tried spending money. We are spending more than we have ever spent before and it does not work. . . . [We] have just as much unemployment as when we started . . . and an enormous debt to boot!"

Before we move on to the next section, I leave you with some food for thought. We are now reaching unprecedented levels of public debt. Government may soon begin issuing bonds just to keep up with its interest payments. Sound familiar? It should. It's a Ponzi scheme, and it can land you a lifetime in prison, like Bernard Madoff, or make you a hero, like FDR.

## Conclusion

The real evil of public finance is that it enables government to commit all of its atrocities against the individual. It is its lifeblood. Chodorov writes,

> When you examine any species of government intervention you find that it is made possible by revenues. A government is as strong as its income. Contrariwise, the independence of the people is in direct proportion to the amount of their wealth they can enjoy.

Although I have argued that taxation itself is inherently evil in that it is nothing more than institutionalized theft, it is of course possible that government can spend those tax revenues on good causes which really do benefit the public. However, whether or not we are to trust government with money reverts back to the more essential question of whether we can trust government at all to handle power responsibly. If there is any lesson to be gotten from this book, it is that we cannot, and money is the most essential, brutally effective kind of power we the people could ever vest in the government. If we do so, then we sow the seeds of our own slavery. Although one may argue that the public necessity requires taxation, the reader must remember that it was precisely this mode of thought which enabled the atomic bomb to be developed and deployed. One who is convinced that we can somehow engineer a large government while avoiding such catastrophes is blinding himself to the lessons of history.

Does the government exist to protect our freedoms, or do we exist to serve it? It takes our property and our money against our will. Anyone willing to see through Big Government and unafraid to challenge it can answer that question. If the government derives its powers from the consent of the governed, as the Declaration of Independence declares, and if the governed cannot take their neighbor's property against the neighbor's will without violating the Natural Law, how can the governed have created a government that can morally do so?

# Chapter 14

# A Ride on Dr. Feinberg's Bus:

*The Right to Be Governed by Laws with Moral Limits*

Imagine catching the bus on your way to class, work, the doctor's office, or coffee with a friend. You hop on board, grab a seat, and proceed to gaze out the window.[1] All of a sudden, the vile stench of a passenger grabs your attention, and you look over to see a strobe light–carrying, stereo-blasting man who plops down in the seat next to yours. He reaches for a chalkboard in his bag and scratches his fingernails across its length. You politely ask him to stop, but he refuses.

As the goose bumps on your arm reach their peak, you make eye contact with a woman seated on the floor who is scratching, drooling, coughing, and burping relentlessly. She is sprawled out on a tablecloth in the aisle of the bus (in the back so as not to create a safety hazard), making a picnic lunch of live cockroaches, soft dog food, and rotten eggs—all sautéed in garlic and onions.

You recoil in disgust and are positive the bus populace cannot get any worse. The bus driver brakes, and a crowd of mourners boards with a coffin in tow. As they saunter past you, a pallbearer's T-shirt comes into view. It is a depiction of Jesus hanging from the cross with the caption: "Hang in there, baby!" One of the other pallbearers is using an American flag as a shawl, wiping her tears and blowing her nose into the stars and stripes.

You attempt to ignore the chaos that surrounds you when a couple directly across the aisle catches your eye. They are kissing, hugging, petting, and fondling one another with sound effects to accompany their grossly inappropriate visual. The man takes off articles of his girlfriend's clothing, leaving little to be imagined.

To avoid the peep show, you stand up and move forward a few benches. A loud and boisterous young man approaches and asks if he can take a seat. "Of course," you respond. He proceeds to rant *ad nauseam* about the weather, politics, his favorite TV show, the bus's leisurely speed, and the burnt toast he ate for breakfast. You take out your newspaper to hint you have no desire to chat, but you are unable to make him stop. To add to your torment, two nasally voices are screeching at an ungodly decibel in the seats behind you.

Head pounding and searching for some kind of relief, you look toward the bus driver whose reproachful eyes signal the entrance of a group of teenage hooligans. Attempting to put the other bus passengers in fear of their lives, the first teenager pretends to pull the pin on a (very realistic) hand grenade, while the second teenager stabs his friends with a fake, rubber knife. The third, fourth, and fifth teenagers—all wearing armbands with emblazoned swastikas—carry cardboard signs with utterly offensive racial and ethnic slurs that denigrate Catholics, blacks, Jews, and Hispanics.

Now ask yourself: Is any of this conduct so reprehensible that it can be considered harmful enough to justify criminal punishment? The late Professor Joel Feinberg, who taught me philosophy at Princeton University, depicted this motley cast of characters as part of a classic study on the types of conduct which can merit criminal punishment, and the types which cannot. As we shall explore below, conduct must not merely offend, but cause actual harm for the state to seek to punish it as being criminal. Moreover, that conduct must be so severe that it can properly be considered a harm not just to the individual, but also to the freedom of all individuals. When is an individual free to pursue a remedy in civil proceedings, and when is it the public itself which prosecutes a crime and punishes a criminal? Any restriction of liberty in the form of criminal punishment is wholly illegitimate unless the exercise of liberty was intended to cause harm and actually did cause harm.

Sadly, the federal government has engaged in a profligate spree of criminalization of harmless behavior. We currently live under the oppression of a government which passes 56.5 new criminal laws a year, or 565 per decade.[2] The United States Government Printing Office, whose core task is to provide "publishing and dissemination services . . . to Congress, federal agencies, federal depository libraries, and the American public," is itself unable to calculate the number of pages in the Code of Federal Regulations. Even the American Bar Association's Task Force on the Federalization of Crime has stated that "so large is the present body of federal criminal law that there is no conveniently accessible, complete list of federal crimes."[3] Stated in financial terms, as of 2006, the federal government and all state governments spent a staggering $109 billion annually on feeding, clothing, and confining imprisoned adults, as well as nearly $98 billion on police services and $47 billion for prosecutions.[4] Although America has approximately 5 percent of the global population, 25 percent of the world's prisoners reside here!

The net result of this irreverent legislation and regulation is a violation of the principles enumerated elsewhere in this book, and a contravention of the Constitution's extremely limited authorization to criminalize conduct. Thus, only a small fraction of the federal government's criminal code can be considered truly legitimate, and it is the government, and not the individuals it prosecutes, that is guilty of the greater unlawful conduct. It is high time that we utilize the criminal law for its one and only true purpose: To safeguard our liberties, not restrain them.

## What Is *Harm*?

I never hurt nobody but myself and that's nobody's business but my own.
—BILLIE HOLIDAY

As mentioned above, in a society that respects natural rights, only conduct which can properly be described as harmful, and not merely offensive, can be criminalized. *Harm* can be defined as "an intentional nonconsensual physical violation of another person's natural rights." It should be clear at once that only actual injuries which fit this description can justifiably be punishable by the government. Should an individual who has never before suffered an epileptic attack be sentenced to life in prison when an unprovoked and unpredictable seizure causes him to swerve off the road and hit a pedestrian? Certainly not. By contrast, rape, murder, and theft are all actions which intentionally cause actual harm to natural rights and thus deserve to be punished as crimes.

More specifically, we can think of harm as requiring that there be an actual victim. A prime example of a victimless crime is the private consumption of alcohol, or any drug for that matter. These substances surely affect one's person, but in what way are they invading or assaulting another's body, rights, or property? One might argue that they lead to dangerous behavior when one is in an altered state, but until a person whose judgment is impaired actually invades or assaults another's body, rights, or property, he should not be punished, and the act of consumption itself should be free from regulation as an application of the right to do to one's body as one chooses. The criminalization of a victimless activity itself is by no means a necessary restriction of liberty, as all restrictions of liberty must be.

And in any event, does not the action of watching an intense football rivalry increase the chance that an individual will harm another? Is the violence in football morally acceptable because the government permits it, or because the participants choose to waive certain natural rights? Lest one think that the government would have the sense to stop at criminalizing drunk driving and leave activities such as attending football rivalries unregulated, consider that many jurisdictions ban the ownership of German shepherd dogs, a breed described by the American Kennel Club as "energetic and fun-loving . . . very fond of children . . . a loyal family pet and a good guard dog, the ideal choice for many families." If German shepherd dogs can be banned, then what other breeds as well? Golden retrievers? Beagles? Chihuahuas? Dogs altogether? The purpose behind this discussion is that justifying the criminalization of certain actions on the grounds that they increase the likelihood of harm to others, but fall short of causing actual harm, is hopelessly subjective and opens the door to the regulation of practically any activity the government chooses. It opens the door to totalitarianism.

More fundamentally, why should the government be criminalizing activities, such as driving without a seatbelt, which are merely risky to ourselves? Laurence M. Vance writes,

> Seat belt, helmet, and texting laws are predicated on the idea that we need the state to protect us from doing something stupid. But it is families and friends that should be the ones persuading people to buckle up, wear a helmet, or turn off their cell phone, not the state. But they won't do it, some say, and therefore the state has to do it. But this presupposes that the state cares more about an individual than do his family and friends—a very dubious proposition.[5]

Why should this sphere of activity—convincing our loved ones to lead healthier and safer lives—come within the coercive power of government? What's next? Government-mandated marriage counseling sessions?

A particular type of victimless crime demands particular attention: Crimes which punish consensual actions between individuals. In order to be considered harm, a "violation" of natural rights must be nonconsensual, since if the recipient of that "violation" consented (assuming he was mentally capable of doing so), he was simply exercising his own liberties, and there can therefore be no victim and no violation of natural rights and hence no crime. This accounts for the difference between consensual sexual conduct and rape, and tackling during a football game and aggravated assault.

Sadly, the criminalization of consensual conduct has historically been one of the primary means by which societies have enforced their own moral values upon others. Such was the case for centuries with sodomy laws, which punished the intimate sexual actions of consenting adults. What legitimate interest could society possibly have in regulating what types of harmless physical interaction may be engaged upon in the privacy of the home? Not only is the public not affected by such actions, but the public would not even know that such actions were taking place. Such laws have nothing to do with preventing harm, or even benefitting a certain group, but merely imposing the collective values of the majority upon the minority in an area of human behavior that should be immune from government regulation, as it does not assault natural rights.

Thus, they are at their base arbitrary restrictions of fundamental liberties, that is to say, restrictions which do not address harm.

## What Is *Offense*?

*Offense*, on the other hand, is merely an affront to another person's senses or subjective sensibilities. This difference is related to the distinction between *malum in se* and *malum prohibitum*. *Malum in se* refers to an action which is "evil in itself"; it is a violation of the Natural Law, and therefore needs no explanation or justification for why it is evil. Its evil is, in other words, *self-evident*. Why is infanticide evil? Although one could write volumes reasoning why it should be criminalized, every single human inherently recognizes its evil. *Malum prohibitum*, by contrast, refers to an action which is wrong merely because the government tells us it is wrong. Harm falls into the former category, whereas offense falls into the latter; it is offensive to us merely because of our cultural upbringing, or because someone in the government simply told us that we should be offended by it. Why should sautéed cockroaches be offensive for any reason other than our dietary customs? One of my Fox colleagues knows a Vietnamese lady who was offended and disgusted by cheeseburgers when she first immigrated to America!

Let us return to Feinberg's bus and its unsavory passengers. While the passengers' conduct is, at times, highly offensive and extremely unpleasant, their conduct is ultimately harmless, or in other words, it falls short of violating any natural right. Although their actions may be quite reprehensible, the characters on that bus are no more deserving of criminal punishment than putting one's elbows on the table during dinner.

According to Professor Feinberg in his magnum opus *The Moral Limits of the Criminal Law*, the unpunishable offenses perpetrated on the bus can be categorized in six ways. The malodorous, strobe light–carrying, stereo-blasting man is an affront to the senses. This infliction to the senses may be annoying and perturbing, but you can plug your nose, close your eyes, and cover your ears—or more simply, catch the next bus.

The second category compels feelings of disgust and revulsion in the spectator and includes the drooling, burping picnicker of cockroaches and rotten eggs. These unfortunate reactions are not affronts to the senses, but rather affronts to subjective sensibilities. You may be sickened or nauseated, but the behavior does not, however, add up to harm. While disgust and revulsion are disagreeable emotional effects, again, one can look away from the woman so as to avoid a sour stomach or catch the next bus. Moreover, such subjective sensibilities are often the product of one's local culture and familial upbringing. It is no more logical to criminalize the picnicker's conduct than to criminalize the selling of foie gras (as Chicago did in 2006),[6] fried frog legs, or bull testicles (euphemistically known as rocky mountain oysters), as repulsive as they may seem to some of us. Not surprisingly, the criminalization of offenses can be used to discriminate against cultures which cannot command a political majority, such as when Parliament banned the playing of Scottish bagpipes in 1747 after the final suppression of the Jacobite risings one year earlier.

While the second category could be called affronts to "lower order sensibilities," the third category involves shock to moral, religious, and patriotic sensibilities, or "higher order sensibilities." These are higher emotional responses digging deeper than mere gut reactions such as disgust and revulsion. This type of offense is a gross violation of some kind of neighborhood principle, including the bus's pallbearer who wears offensive religious clothing or who desecrates the country's treasured symbol. As a religious individual, you may be deeply offended by the religiously offensive T-shirt worn by the youth; however, his behavior in no way harms you personally. Moreover, since desecration of the American flag is purely symbolic, criminalizing it is really just another way of punishing a thought and the expression of an idea. It is a flag burner's distaste for the United States, and not the actual destruction of a material thing, which people find so repulsive. And if the government has the ability to regulate our thoughts—the innermost realm of the individual—then we truly have no freedom whatsoever.

Extreme deviations from prevailing standards of "normalcy" induce feelings of shame, embarrassment, and anxiety, which are encompassed in the fourth category of un-punishable offense. The overly affectionate and sexually inappropriate couple on the bus is a prime example. Their actions constitute ordinary and acceptable ways of deriving sexual pleasure when done in private;

however, in public, a viewer may feel temptations of voyeurism, which trigger feelings of shame, embarrassment, anxiety, and envy. Your body, your rights, your property, however, are not violated as a witness.

Next among un-punishable offenses is the category of annoyance, boredom, and frustration. To be fair, the mental states provoked by loud, boisterous, and incessantly talking seatmates or the two women with high-pitched, nasally voices can be almost as painful and difficult to tolerate as the examples from other categories. But nonetheless, there is no natural right to be free from screeching voices.

And finally, fear, resentment, humiliation, and anger can be the reasonable reaction to the hand grenade–waving, rubber knife–brandishing, swastika–wearing teenagers who deliberately seek to cause these unwanted emotions. In a way, these behaviors are the most offensive and disturbing of the categories. This type of conduct induces sentiments that are sometimes the most difficult to handle and control, particularly to those who are part of the targeted group—on Feinberg's bus in particular, Catholics, blacks, Jews, and Hispanics. Yet again, it is clear that these thoughts cannot be criminalized, so why could simply making others aware that they possess those thoughts be any different, and more deserving of punishment? No thoughts can morally be criminalized. After all, a member of any ethnic or religious group certainly knows that there are those out there who harbor ill will toward him. Why is it any more "harmful" to know that one of those individuals happens to be riding the same bus as he is? Moreover, once again, this offense can be avoided. The offended individual may look away, or take a deep breath, signal the bus driver to stop, and get off the bus.

## But Is Refraining from Punishing Offense Really Worth It?

At the age of twenty, Osvaldo Hernandez was arrested and prosecuted for possession of a small pistol, a felony under New York state law. Hernandez, who grew up in a dangerous neighborhood in Queens, New York, claimed the handgun was for self-defense. Yet, despite his plea, the court convicted and sentenced him to a year in jail on Rikers Island. After eight months, the government released Hernandez on good behavior, after which he enlisted in the United States Army.

After three years with the 82nd Airborne Division, Hernandez was deployed to Afghanistan, as a member of an elite paratrooper group, and served a fifteen-month tour overseas. Upon completion of his deployment to Afghanistan, Hernandez sought to become a member of the New York City Police Department (NYPD). However, his previous felony conviction prohibited him from joining the NYPD because of the department's blanket prohibition against hiring individuals with prior felony convictions. Fortunately, on December 29th 2009, New York Governor David Paterson pardoned Hernandez's felony conviction in order for him to achieve his lifelong dream of becoming a police officer. What was Hernandez's response to the pardon? He thanked the governor for "giving [him] back his life."[7] In what kind of world can a man serve his country abroad as a soldier but domestically be unable to defend its citizens as a police officer without a court battle? Could there possibly be a legitimate justification for taking Osvaldo Hernandez's lifelong dream away from him on the grounds that he possessed a dangerous weapon for self-defense in a dangerous neighborhood? Stated differently, did his mere possession of the pistol harm anyone? No.

Let us return to Professor Feinberg's bus again. Note that you, the passenger, have several options for avoiding the offensive behavior: You could look away, get off the bus, or lobby your local government to ban or to criminalize those particular types of conduct. Indeed, one might sensibly wonder why it is that passengers should have to get another bus in order to avoid such repulsive actions. After all, is not freedom about the ability to choose one's profession, start a family, and worship the God of one's choosing, and not eating live cockroaches and rotten eggs on a public bus? In other words, aren't there certain types of offenses which don't deserve protection as fundamental liberties, at least when compared with the inconvenience required to avoid them? Are you justified in demanding legal protection at the cost of the mourners', the teenagers', and the picnicker's liberty?

Most fundamentally, the criminalization of victimless offenses rests upon the doctrine of legal paternalism. Under the legal paternalism concept, the government views itself, and not us, as in the best position to regulate our daily conduct. Thus, where this concept prevails, like in New York City, for example, we have the Nanny State (too much salt in your food, too much trans fat in your diet, wasteful light bulbs in your lamps, etc.). However, this directly violates the Natural Law principle that no government can be above the individual, since a government is a human creation, and the creature is always subservient to its creator. Additionally, the content of those laws themselves will be the product of the moral tides of the day, and not immutable Natural Law principles which inhere in the order of things.

Moreover, to illustrate the practical impropriety of legal paternalism, consider criminal prohibitions on various forms of gambling, for example. At what point in time did the government decide that it is in the best position to tell you how to handle your finances and restrict your ability to gamble? Was it in September of 2007, when our nation's national debt began to rise on an average of $4.13 billion per day?[8] If you were to mimic the government's handling of its finances, how balanced would your budget be?

The central evils of criminalizing offensive behavior, however, are the exaltation of the state over the individual and the use of this exaltation as the primary mechanism to assert control over persons. By limiting what you can or cannot do, the government's criminalization of harmless conduct restricts liberty and freedom on a daily and constant basis. At any point in time, it is astonishing how many criminal codes we are subject to. You want to jaywalk to make your dentist appointment on time? You can't. You want to sit on a park bench and eat your dinner after sunset? You can't. You want to ride your bike to the grocery store without lugging along a helmet? You can't. You want to skateboard in front of the courthouse? You can't. You want to bet money with your favorite bookie on your favorite baseball team? You can't. You want to buy a drug not approved by the FDA? You can't. You want to cool off with a beer on the beach? You can't. You want to talk on your cell phone while driving safely? You can't. You want to paint the fire hydrant (on your property) in front of your house green to match the grass? You can't. You are on an empty subway car, and you want to put your packages on the seat next to you. You can't. You want to collect rainwater on your own property for your own consumption? You can't. The bottom line is every law, regulation, rule, and ordinance made by the state affects your behavior in some way, and the government has more control over you than you could ever imagine. And there can be no more effective way of controlling your moral and behavioral standards than by threatening to brand you with society's most powerful stigma, as a criminal, thus destroying life projects, careers, and family ties. Everything that the government does either compels or restrains, under the threat of force. Government is the negation of liberty.

Moreover, the aggregation of control may seem like a small issue today, but could end up being a larger and more invasive issue tomorrow. With the lengthening and growing complexity of the criminal code, the criminalization of the subjective whims and sensibilities of the Congress may become status quo. And then we will never know what it feels like to truly be free. In this way, the government is also able to aggrandize power in itself by increasingly controlling the lives of its citizens.

Finally, the simplicity and ease of avoiding the problem without criminalizing conduct cannot be overstated. Justice John Marshall Harlan, writing for the Supreme Court in *Cohen v. California* (1971), discussed just such a solution.[9] In that case, the defendant wore a jacket bearing the words "F—the Draft" inside a Los Angeles courthouse. While the police and the prosecutors were clearly offended by the display, the Supreme Court found in favor of a Vietnam War protester's First Amendment right to express disfavor of the draft. Justice Harlan's response to the offended individuals? He suggested the observers "effectively avoid further bombardment of their sensibilities simply by averting their eyes." Or, as discussed before, they could simply catch the next bus.

Understood in this light, the push to criminalize a certain activity can be understood as an application of a recurrent theme in this book: Individuals so often prefer to have the state, and not themselves, solve their problems for them because doing so is much more "convenient," even if it comes at the expense of liberty. Further compounding this problem is the fact that those from whom they demand legal protection are often the least respected, most misunderstood, and hated members of society. Moreover, today's controversy is often tomorrow's mainstream culture. How soon we forget the initial public backlash to the music of the Beatles, or even contemporary pushes to ban *Harry Potter* (for teaching children about witchcraft). In sum, certainly it is inconvenient to carry around earplugs or catch the next bus, but we simply cannot sacrifice liberty for the sake of convenience. Or even worse, sacrifice another's liberty for the sake of our own convenience.

## What Did the Founders Have to Say?

Given these dangers of profligate criminalization, it should come as no surprise that the Founders enshrined an extraordinarily limited ability for the federal government to make crimes. Article I, Section 8 provides that Congress can only punish treason, "counterfeiting the Securities and current Coin of the United States," "Piracies and Felonies committed on the high Seas, and Offenses against the Law of Nations." Moreover, Thomas Jefferson famously wrote that all "acts which assume to create, define, or punish crimes other than those so enumerated in the Constitution are altogether void and of no force."[10] In clear contravention of these principles, the federal government is currently able to criminalize whatever it wishes.

As an example, the Supreme Court held in *Gonzales v. Raich* (2005) that Congress's constitutional authorization to regulate interstate commerce also grants it the power to criminalize homegrown medicinal marijuana; that is, marijuana not procured through any commercial transaction. In her dissent, Justice O'Connor noted the impropriety of such a law:

Relying on Congress' abstract assertions, the Court has endorsed making it a federal crime to grow small amounts of marijuana in one's own home for one's own medicinal use. This overreaching stifles an express choice by some States, concerned for the lives and liberties of their people, to regulate medical marijuana differently.[11]

Thus, ultimately the government's criminalization of harmless or merely offensive conduct not only deprives individuals of their natural right to choose private behavior; it also allows the government to acquire more power than was granted to it by the Constitution.

In sum, the answer to the question posed earlier about NYPD Officer Osvaldo Hernandez is: No. There cannot be a legitimate justification for cases such as Osvaldo Hernandez's. In fact, his story precisely illustrates the evil and tyranny of criminalizing harmless, victimless behavior! We must demand that governments abide by the Natural Law if we are to prevent the government from controlling our lives, aggrandizing power to itself, and at the end of the day, ourselves from sacrificing liberty for convenience.

## Private Harm versus Public Harm

We have discussed up to this point the difference between offense and harm, and found that only harms are eligible for criminalization under a governmental scheme that protects natural rights. However, there is an additional requirement which must be satisfied before harm can be criminalized: It must be a harm against the general public, and not just a private individual. Thus, although it should be a crime to steal a car, it is not a crime if your dog urinates on a neighbor's bush, thus killing it. We can therefore say that being a harm is a necessary prerequisite for criminalization, but it is not sufficient. But how can we distinguish between these public and private harms?

Before delving into what constitutes harm against the public, it is helpful to review briefly the difference between crimes and torts. Our legal system can be divided into two principal parts: The civil law and the criminal law. The civil law addresses *torts* and contractual relations: Breaches of a duty owed by one individual to another individual. By duty owed to an individual, it is meant that someone is obligated not to act in a certain way as to a particular person or entity, such as a business. Thus, I owe a duty to you not to ruin your bush by letting my dog urinate on it. When that duty is breached, the harmed individual has what is called a *cause of action*, or the ability to pursue a remedy for that wrong in a court of law. In the particular case of the dog and the bush, the remedy would be monetary compensation equal to the value of the bush that was destroyed, no more and no less.

By contrast, the criminal law involves breaches of duties owed not just to an individual, but to all individuals; we all owe a duty to society not to attack innocent civilians wantonly, for example. When this duty to the general public has been breached, then the general public, in the form of the government, can bring those alleged to have perpetrated the breach to court and pursue not compensation, but actual punishment. This is, if you have ever wondered, why criminal cases have names such as *State v. Rockwell* or *United States v. Rothbard*. By contrast, civil cases have names such as *Chodorov v. Von Mises* or *Napolitano v. Beck*.

In order to understand this difference better, think of a child who recklessly throws a baseball into a neighbor's window, thus causing $200 worth of damage. The neighbor should, of course, be able to recover the $200 to replace the window, and thus be "made whole." The neighbor has an interest in recovering $200 to undo the harm that has been committed against him, no more and no less. This can be considered the *civil* component of the child's harm. However, because the action was so reckless, the "authority figures" in the child's life (i.e., his parents) may be justified in punishing the child by requiring him to mow the lawn every Saturday for the next four months. Why? Because the entire neighborhood benefits from, and has a legitimate interest in, having the child taught a lesson about responsibility and respect for others' property. This represents the *criminal* component of the child's harm.

Note in particular that this punishment, although arising from the same action of breaking a window, can be considered entirely different from the $200 compensation to the neighbor, as can the reasons for imposing those separate remedial measures upon the child. It would make no sense to require the child, in addition to paying the neighbor $200, also to mow the neighbor's lawn; mowing the lawn is intended to teach the child a lesson, rather than compensate the neighbor for his wrong. If the neighbor could have his lawn mowed in addition to receiving $200, then in effect, he is receiving something he is not entitled to, and would actually become enriched by the whole ordeal. Moreover, it would be equally nonsensical to give the $200 to the child's parents, but not the neighbor; then the parents (i.e., the government) are receiving something they are not entitled to—the value of the window—and the neighbor is left $200 in the hole. Thus, there is a compelling reason to have two separate systems, a civil and a criminal, which serve two very distinct purposes.

So what then can be considered a mere tort, and what rises to the level of a crime, which can be justifiably punished by the government? That is a question which has vexed legal scholars for as long as there have been two separate systems. To be considered a tort, I would argue that the conduct must be a violation of the Natural Law, and thus an actual harm. The criminal law, however, involves a special breed of violations of the Natural Law, where society itself is justified in punishing the wrongdoer, as opposed to just giving the harmed individual a right to recover damages. Society is justified in punishing a wrongdoer when it has a compelling interest in (1) deterring future crime, (2) rehabilitating the individual, or (3) incapacitating the individual from committing further wrongs against others. Unless at least one of these requirements is convincingly met, then punishment is completely unwarranted, and the government is intermeddling in an essentially private civil matter between two or more persons. Recall that we stated that the purpose of the criminal law is to safeguard our liberties: These requirements ensure that the criminal law is not imposing needless or arbitrary punishment, and is actually serving that one true purpose.

As for deterrence, there must be a need to prevent future harms by imposing penalties which discourage subsequent misconduct. Recall the child who broke his neighbor's window: We can agree that errant children pose a significant risk of doing further property damage, and thus the entire neighborhood is justified in discouraging them by imposing a penalty. When the child learns that he will be forced to mow his parents' lawn every Saturday for four months, he is much less likely to break other windows in the future. Similarly, when a thief steals and resells a car, if he was only required to repay the market value of the stolen car, then he would be no worse off as a result of having committed the crime, and thus have no incentive not to continue to steal cars. Moreover, provided he can resell each car before he is caught, and assuming he will only be caught a fraction of the time, he will actually be making a net profit off of a criminal career. Thus, there it is a social necessity that the government punish him in order to deter future theft.

As for rehabilitation, requiring the child to mow lawns can not only deter future crime, but also teach the child the error of his ways. By having his Saturdays "stolen" from him, he can experience for himself what it is like to be the victim of crime. Thus, by being brought to justice, he is more likely to grow up to become a healthy individual who will not continue to destroy property. Michael S. Moore, a professor of law at the University of Illinois, notes that the proper ideal of rehabilitation is to "make criminals safe to return to the streets. This sort of rehabilitative theory justifies punishment, not by appeal to how much better off criminals will be at the end of the process, but rather by how much better off all of us will be if 'treatment' is completed because the streets will be much safer."[12]

It is important to note that Professor Moore distinguishes between rehabilitation for the criminal's sake and for our sake, as a society. If society is determining what is best for the criminal himself, that involves just the sort of legal paternalism which we have discussed and rejected earlier in this chapter. By contrast, only rehabilitation for the sake of society is proper, and squares with the entire purpose of the criminal law. And in any event, if helping individuals to become self-sufficient members of society for their own sake is our goal, why is it that we would choose to spend scarce resources on rehabilitating car thieves instead of autistic children? Those who argue for this justification of punishment must argue why criminals are somehow more deserving of our help than the disenfranchised.

Finally, incarceration of one who gives up his own natural rights serves the natural rights of all by keeping aggressors off the streets, where they can continue to inflict future harm. By contrast, unless it is convincing that they will continue to do harm, there can be no justification for criminalization. If I am required to compensate my neighbor for the lost value of his bush, I will almost certainly not allow it to happen again, and there can be no justification for incapacitating me or my dog, Gina.

Thus, unless at least one of these requirements is met, there cannot be a moral justification for government punishing an individual for wrongdoing, and thus, there is no concurrent justification for criminalization. It is absolutely essential to the ideal of limited government, and the pursuit of freedom, to limit the criminal law to only what is necessary to safeguard our liberties, and that means only prosecuting those who intentionally cause real harm by violating another's natural rights without his consent and without moral justification.

## Conclusion

In sum, although the ostensible purpose of the criminal law might be to protect us from harm, too much prosecution is a far greater evil than too much crime. "Why?" you might ask. If you fear crime, then you are free to help yourself by locking your doors and buying a gun. Every sound adult human possesses the natural right to self-defense and all the intelligence and strength needed to exercise that right. If, by contrast, you fear unlawful prosecution, there is no feasible way to resist the coercive power of the state. How long will it be until the state's long, powerful arm eventually reaches you? How long was it until an unstoppable tide of federal government evicted Native Americans from their homelands? How long was it until the government could command how much wheat you grow in your backyard? *It is dangerous to be right when the government is wrong.*

No, my reader, the government cannot be constrained, and liberty preserved, by pistols and door locks alone. It is only with laws that we can ensure enduring freedom and the enforceability of natural rights. The Founders recognized this inescapable truth. Certainly, they fought a long and bloody war to escape tyranny. But what did they leave us when the war had been fought, the battles won, and the enemy had retreated from our shores? They left us with a *Constitution*—a set of laws binding the government based upon the Natural Law—and a hope that it would be honored in perpetuity.

Sadly, since the day of its ratification that Constitution has been battered and worn down to its very bones—a mere skeleton of the liberty our Founders promised us. But, my reader, all the injustice in the world can never destroy the hope of restoring freedom, just as all the darkness in the world can never extinguish the flame in our hearts.

The Founders' dream lives in each and every human being, as does the power to turn it into a reality. Although it is dangerous to be right when the government is wrong, that danger is imperceptible when compared to the danger of languishing for the remainder of our lives in the physical and spiritual chains of tyrants.

# Chapter 15

# Ignoring Stupidity:

*The Right to Reject the State*

Since the government derives its powers from the consent of the governed, the final, and capstone natural right, is the right not to consent to any government. When the state has assaulted freedom and offered no accountability, are we simply to relinquish any and all interest in the matter as a lost cause? No, my reader, we must do just as the colonists did in 1776: Alter or abolish the government and institute a new system of laws which allows us to pursue our natural yearnings.

If the government itself came about in America by seceding from Great Britain, if the government itself exists only because free persons have freely given some of their natural freedoms to it, if the sole moral underpinning of the government in America is the free consent of the governed, what becomes of the government when that consent is withdrawn?

This is not the lesson or the argument of the Civil War, though lessons there are. This is the concept of a social compact. Since the federal government came about by the states freely ceding limited powers to it, why can't they take those powers back? Since a dozen counties in western Virginia left that state and formed a new one during the Civil War, what is to prevent that from happening elsewhere in America today? And if I can no longer consent to the government that lies, cheats, steals, and kills in my name, why can I simply not withhold my consent and ignore it?

## The Positive Moral Duty to Disobey Stupidity

How did Thomas Paine and Thomas Jefferson view the right to disobey the government? Paine recognized dangers of a system which resulted in more and more British elites benefitting from the British government, and being given land in America. This would lead to a situation where there would be a growing population in the colonies, and the rest of the continent, and this population would be much less likely to seek independence, and much more likely to take up arms to resist an independence movement. This would severely hamper the prospects of uniting the entire population for the common goal of gaining independence, as well as introduce America to many more enemies of the independence movement, and it is why he called for imminent action.

Paine was very well aware that he and his fellow residents of the New World had a positive moral duty to act quickly to disobey the unjust laws of the British government, for if they let any more time pass, the unjust system could have bred an opposing force that was too strong for the colonists to defeat. Thus, he knew that one of the greatest, if not ultimate, dangers to liberty was infringements upon this right.

What did Thomas Jefferson have to say in the Declaration of Independence about government exercising unjust powers?

[W]henever any Form of Government becomes destructive of these Ends [the protection of our natural rights], it is the Right of the People to alter or to abolish it, and to institute new Government, laying its Foundation on such Principles, and organizing its Powers in such Form, as to them shall seem most likely to effect their Safety and Happiness.[1]

In other words, once a government strays from its just powers, it is the right of the people to remove the government, by altering or abolishing it; or in the colonists' case, to fight a war for independence, and implement a new and just government. When government becomes the enemy of rights, it can be tossed out. Rights are permanent, inherent features of all humans; governments are devices that can come and go according to the wishes of those who cede power to them. *Our natural rights cannot be changed or abolished, but governments can.*

Jefferson went to the heart of Paine's argument calling for imminent action by the colonists:

> Prudence, indeed, will dictate that Governments long established should not be changed for light and transient Causes; and accordingly all Experience hath shewn, that Mankind are more disposed to suffer, while Evils are sufferable, than to right themselves by abolishing the Forms to which they are accustomed.[2]

Jefferson here is paternal: Do not get upset by immaterial and momentary problems that can be solved peacefully. However, since mankind is prone to suffering, we must constantly stay on guard and make sure the shackles of tyranny do not chain us down. Jefferson understood that this document preached a political ideology that would cause rebellions in many other places in the world. Since he wished to maintain good diplomatic ties with other European nations, he pointed out that revolutions should not be started for trivial reasons, but only when governments become despotic or tyrannical. At the same time he issued a warning against complacency, because as he explained, "Eternal vigilance is the price of liberty."[3]

But, when should you start to get upset?

> When a long Train of Abuses and Usurpations, pursuing invariably the same Object, evinces a Design to reduce them under absolute Despotism, it is their Right, it is their Duty, to throw off such Government, and to provide new Guards for their future Security.[4]

Here, Jefferson is saying, when a government engages in behavior designed to obscure or deliberately ignore your rights, and when the government becomes the important item which turns you, the individual, into an unimportant item, and that its function is not to serve you but to master you, you not only have a right to get rid of the government, but you have a positive moral duty to get rid of it; put differently, "The tree of liberty must be refreshed from time to time with the blood of patriots and tyrants."[5]

## I Had a Dream Today, That My Brothers and Sisters Overthrew the Government

Just as it was Thomas Paine's positive moral duty to organize mass disobedience of unjust laws by spreading the message of independence, individual liberty, and natural rights, and thus to expose the unjust actions of the British government, it is our duty to spread this same message, and expose the unjust actions of the current American government. Most importantly, we must engage in peaceful civil disobedience of those unjust laws. Just think of the world we would be living in today if the American colonists did not fight for independence and disobey the British laws, or if Rosa Parks did not think she had a duty to violate the unjust law which made it illegal for her to sit in the front of the bus, or if Dr. Martin Luther King Jr. did not find it his duty to fight injustice.

Not surprisingly, the right to ignore or disobey an unjust government has been articulated by many powerful American thinkers throughout our history, each responding to a different moment in a long train of abuses. Consider the examples of Henry David Thoreau and Dr. King. As explained by Thoreau, this positive moral duty of civil disobedience to unjust laws comes from the reasoning that if no action is taken by an individual to disobey and change an unjust law or legal system, the individual in turn practically becomes a supporter, an enabler of the unjust law or legal system, and anyone who supports an unjust law or legal system is acting in violation of the morality set forth by the Natural Law.

Dr. King clearly understood the necessity of acting upon the positive moral duty of civil disobedience, and he stated this reason in his "Letter from Birmingham Jail," where he wrote, "I cannot sit idly by in Atlanta and not be concerned about what happens in Birmingham. Injustice anywhere is a threat to justice everywhere." No longer shall Americans sit idly by at home and accept the status quo while injustice surrounds us. It is time to start peacefully fighting the injustice that takes place in our state legislatures as well as in Washington, D.C.

## You Say You Want a Revolution

The entire collapse of human liberty we have seen in this book is precisely what happens when unjust laws are enforced by states and obeyed by persons in those states for too long. Since not enough members of society exercise their positive moral duty of civil disobedience, they have allowed this immoral and unjust system of legalized wealth redistribution and theft to go on for so long and grow so large that it has gained so many allies whose dependence on the system for survival has forced them to oppose and resist any true change. This is the precise scenario Paine warned the colonists about in regards to the war for independence, why he urged imminent disobedience to unjust laws.

It is the duty of moral persons to study the ideas espoused by classical liberal philosophers such as John Locke, Thomas Jefferson, and Thomas Paine. We must learn the lessons taught in *Common Sense*, demanded in the Declaration of Independence, and promised in the Bill of Rights, and we must stop obeying the unjust laws with which the government enslaves. It is time for us to elect new members of Congress who will codify these classical liberal ideals into law, and create a Declaration of Individual Liberty. No longer shall we sit idly by while the shackles of tyranny hold us down. We must stand up and fight, fight for our right to be free.

## Conclusion

Why is it dangerous to be right when the government is wrong? While I have been writing this book, the United States experienced a bitter and divisive congressional election, an unchecked assault on privacy and bodily integrity at the Security areas of major airports, and the death of Osama bin Laden.

The congressional elections resulted generally in numerical victories for

Republicans. In the House of Representatives, control shifted from Big Government Democrats to Big Government Republicans. In the Senate, the Republicans acquired enough seats to enable them to filibuster virtually any proposal put forward by the White House or by congressional Democrats.

During the campaign in the fall of 2010, Republican candidates for federal office ran, almost to a person, vowing to shrink the government, slow federal spending, impede the march toward socialism, and restore individual liberty. These would be many of the same Republicans who, when they ran the Congress and took direction from President George W. Bush just a few years ago, authorized unlawful and unconstitutional wars, directly assaulted personal freedoms via the so-called Patriot Act (the most offensive legislative attack on constitutionally guaranteed freedoms since the Alien and Sedition Acts in 1798), federalized education, bailed out banks they liked and rejected the entreaties of those they disliked, and ran up trillions in debt. I have argued, however, that divided government can lead to transparency, debate, and exposure. We shall see. The same folks who have endured the government administered pornographic photographs and sexual groping at our airports spasmodically rejoiced at the killing of Osama bin Laden. While the emotional and patriotic sides of me rejoice that this monster is dead, the moral and legal sides of me are compelled to warn that this business of the President deciding to kill people is very dangerous. Put aside that governmental assassination is a violation of the Constitution, that all killing except in self-defense is immoral, the President cannot order any killing absent a declaration of war from Congress. If the President can kill a popularly perceived monster, can he kill one not yet known or feared? When will the killing stop?

During my writing of this book, we have also seen the advent of the Tea Party—a grassroots movement reminiscent of the Goldwater movement in the early 1960s—which heralds sound money, personal freedom, reduced taxes, and a general return to respect for the Constitution. It is, of course, easier for Republicans to advance these ideas when a liberal Democrat—or even a socialist—occupies the White House, than it is when one of their own does. It remains to be seen if we shall experience an enhancement of human freedom via a reduction in the behavior of government.

Do we have a two-party system in America today? I think not. We have one Big Government Party. It has a Republican wing that prefers war, deficits, assaults on civil liberties, and corporate welfare; and a Democratic wing that prefers war, taxes, assaults on commercial liberties, and individual welfare. Neither wing is devoted to the Constitution, and members of both wings openly mock it. Will the Tea Party Republicans be devoured by the Big Government Republicans? I hope not; but I fear so.

My fear is based on the truism that in America, people go into government in order to utilize its powers to tell others how to live their lives. Very few persons—Congressman Ron Paul and Senator Rand Paul are the exceptions here—go into government in order to shrink and to restrain the government.

It is dangerous to be right when the government is wrong because government in America today is not logic or reason, it is not fidelity to the Constitution, and it is not compliance with the Rule of Law: Rather, *it is force*. Government today steals liberty and property in the name of safety. It restricts your ability to express yourself, to defend yourself, to be yourself; and it uses fear to keep the people submissive. Government rejects its moral and legal obligations, insulates itself from litigation, breaks it own laws, makes its own rules, declares worthless paper to be money, and then devalues even that. Government will not hesitate to use force upon those who challenge it. Government has made it unlawful to resist its uses of force even when those uses are patently and unconditionally wrong.

But Americans have accepted danger before. And there are stirrings in the land that enough is enough. Wise folks are buying guns and gold. States are blatantly telling the federal government that they simply cannot and shall not obey federal commands that they cannot afford or are not grounded in the Constitution. Even many police have taken public oaths to disobey the orders of their superiors when those orders violate constitutional guarantees. And many thinking Americans—though apparently not the flying public—have seen through the false promises of safety.

The government's sole moral obligation is to preserve freedom. And freedom is the unfettered ability to choose to follow your own conscience and free will, not that of someone in the government. If the government keeps us safe but not free, the government will have become tyrannical and it will be as illegitimate as was the government of King George III in 1776. And it will be time for it to go.

It has been almost 240 years since last we dispatched tyranny from America. Is the spirit that animated the Founders in 1776 still alive? Are there those among us who unambiguously declare that liberty trumps safety? Is life so sweet and peace so dear that we would prefer to live as slaves rather than risk perishing for freedom?

# Acknowledgments

I owe much gratitude and write to express my deep appreciation for those whose work, encouragement, and faith helped the concept of this book to become reality.

My researchers are all, at this writing, bright, happy law students who attacked the assignments I gave them with great zeal and much patience. They are Timothy P. W. Sullivan, Sarah B. Vander Woude, Daniel Podvesker, and Erin Sullivan; they worked well and hard, and I thank them. My Fox colleagues and buddies Glenn Beck, Stuart Varney, and Charles Gasparino challenge and encourage my work every day. My ideological soul mates Lew Rockwell and Tom Woods have given me much intellectual sustenance. My friend James C. Sheil meticulously edited this book and challenged many of its premises. Having Jim edit your book is akin to running it through a grammar machine—if only such a device existed. And my boss at Fox, who gave me a platform and a megaphone with which to advance the ideas of freedom, has given me more than I can ever repay. Roger Ailes is not only a media giant and genius; he is patient, hilarious, and a hell of a nice guy.

Whatever merits, if any, this book has are the result of all those whose intellects I consulted. Whatever faults it has are mine and mine alone.

# Notes

## Introduction

1. *On Free Choice of the Will*, book one, section 5.
2. Andrew P. Napolitano, *Dred Scott's Revenge: A Legal History of Race and Freedom in America* (Nashville: Thomas Nelson, 2009), 252.
3. Randy E. Barnett, "The Imperative of Natural Rights in Today's World," *The Good Society* 12, no. 3 (2003).
4. Murray N. Rothbard, *The Ethics of Liberty* (Atlantic Highlands, NJ: Humanities Press, 1982).
5. *Supra* note 2.
6. *Summa Theologica*: "Of Human Law," trans. 1947 by Fathers of the English Dominican Province.
7. Dr. Martin Luther King Jr., "I Have a Dream" speech, 1963, http://www.usconstitution. net/dream.html, emphasis added.
8. Declaration of Independence, para. 1, 1776.
9. *V for Vendetta* (Warner Bros., 2006).

## Chapter 1

1. Ayn Rand, *The Fountainhead* (New York: Bobbs-Merrill, 1943).
2. *Law Notes*, vol. 5 (1902), http://google.co.uk/books?id=wxwqA.
3. "When Pure Democracy Fails," *The Green Libertarian*, August 7, 2010, http:// greenlibertarian.net/index.php/news/301-when-pure-democracy-fails.
4. James Madison, *Federalist* No. 10, 1787.
5. This full interview is available at http://www.youtube.com/watch?v=p-5_pv8csMY.
6. Declaration of Independence, para. 2, 1776.

## Chapter 2

1. David King, "Eminent Domain Changes Seek to Limit State's Power to Seize Property," *Gotham Gazette*, February 4, 2010.
2. Ibid.
3. Karen Freifeld, "Columbia University's Harlem Expansion Is Upheld by New York's Top Court," *Bloomberg*, June 25, 2010.
4. James V. DeLong, *Property Matters: How Property Rights Are Under Assault—and Why You Should Care* (New York: Freedom Press, 1997).
5. Roger Pilon, *Cato Handbook for Congress: Policy Recommendations for the 108th Congress* (Washington, DC: Cato Institute, 2003).
6. Tarso Ramos, "Regulatory Takings and Private Property Rights," Political Research Associates, 1995, www.publiceye.org/eyes/privprop.html.
7. Walter Block, "Rent Control," Library of Economics and Liberty, http://www.econlib. org/library/Enc/RentControl.html.
8. Ibid.

## Chapter 3

1. *Beauharnais v. Illinois*, 343 U.S. 250, 287 (1952).
2. James Madison, "The Question of a Bill of Rights," 1788, http://www.constitution.org/jm/17881017_bor.htm.
3. Geoffrey R. Stone et al., *The First Amendment* (New York: Aspen Publishers, 2008), 20.
4. *Schenck v. United States*, 249 U.S. 47 (1919).
5. *Frohwerk v. United States*, 249 U.S. 204 (1919); *Debs v. United States*, 249 U.S. 211 (1919).
6. *Frohwerk v. United States*, 249 U.S. 204 (1919).
7. *Supra* note 3 at 30.
8. *Brandenburg v. Ohio*, 395 U.S. 444, 446 (1969).
9. Ibid., emphasis added.
10. *Citizens United v. Federal Election Committee*, 130 S. Ct. 876 (2010).
11. *Holder v. Humanitarian Law Project*, 130 S. Ct. 2705 (2010).

## Chapter 4

1. Dan Ackman, "The Case of the Fat Aerobics Instructor," *Forbes*, May 9, 2002, http://www.forbes.com/2002/05/09/0509portnick.html.
2. Ibid.
3. Ibid.
4. George Getz, "Fat Law Should Be Repealed," Ifeminists.com, May 14, 2002, http://www.ifeminists.com/introduction/editorials/2002/0514b.html.
5. U.S. Const., Amend. I.
6. John Rawls, *Political Liberalism* (New York: Columbia University Press, 1993).
7. Thomas Paine, *Rights of Man*, 1791.
8. Walter E. Williams, "The Right to Discriminate," Townhall.com, June 2, 2010, http://townhall.com/columnists/WalterEWilliams/2010/06/02/the_right_to_discriminate.
9. Laurence M. Vance, "Discrimination and a Free Society," Lewrockwell.com, June 5, 2010, http://www.lewrockwell.com/vance/vance205.html.
10. Roger Pilon, "Crucial Line Between Public, Private Discrimination Missing from Law," Cato Institute, May 30, 2003, www.cato.org/pub_display.php?pub_id=3129.
11. *Plessy v. Ferguson*, 163 U.S. 537 (1896). It held that "separate, but equal" train cars for blacks and whites are constitutional. It has since been overturned by *Brown v. Board of Education*, 347 U.S. 483 (1954).
12. John Stossel, "Fight Bigotry without Government," *Reason*, June 3, 2010, http://reason.com/archives/2010/06/03/fight-bigotry-without-government.
13. Ibid.
14. Jacob Hornberger, "Rand Paul, Civil Rights, and More Liberal Hypocrisy on Race," Campaign for Liberty, May 22, 2010, http://www.campaignforliberty.com/article.php?view=875.
15. John Stossel, "O'Reilly Tonight: Freedom of Association," Foxbusiness.com, May 25, 2010, http://stossel.blogs.foxbusiness.com/2010/05/25/oreilly-tonight-freedom-of-association/.
16. Krissah Thompson and Dan Balz, "Rand Paul Comments About Civil Rights Stir Controversy," *Washington Post*, May 21, 2010.
17. Charles W. Baird, "On Freedom of Association: Why Doesn't Freedom of Association Apply in Labor Markets?" *The Freeman: Ideas on Liberty* 52, no. 7 (July 7, 2002).
18. Ibid.
19. Ibid.
20. Ibid.
21. Ibid.
22. Ibid.
23. Ibid.

24. Walter E. Williams, "The Right to Deal," George Mason University, September 22, 2003, http://econfaculty.gmu.eu/wew/articles/03/deal.html.

## Chapter 5

1. "TSA Detains Official from Ron Paul Group," *Washington Times*, April 6, 2009.
2. *Saenz v. Roe*, 526 U.S. 489 (1999).
3. *Shapiro v. Thompson*, 394 U.S. 618 (1969).
4. Ibid.
5. Robert Higgs, *Resurgence of the Warfare State: The Crisis Since 9/11* (Oakland, CA: Independent Institute, 2005), 36.
6. Ibid., 38.
7. "Bomb Parts Pass Checkpoints at 21 U.S. Airports," ABCnews.com, March 17, 2006, http://abcnews.go.com/US/story?id=1735898.
8. Ibid..
9. Becky Akers, "Unshakable Faith," Lewrockwell.com, January 11, 2010, http://www.lewrockwell.com/akers/akers118.html.
10. *New York City Transit—History and Chronology*, Metropolitan Transportation Authority, http://www.mta.info/nyct/facts/ffhist.htm.
11. Joan Gralla, "NY Subway Fares to Rise; Most Service Cuts Spared," Reuters, May 11, 2009, http://uk.reuters.com/article/idUKTRE54A5QF20090511.
12. Albor Ruiz, "Immigration Laws Are Breaking Families Apart, Deporting Too Many Parents with US-born Children," *New York Daily News*, July 9, 2009, http://www.nydailynews.com/ny_local/brooklyn/2009/07/09/2009-07-09_immigration_laws_are_breaking_families_apart_deporting_too_many_parents_with_usb.html.
13. David R. Henderson, "Raising the Minimum Wage Will Discourage Migration? It Just Ain't So!" *The Freeman: Ideas on Liberty* 56, no. 9 (November 2006).
14. Dr. Ron Paul, "Immigration and the Welfare State," Lewrockwell.com, August 9, 2005, http://www.lewrockwell.com/paul/paul269.html.
15. Steve Chapman, "Immigration and Crime: There's Nothing to Fear from Illegal Immigrants," *Reason*, February 22, 2010, http://reason.com/archives/2010/02/22/immigration-and-crime.
16. Ibid.
17. Steve Chapman, "Legalize Immigration: It's Time to Focus on Letting Illegal Immigrants In," *Reason*, May 31, 2010, http://reason.com/archives/2010/05/31/legalize-immigration.
18. Ibid.
19. Thomas Kaplan, "Bid for Trophy Becomes a Test of Iroquois Identity," *NewYork Times*, July 12, 2010, A16.

## Chapter 6

1. Charlie D'Agata, "Bloomberg Wants 'Big Brother Britain' for NYC," *LA Overview*, May 12, 2010, http://www.laoverview.com/a7827-mayor-bloomberg-wants-big-brother-britain-for-nyc.
2. "Arizona Governor Proposes Ballot Measure to Save Speed Cameras," The truthaboutcars.com, January 18, 2010, http://www.thetruthaboutcars.com/arizona-governor-proposes-ballot-measure-to-save-speed-cameras/.
3. Ibid.
4. Thom Hartmann, "Dear Clarence Thomas: It Happened on July 4, 1776," *Liberty Mulch*, July 4, 2003, http://www.libertymulch.org/articles/030703_hartman_thom.html.
5. U.S. CONST. AMEND. IV, emphasis added.
6. U.S. CONST. AMEND. IX.

7. See Randy Barnett, "A Law Professor's Guide to Natural Law and Natural Rights," 20 Harv. J.L. & Pub. Pol'y 655 (1997).

8. *Whalen v. Roe*, 429 U.S. 589, 598–600 (1977).

9. Despite Justice Brandeis's progressive thinking on many issues, and whose views I rarely agree with, he was dead-on in his views of privacy.

10. Samuel D. Warren and Louis D. Brandeis, "The Right to Privacy," 4 Harv. L. Rev. 1931890.

11. Ibid., 195.

12. *Olmstead v. United States*, 277 U.S. 438, 478 (1928) (emphasis added).

13. *Loving v. Virginia*, 388 U.S. 1 (1967).

14. Stephanie Coontz, "Taking Marriage Private," *New York Times*, November 26, 2007, www.nytimes.com/2007/11/26/opinion/26coontz.html.

15. Ibid.

16. Ellis Cose, "One Drop of Bloody History," *Newsweek*, February 13, 1995, 70.

17. See *supra* note 13.

18. Ibid., 12.

19. *DOMA Watch*, http://www.domawatch.org/index.php.

20. Ibid.

21. *Gill v. Office of Pers. Mgmt.*, 2010 U.S. Dist. LEXIS 67874 at *11 (D. Mass. July 8, 2010).

22. Ibid.

23. Igor Volsky, "Court Finds DOMA Unconstitutional, Say It Forces MA to 'Violate the Equal Protection Rights of Its Citizens,'" ThinkProgress.org, July 8, 2010, http://thinkprogress.org/2010/07/08/mass-doma-case/; see also *Massachusetts v. United States HHS*, 2010 U.S. Dist. LEXIS 67927 (D. Mass. July 8, 2010) and *Gill v. Office of Pers. Mgmt.*, 2010 U.S. Dist. LEXIS 67874 (D. Mass. July 8, 2010).

24. U.S. CONST. AMEND. X.

25. *Massachusetts v. United States HHS*, at 11.

26. Ibid. 39.

27. Ibid., 50.

28. *Griswold v. Connecticut* 381 U.S. 479, 500 (1965).

29. Ibid., 485.

30. See Senator Feingold's Web site, http://feingold.senate.gov/issues_patriot.html.

31. Final Vote Results for Roll Call 398, http://clerk.house.gov/evs/2001/roll398.xml.

32. U.S. CONST. AMEND. IV.

33. Federal Bureau of Investigation, press release, http://www.fbi.gov/pressrel/pressrel07/nsl_faqs030907.htm.

34. Ibid.

35. Ibid.

36. Andrew P. Napolitano, "How Congress Has Assaulted Our Freedoms in the Patriot Act," Lewrockwell.com, December 15, 2006, www.lewrockwell.com/orig6/napolitano2.html.

37. *Supra* note 33.

38. Kim Zetter, "FBI Use of Patriot Act Authority Increased Dramatically in 2008," *Wired*, May 19, 2009, http://www.wired.com/threatlevel/2009/05/fbi-use-of-patriot-act-authority-increased-dramatically-in-2008/.

39. H.R. 3162, 107th Cong. (2001).

40. Douglas MacMillan, "Google Details Governments' Data Demands," *Bloomberg BusinessWeek*, April 21, 2010.

41. Ibid.

## Chapter 7

1. Tom Knighton, "Prostitution: The Other Prohibition," United Liberty, June 24, 2010, http://www.unitedliberty.org/articles/6176-prostitution-the-other-prohibition.

2. Paul Armentano, "The Case for Legalized Prostitution," The Future of Freedom Foundation, December 1993, http://www.fff.org/freedom/1293e.asp.
3. "New York City Passes Trans Fat Ban," MSNBC, December 5, 2006, http://www.msnbc.msn.com/id/16051436/.
4. John Coté, "Sugary-drink Ban Starts to Affect S.F. Sites," Sfgate.com, July 6, 2010, http://articles.sfgate.com/2010-07-06/bay-area/21939137_1_vending-machines-soda-obesity.
5. Mary Katherine Ham, "Nanny State Looks to Ban Salt in NY," The Weekly Standard, March 11, 2010.
6. Ibid.
7. Eric Felten, "Thin Edge of the Wedge: A Fat Kid," Wall Street Journal, April 30, 2010.
8. Ibid.
9. Dr. Sally Satel, "The Waiting Game," American Enterprise Institute for Public Policy Research, June 26, 2006, www.aei.org/docLib/20060607_SatelQF.pdf.
10. The Organ Procurement and Transportation Network provides further information: http://optn.transplant.hrsa.gov/data/.
11. Ibid. You can watch the ups and downs of the organ list.
12. Ibid.
13. Dr. Sally Satel, "About That New Jersey Organ Scandal," American Enterprise Institute for Public Policy Research, July 26, 2009, www.aei.org/article/100806.
14. Benjamin E. Hippen, "Organ Sales and Moral Travails: Lessons from the Living Kidney Vendor Program in Iran," Cato Institute, Policy Analysis no. 614, March 20, 2008.
15. Supra note 13.
16. David E. Harrington and Edward A. Sayre, "Paying for Bodies, But Not for Organs," Cato Institute, 2006, http://www.cato.org/pubs/regulation/regv29n4/v29n4-1.pdf.
17. Supra note 9.
18. Ibid.
19. Alex Tabarrok, "The Meat Market," Wall Street Journal, January 8, 2010.
20. Supra note 13.
21. Ibid.
22. Supra note 19.
23. Ibid.
24. Ibid.
25. "Number of U.S. ESRD Patients Exceeds 500,000," Renal Business Today, September 19, 2008, http://www.renalbusiness.com/hotnews/half-million-esrd-patients.html.
26. Dr. Sally Satel, "Organs for Sale," November 2006, http://www.sallysatelmd.com/html/a-amer01.html.
27. Virginia Postrel, ". . . With Functioning Kidneys for All," The Atlantic, http://www.theatlantic.com/magazine/archive/2009/07/with-functioning-kidneys-for-all/7587/.
28. Ibid.
29. Gary S. Becker and Julio Jorge Elías, "Introducing Incentives in the Market for Live and Cadaveric Organ Donations," University of Chicago, 2002, http://home.uchicago.edu/~gbecker/MarketforLiveandCadavericOrganDonations_Becker_Elias.pdf.
30. Supra note 19.
31. Ibid.
32. Ibid.
33. Ibid.
34. Supra note 9.
35. Ibid.
36. Jon Gettman, "Lost Taxes and Other Costs of Marijuana Laws," Drugscience.org, http://www.drugscience.org/Archive/bcr4/3Availability.html.
37. "The Alcohol Link," Uncle Mike's Library, April 13, 2009, http://www.unclemikesresearch.com/the-alcohol-link/.

38. Ibid.

39. John Stossel, "End the Drug War," Creators.com, http://www.creators.com/opinion/john-stossel/end-the-drug-war.html.

40. Ibid.

41. Ibid.

42. Dr. Jeffrey A. Miron, "The Budgetary Implications of Marijuana Prohibition," Marijuana Policy Project, June 2005, http://www.prohibitioncosts.org/mironreport.html.

43. Ibid.

44. http://www.prohibitioncosts.org/.

45. Randy Balko, "A Drug Raid Goes Viral," *Reason* August 2010, http://reason.com/archives/2010/07/16/a-drug-raid-goes-viral.

46. Ibid.

## Chapter 8

1. James A. Donald, "Natural Law and Natural Rights," Jim.com, http://jim.com/rights.html.

2. *McDonald v. City of Chicago*, 2010 U.S. LEXIS 5523, at *47 (2010).

3. For a historical overview of Kristallnacht and the 1938 pogroms please see the United States Holocaust Memorial Museum's exhibition, http://www.ushmm.org/museum/exhibit/online/kristallnacht/frame.htm.

4. Michael Berenbaum, "Kristallnacht," Encyclopaedia Britannica Online, http://www.britannica.com/EBchecked/topic/323626/Kristallnacht.

5. Kathy Chang, "Those Who Were There Remember Kristallnacht, Holocaust," *Greater Media Newspapers*, http://ws.gmnews.com/news/2009-12-16/front_page/006.html.

6. *Supra* note 3.

7. Robert Faurisson, "The Warsaw Ghetto 'Uprising': Jewish Insurrection or German Police Operation?" *Journal of Historical Review* 14, no. 2 (March 1994): 2–5.

8. James T. Areddy, "Staring Down the Barrel: The Rise of Guns in China," *Wall Street Journal*, October 14, 2008.

9. Information from the Stockholm International Peace Research Institute (SIPRI), http://www.sipri.org/. Please see the databases for yearly data.

10. Ibid.

11. Report of the Subcommittee on the Constitution of the Committee on the Judiciary, United States Senate, 97th Cong., 2d Sess. (1982), SuDoc# Y4.J 89/2: Ar 5/5, emphasis added.

12. Brady Handgun Control Act, 103rd Cong. (Pub.L. 103-159, 107 Stat. 1536), (1993).

13. John R. Lott Jr., *More Guns, Less Crime: Understanding Crime and Gun Control Laws* (Chicago: University of Chicago Press, 2010), 237 (for a complete statistical analysis of gun control laws and the negative impact they have on the country and local communities).

14. Gary Kleck, *Point Blank: Guns and Violence in America* (Piscataway, NJ: Aldine Transaction, 1991), 47–48.

15. Dr. Paul H. Blackman, "The Armed Criminal in America," National Rifle Association Institute for Legislative Action, September 9, 2003, http://www.nraila.org/issues/articles/read.aspx?id=117.

16. *Supra* note 1.

17. Nicole Marshall and Matt Barnard, "Intruder Who Was Shot, Killed by Tulsa County Homeowner Identified," *Tulsa World*, April 2, 2010, http://www.tulsaworld.com/news/article.aspx?subjectid=11&articleid=20100402_11_0_TURLEY322310.

18. *Supra* note 13 at 241.

19. Ibid.

20. "When Mass Killers Meet Armed Resistance," Freestudentsblogspot.com, April 18, 2007,

http://freestudents.blogspot.com/2007/04/when-mass-killers-meet-armed-resistance.html.

21. Massad Ayoob, "Meet Otis McDonald," *Backwoods Home Magazine*, March 17, 2010, http://backwoodshome.com/blogs/MassadAyoob/2010/03/17/meet-otis-mcdonald/.
22. Ibid.
23. *Supra* note 2 at 15.
24. Ibid., 43.

## Chapter 9

1. Joseph R. Strayer, *On the Medieval Origins of the Modern State* (Princeton, NJ: Princeton University Press, 1973), 18.
2. 4 Parl. Hist. Eng. 1774 (1700).
3. "Seditious Libel," *The Free Dictionary*, http://legal-dictionary.thefreedictionary.com/Seditious+Libel.
4. 10 H.C. Jour. 1688–93, at 1 (1803), given at the Court in the Hague, October 10, 1688.
5. Stephen A. Higginson, "A Short History of the Right to Petition Government for Redress of Grievances," 96 Yale L.J. 142, 153 (1986).
6. Ibid., 149.
7. "A Petition Clause Analysis of Suits Against the Government: Implications for Rule 11 Sanctions," 106 Harv. L. Rev. 1111, 1115 (1993).
8. *Commonwealth v. Beaumarchais*, 7 Va. 122 (1801) (opinion of Edmunton, C.J.), emphasis added.
9. *Bi-Metallic Investment Co. v. State Board of Equalization*, 239 U.S. 441 (1915).
10. W. Channing, *Remarks on the Slavery Question, in a Letter to Jonathan Phillips, Esq.* (Boston: J. Munroe, 1839), 15, 17.
11. *Supra* note 5 at 158.
12. www.mlkonline.net/dream.html.

## Chapter 10

1. This anecdote is based on Robert B. Stinnett, *Day of Deceit: The Truth About FDR and Pearl Harbor* (New York: Free Press, 2000).
2. "The McCollum Memo," Whatreallyhappened.com, October 7, 1940, http://whatreallyhappened.com/WRHARTICLES/McCollum/index.html.
3. Laurence M. Vance, "Rethinking the Good War," Lewrockwell.com, 2009, http://www.lwerockwell.com/vance/vance181.html.
4. Ibid.
5. Bettina Bien Greaves, "Japan's Gift to FDR," Lewrockwell.com, June 29, 2010, http://www.lewrockwell.com/orig11greaves1.1.1.html.
6. Anne Leland and Mari-Jana Oboroceanu, *American War and Military Operations Casualties: Lists and Statistics*, Congressional Research Service, February 26, 2010, http://fpc.state.gov/documents/organization/139347.pdf.
7. Robert Higgs, *Resurgence of the Warfare State: The Crisis Since 9/11* (Oakland, CA: Independent Institute, 2005). Much of the content for this chapter is inspired by this book, which is both brilliant and provocative in its exploration of the 9/11 crisis.
8. Ibid., 24.
9. Robert Higgs, "What's So Special About Those Killed by Hijackers on September 11, 2001?" Lewrockwell.com, September 13, 2003, http://www.lewrockwell.com/higgs/higgs21.html.
10. *Supra* note 7 at 67.
11. Robert Higgs, "If We're Really in Danger, Why Doesn't the Government Act as If We're in Danger?" Independent Institute, October 28, 2002, http://www.independent.org/

newsroom/article.asp?id=114.
12. Ibid.
13. *Supra* note 7.
14. Ibid., 24.
15. Ibid., 43.
16. *Backgrounder: Soldiers at War*, PBS, October 16, 2008, http://www.pbs.org/pov/
    soldiersofconscience/special_background.php. (Web site provides additional data
    regarding conscientious objectors.)
17. *Supra* note 9 at 12.
18. William H. Rehnquist, *All the Laws but One: Civil Liberties in Wartime* (New York: Knopf,
    1998), 192.
19. *Supra* note 7 at 11.
20. Ibid., 10.
21. Ibid.
22. Ibid., 25.
23. Ibid., 4.
24. Ibid., 96.
25. Ibid., 61.
26. Ibid., 63.
27. Ibid., 59.
28. Robert Higgs, "Wartime Prosperity? A Reassessment of the U.S. Economy in the 1940s,"
    Independent Institute, March 1, 1992, http://www.independent.org/newsroom/article.
    asp?id=138.
29. Ibid.
30. *Supra* note 7 at 79.
31. Ibid.
32. *Supra* note 9.
33. Ibid., 145.
34. Ibid., 223.

## Chapter 11
1. James Madison, *Notes of Debates*, 336–37 (statement of J. Wilson).
2. James Madison, speech before the U.S. House of Representatives, June 8, 1789.
3. Trial Record from Zenger's *A Brief Narrative of the Case and Trial of John Peter Zenger*
   (1736), http://law2.umkc.edu/faculty/projects/ftrials/zenger/zengerrecord.html.
4. Ibid.
5. Burton Alva Konkle, *The Life of Andrew Hamilton, 1676–1741: "The Day-Star of the American
   Revolution"* (Philadelphia: National Publishing Co., 1941), 104.
6. For a further discussion of this issue, see Andrew Bacevich, *The Limits of Power: The End
   of American Exceptionalism* (New York: Metropolitan Books, 2008).

## Chapter 12
1. Murray N. Rothbard, *The Case Against the Fed* (Auburn, AL: Ludwig von Mises Institute,
   1994).
2. http://quotes.liberty-tree.ca/quotes_by/andrew+jackson.
3. Ludwig von Mises, *Theory of Money and Credit* (1912); for a more recent edition, see the
   2009 edition (Orlando: Signalman Publishers). Mises explained monetary and banking
   theory by applying the marginal utility principle to the value of money and then
   proposing a new theory of industrial fluctuations. Hayek used this as a foundation to
   build a new theory of the business cycle, which is what later became known as the
   "Austrian Business Cycle Theory." See Friedrich Hayek, *Prices and Production* (London: G.

Routledge, 1931) and Friedrich Hayek, *The Pure Theory of Capital* (London: Macmillan, 1941).

4. For a complete account of the formation of the Federal Reserve System, the following books are highly suggested: Ron Paul's *End the Fed* (New York: Grand Central Publishing, 2009); Murray N. Rothbard's *The Case Against the Fed, supra* note 1; and G. Edward Griffin's *The Creature from Jekyll Island* (Appleton, WI: American Opinion,1994).

5. *Supra* note 1.

6. Ron Paul, *End the Fed*.

7. Executive Order 6102 was an Executive Order signed on April 5, 1933, by U.S. President Franklin D. Roosevelt "forbidding the Hoarding of Gold Coin, Gold Bullion, and Gold Certificates" by U.S. citizens.

8. Mike Hewitt, "Ben's Helicopters Are Here!" DollarDaze, December 1, 2008, http://dollardaze.org/blog/?post_id=00523.

## Chapter 13

1. Murray N. Rothbard, "The Myth of Neutral Taxation," Lewrockwell.com, http://www.lewrockwell.com/rothbard/rothbard36.html.

## Chapter 14

1. Joel Feinberg, *The Moral Limits of the Criminal Law* (Oxford, England: Oxford University Press, 1984). My former professor and great philosopher, Joel Feinberg, inspired this chapter. His four-volume treatise on the moral limits of the criminal code provides great insight as to how the government criminalizes acts which cause no harm. Specifically, direct credit must be given for the bus concept, or as I refer to it, "Feinberg's bus." While our views diverge at many points, Feinberg's treatise is a must read for anyone interested in philosophical views of the criminal law in a free society.

2. John Baker, "Revisiting the Explosive Growth of Federal Crimes," Heritage Foundation, June 16, 2008, http://www.heritage.org/Research/Reports/2008/06/Revisiting-the-Explosive-Growth-of-Federal-Crimes.

3. Ibid.

4. Bureau of Justice Statistics, *Key Facts at a Glance: Direct Expenditures by Criminal Justice Function, 1982–2006*, http://bjs.ojp.usdoj.gov/content/glance/tables/exptyptab.cfm.

5. http:www.lewrockwell.com/vance/vance204html.

6. Francie Grace, "Foie Gras Banned in Chicago," CBS News, April 27, 2006, http://www.cbsnews.com/stories/2006/04/27/national/main1550028.shtml.

7. Glenn Blain et al., "Gov. Paterson Pardons Army Veteran Osvaldo Hernandez of Felony that Blocked Him from Joining NYPD," *New York Daily News*, December 29, 2009.

8. U.S. National Debt Clock, http://www.brillig.com/debt_clock/ (accessed August 4, 2010).

9. *Cohen v. California*, 403 U.S. 15 (1971).

10. Kentucky Resolutions, adopted November 10, 1798.

11. *545 U.S.* at 45.

12. Michael S. Moore, *Law and Psychiatry: Rethinking the Relationship* (New York: Cambridge University Press, 1984).

## Chapter 15

1. Declaration of Independence, para. 2, 1776.

2. Ibid.

3. Source not known.

4. Declaration of Independence, para. 2, 1776.

5. Letter of Thomas Jefferson to William Stephens Smith, 1787.

# Index

# About the Author

A graduate of Princeton University and the University of Notre Dame Law School, Judge **Andrew P. Napolitano** is the youngest life-tenured Superior Court judge in the history of the State of New Jersey. He sat on the bench from 1987 to 1995, when he presided over more than 150 jury trials and addressed thousands of motions, sentencings, and hearings. He taught constitutional law at Seton Hall Law School for eleven years, and he returned to private practice in 1995. Judge Napolitano began television work in the same year.

As the Senior Judicial Analyst for Fox News, Judge Napolitano broadcasts nationwide on the Fox News Channel (FNC) and the Fox Business Network (FBN) throughout the day, Monday through Friday. He hosts *Freedom Watch* on FBN on weekdays, and he is the one of the rotating hosts for *The Five*, weekdays on FNC.

Judge Napolitano is a nationally recognized lecturer on the U.S. Constitution, the rule of law, civil liberties in wartime, and human freedom. He has been published in the *New York Times*, the *Wall Street Journal*, the *Los Angeles Times*, and numerous other publications. This book is his sixth on the U.S. Constitution.